# love
# factually

## For Single Parents
## [& Those Dating Them]

# DUANA C. WELCH, PHD

LoveScience Media, LLC, publisher, Eugene, Oregon, USA.

First edition, 2019.

The stories, letters, comments, and examples in this book are real. However—except for the author and her husband Vic Hariton, and the scientists, authors, and sources identified by last name—everyone else's names and identifying details have been changed, and their quotes and letters have been edited, to protect their privacy and dignity.

The e-version of this book may contain affiliate links to some of the recommended reading and books and works used in writing *Love Factually for Single Parents [& Those Dating Them]*. Purchasing through these links provides a small sales commission to the author. However, the author was not approached by any of these authors or publishers to include their work in this book; Duana Welch's decision to include these books is based solely on the works' merit and usefulness in her experience. Readers should examine the books to determine their value to them before making any purchase.

If you want to communicate with Duana, email her at Duana@LoveSciencemedia.com. As with content at her blog, your letter may be published, either on-site at LoveScienceMedia.com, and/or in a future book. If your letter is chosen, your name will be changed, your other identifying information will be removed and/or changed, and prior to publication the letter may be edited for brevity or to maintain your anonymity.

# Dedication

" Everyone deserves love, including you! *Love Factually for Single Parents [& Those Dating Them]* gives you actionable, practical strategies to take control and successfully navigate the classic dating challenges of a single parent, based on solid relationship science that will prepare you for a great relationship. So don't sit back and hope love happens. Instead, get the facts for you and your children. You will love reading this book!"

~ DR. TERRI ORBUCH (PH.D.), AUTHOR OF *5 SIMPLE STEPS TO TAKE YOUR MARRIAGE FROM GOOD TO GREAT* AND *FINDING LOVE AGAIN: 6 SIMPLE STEPS TO A NEW AND HAPPY RELATIONSHIP*

" We don't get this mating training at home growing up. Either we educate ourselves about the science that is invisibly impacting us, or we continue to grope in the dark wondering why we can't find the right mate. Add children to the equation and people definitely need this wonderfully specialized book."

~ JOAN NORTON, ATTORNEY-MEDIATOR, FAMILY LAW

" A must read for single parents seeking a lifetime relationship. *Love Factually for Single Parents [& Those Dating Them]* is an insightful, encouraging, no-nonsense, research-based guide that provides all the knowledge, skills, and tools people need to succeed at the complicated task of creating lasting love."

~ TIM COLE, PH.D., AUTHOR OF *BROKEN TRUST: OVERCOMING AN INTIMATE BETRAYAL*

" What a gift this book is! With Dr. Duana Welch by your side, you'll find laughter, healing, and balance as a parent and a person; learn to embrace happiness and fulfillment while safely and effectively navigating the dating process for yourself and your children; and ultimately, find a partner to fearlessly love. As a licensed professional counselor working with people facing these very challenges, and as a single parent myself, I highly recommend this book!"

~ CARRIE LYNNE PIETIG, LICENSED PROFESSIONAL COUNSELOR

" This book is a ray of hope in a world of cynicism. Even better, it's hope founded on fact. In my twenty-plus years writing about and helping couples find and keep good partnerships, I've seen an increase in fear, a major roadblock to love. Readers of this book will learn why holding onto hope is realistic, as well as how to move through their fears, create lasting love, and feel better about themselves in the process. *Love Factually* is a helping, healing journey."

~ SUSAN PAGE, AUTHOR, *IF I'M SO WONDERFUL, WHY AM I STILL SINGLE?*

" If you want to transform your dating life into an effective search that significantly increases your odds of meeting the right person, *Love Factually* is a must read. Dr. Duana Welch is like having a kind, gentle, funny, and firm love guide/guru beside you as you traverse the rocky trail of being able to fully embrace a healthy, deeply fulfilling, satisfying and enriching relationship. I recommend this book to my clients, and to men and women who are serious about investing in themselves in order to become, and attract, the person they want and deserve."

~ CARRIE LYNNE PIETIG, LPC-S, USING GOTTMAN METHOD COUPLES THERAPY IN PRIVATE PRACTICE

" *Love Factually* is like having Malcolm Gladwell and Brené Brown gene-splice with Dear Abby and The Rules. The Steps here are fantastic, and it's a great, fun read we highly recommend!"

~ ELLEN FEIN & SHERRIE SCHNEIDER, AUTHORS OF *THE RULES, ALL THE RULES, AND NOT YOUR MOTHER'S RULES*

" *Love Factually* is a sure bestseller you won't be able to put down until you've read it cover-to-cover. Duana Welch's wise counsel, warm voice, and fact-based approach ensure that men and women alike will never again have to suffer the stomach-churning pain of yet another relationship gone wrong. *Love Factually* offers encouragement, hope, and well considered, proven answers for all who want to know how to find and sustain a loving and secure relationship."

~ DEREK COLLINSON, HOWDOIDATE.COM

# CONTENTS

# INTRODUCTION

N early 15 years ago, on a plane bound for San Antonio with my toddler, I met a very kind man who told me that everything would be okay.

I needed to borrow his faith. I had run away from my home in California, where my then-husband was a danger to himself, to me, and to our two-year-old, who had recently been diagnosed with a chronic condition. I pretended to be leaving for a long family visit, and we never went back.

I ran to my family in Texas—leaving behind a research and academic career, pets, community, friends, colleagues, students, and the first house I'd ever bought. A suitcase and a case of pneumonia went with me.

It was the lowest point of my life, admitting defeat and leaving so much I loved, including the father of my child, a good man with a bad problem. I was unemployed for over a year, and wondered who I was. After all, my life from age 17 onward was dedicated to developing a career I now couldn't hope to replicate. It felt like I would never feel cheer or humor or love again. I went to therapy and was on antidepressants...for years.

Many people helped us. A few were: my mom and stepdad, who opened their house to us for eight months and gave my child a solid family where he was continually safe, cherished, and cared for; women in the community, who actively included us in their lives and who showed compassion without judgment; doctors who assured me I was doing fine keeping my child safe, and who treated me as a peer as I sought help for my own depression; the priest-turned-lawyer who made sure I got unemployment benefits even though I'd left my job voluntarily, "because you did the only thing a good parent had a choice to do;" the small-business owner who made me president of her company, and who remains a close friend; and that very kind man on the plane, who knew nothing of my situation but could see that I was suffering and assured me there were brighter days ahead.

Ultimately, and most vitally, there was Vic Hariton, who saw everything we could be, and what I could do, and who became my husband and the hero of my story. We met four years into my single-parent journey. Over a decade after our vows, we've created lives, shared and separate, that are filled with meaning and joy and that we wouldn't have dreamed of without the support of the other.

## DATING: BEFORE CHILDREN VS. AFTER CHILDREN

In this book, I delve into real people's challenges and explore my personal trials, too. It's imperative that if I'm going to write about your struggles, I should come clean about my own. I'm not preaching at you from the Mt. Olympus of perfection. I've been tried, found wanting, and recovered from a badly broken heart, not just metaphorically but literally: I required open-heart surgery a few years after leaving my ex. I know the emotional, financial, and physical toll and unique challenges that rebuilding your life while single-parenting can bring.

One of those unique challenges is dating. Because if you've dated Before Children and After Children, you know it's not the same! The book you're now reading is a whole new take for single parents who are committed to getting love right this time around, with information on challenges that specifically deal with your needs.

As a single mom in her 30s wrote to me, "I've really had to reevaluate the people I choose to date and spend time with. Now it's not just my life and time I'm wasting, but potentially my child's (even though so far nobody has made it far enough to be introduced)."

She's right, of course. Think back to your BC dating. Remember the freedom to schedule time together when you wanted, regardless of your mother's babysitting availability? To spend an evening together that neither of you planned? To go where you wanted, and stay out as late as you liked—or even have a spontaneous weekend away? To have someone overnight without wondering how to hide their presence from/explain their presence to your kids? To have sex in the living room, without wondering who might pop in? To Netflix and chill with someone you've just met, without worrying whether it was too soon for them to meet your child?

More seriously, remember what it was like to date without having a difficult ex? To not wonder how much the kids would leak to their other parent, or how much your ex might try to pry out of them? To meet new partners without needing to forgive your ex, or yourself? To consider only yourself and your desires, without fearing what your choices might mean for the lives you've already created? To meld your life with someone else's, without also trying to convince the kids that this is a good idea? To have months or even years as just-you-two? To live together and not consider the impact of the move on your kids' ties to their other parent, grandparents, step-sibs, etc.?

When a marriage comes with an ex and kids, a whole village can be involved in your love life. Bringing two people together isn't nearly as tough as bringing all these people together. Geez. No wonder so many custodial single parents decide to remain single! The complexity, and the struggle, are real.

## CHALLENGES THIS BOOK ADDRESSES

Like many of you, I struggled in my post-separation life. There were many hard times and a lot of work before and after Vic and I met. Luck played its role, but chance favors the prepared—and with a child to consider and a broken heart to fix, this time I made sure I was ready for success. After all, my mistakes would now cost not only me, but my child.

I was determined not to remain alone.

I was equally determined to get it right this time.

The secret of my success was relationship science. Although my Ph.D., laboratory, and professorship at Cal State Fullerton had been devoted to studying successful memory and aging, my new passion was for sciences I could apply to my mate search, from psychology to anthropology, sociology, and biology. Where my professional objective had been to create publishable research, my new research goal was purely personal. The results are my marriage to Vic, my international client practice, the LoveScience blog read in more than 30 nations, and ultimately, the *Love Factually* books.

**This is the first book that relies on science rather than opinion, to help single parents find the right partner not only for themselves but also for their children.** It's the book I needed, wanted, and ultimately never found, and you've been on my mind as I've written it. If you're a single parent, you may have seen that most dating books sound as if the world is child-free, and as though opinion is all that's available. Yet why would we trust our lives and our children's to opinion by itself, when there's science to guide us?

Take meeting someone, for instance. One way to maximize your exposure and quickly find out whether that person fits your must-haves is to date online—an increasingly common way to get happily hitched[1]. But did you know there are dating sites and apps where up to a third of the guys are already married[2]? They're not all created with equal clientele. Knowing who's likely to be where is a key to saving your limited time and emotional bandwidth.

Another example is arguing. All couples disagree at times, and fighting about child discipline can get even more complex when the kids in question aren't yours[3]. But science tells us that some forms of arguing are toxic, while other forms are healing. Across decades, studies have found that happy couples complain even more than unhappy couples do—and that there's a formula for complaining that gets the best results in the moment, as well as over the long haul[4].

Science even tells us at which ages in your children's lives you are likely to more easily and successfully repartner, and how the children's gender affects those efforts[5].

This information has been put to work for me and my clients. Now, it can work for you.

Using research, I found answers for my most pressing questions—and yours. Before writing this book, I wanted to double-check whether the struggles I faced as a dating single parent were the same as those that other men and women—single parents, those dating them, and those raised by them-- were confronting. So I prepared a questionnaire asking those folks to share their challenges, and they responded generously.

As their answers make clear, most of us, regardless of gender, are dealing with many of the same issues. Some that are explored in this book include:

- *How do I deal with, get over, and (maybe) forgive my ex?*

- *How do I keep my kids out of the middle?*

- *How can I face my fears, improve my self-esteem, and take care of myself while dating?*

- *What are the best ways to meet people when my schedule is tight?*

- *How can I find people who are willing and able to meet my needs, and maybe some of my children's needs?*

- *How can I quickly tell whether someone is safe for me/my kids?*

- *(How) can I remember to flirt?!*

- *How much has dating changed? I feel rusty.*

- *When's the right time for an adult sleepover?*

- *When's the right time for my kids to meet someone new?*

- *Should we live together before/instead of making more of a commitment?*

- *What's the best way to blend families? (And what if my kids hate my partner?)*

- *How do I set boundaries on how much parenting my partner does?*

- *How can I tell whether my new relationship is workable?*

- *How can I grow my relationships with my partner and my kids, even when we disagree?*

- *If I have to break up with a new partner, how do I cushion the blow for my children?*

- *How do we move forward together when we're both sure: Yes! This is it!?*

For readers of my first book, you'll find much new information here. *Love Factually for Single Parents [& Those Dating Them]* specifically deals with issues relevant to your situation. Because love can be more complicated the next time around, this new *Love Factually* contains many more Exercises and examples than my first book did. If you haven't yet read the original *Love Factually*, it's the first book to use relationship science to give step-by-step dating guidance so you find the love of your life, whether or not you're a parent. This new book likewise relies on science rather than opinion, but it covers new and different ground—supplementing the first, without replacing it. I recommend reading both, but you can benefit from each book without referring to the other.

# WHO THIS BOOK IS FOR

When I was dating the first time around, I yearned for one solid, lifelong relationship--not a string of them. And that certainly does happen; the current divorce rate for first marriages is around 30%, nowhere near the 50% statistic often cited[6].

Yet ending a mateship is common around the world. From hunter-gatherer tribal cultures to the most developed nations, all have their ways of putting asunder what culture, law, and love had joined together[7]. This means that globally, relationships and families are diverse. Today, about half of American children live in some arrangement other than the iconic nuclear family[8].

The upshot? In many Westernized nations today, stepfamilies are almost as common as intact unions.

What's not the norm is losing your need for sexual union and emotional companionship after a relationship ends. People need people all the way through life, and most of us need one primary adult partnership to thrive at our highest levels emotionally, sexually, and in terms of health, longevity, and wealth[9]. Some longitudinal research even concludes that the most effective way to get over a lost love is to find a new one[10].

So the question isn't whether most single parents can or will love again. Love is likely! Most of you, like me, aren't going to throw in the towel. But success is harder. Largely due to the pressures listed above, After Children unions are significantly likelier to end in divorce than BC marriages are—with up to 75% of couples divorcing if both have children when they repartner[11]. *Let's use science to increase those odds to be more in your favor.*

*This book is for you, single parents:* people who have had children and then either divorced or, if never married, separated from their partner. If this is you, you may feel a need to find not only the right partner for yourself, but for your children, and maybe even for your grand-children. You may be distrustful of yourself and your judgments, and consequently, have trust issues about others, and deeper ambivalence about whether getting into another relationship is worth the risk. Maybe you find yourself taking the very long view of all your relation-ships: marriage sometimes does end, but parenthood is forever, and you want to consider all of this as you make wise and happy decisions. This book will help you sort all these issues out.

This book is also for single parents who never had a mate to begin with, or whose partner has died. In either of these situations, you're likely well-versed in the fears of involving new people in your kids' lives, and the dilemmas of finding someone worthy and good for all of you when your time and energy are at a premium. Relationship science will help you resolve those fears and dilemmas.

This book is for single parents regardless of age or gender or sexual orientation. Although there's a lot more relationship science on cisgender, heterosexual people, I'll incorporate diverse perspectives whenever possible, and suggest how heteronormative science may apply when that's all we've got.

*What if you're not a single parent yourself, but you're dating someone who is?* This book will help you understand your prospective partner's experiences, and it will show you how to make a happy life with them and their entourage. I also present examples of the non-parent's perspective, so your new partner-with-kids can appreciate your experience, too.

*Finally, I hope that friends, parents-of-single-parents, employers, therapists, and others who care about single parents find this an invaluable reference.*

If you're a parent who is already in a marriage or committed partnership and want to know whether to stay or go, you can write to me at Duana@LoveScienceMedia.com and I will point you towards helpful resources to make that weighty decision. And if you're looking for an open relationship, polyamory, or a noncommitted relationship, I am fully in favor of your finding that—but this book won't satisfy you.

I can't candy-coat it: dating After Children is tough. All the challenges you faced BC are likely to be magnified, and new ones pop up with daunting regularity. And yet, because of science, there's every reason to be hopeful that you, yes you, can find love for yourself and your family—and have your happily-ever-after, after all. As one of my clients put it, "In our conversations, one of the most affecting and touching things you communicated to me was that I deserve a healing love; a love that restores me and makes me feel safe and at home. I strongly believe that this is absolutely what any single parent needs to hear, believe, and have wished for them. They already know what's hard."

You certainly do. So although you already may have been through the pain of single parents who've loved and lost, hang in there. Keep reading. Let science help you, as it has so many. And don't give up. Yes, love can hurt. But it heals us, too. Let's find it for you now.

Duana Welch

*August 8, 2018*

Duana C. Welch, PhD

# PART I:

# Getting Ready For Love

# CHAPTER 1:

# Put The Past—And Your Ex—Behind You

hen Amy met her husband Paul, she'd been through years of hell with her ex:

*"There was a significant amount of arguing after the divorce, and sometimes there still is. It was even past arguing and crossed over to emotional abuse and verbal abuse. I still have copies of text messages I transcribed a long time ago if you want some real samples! It was terrible. It doesn't happen much anymore, but boy was it intense for a very long time."*

The fights could be maddening, including this one during Amy's engagement to Paul:

*"My ex threw a fit when we went on a large group camping trip, and Paul and the kids and I slept in the same tent. It's not like we had a double sleeping bag or anything?! Plus, my ex had lived with multiple girlfriends before we had that camping trip...sleeping in the same bed. Multiple women. And he had our kids for overnight visitation when living with them."*

No matter what has happened between you and your ex, you can get into a new, healthy, thriving relationship—like Amy and Paul, now happily married for seven years.

Yet most single parents have a tough time getting a new relation-ship off the ground, in part because most are still in a relationship… with our exes. For one thing, parenting and the laws governing it tend to require interaction. For another, most of us just aren't very good at ending the issues that led up to separation or divorce. Although couples tend to hope that physical separation will end their disputes[1], in most cases the fighting continues and the kids are in the middle[2].

This is particularly true for the one-third of divorces that stem from one or both partners' abuse of substances or people[3]. If that's your scenario, you'll need to build your skills to avoid being stuck in a harmful dynamic. You can't control any abuser, but you can control your reaction and exposure to them.

So I want to start off with a question: *how much more time does your ex get?*

It's a serious inquiry. Lots of people never successfully and happily rebuild their lives after divorce[4]. Between bitterness, anger, hurt, low self-esteem, enmeshment, fights, and fears of change and of making another mistake, it's easy to see how folks can remain stuck in the past. Scientists have seen it again and again[5].

I've seen it, too. I've encountered ex-husbands who wore their wedding rings a decade or more after the divorce, living like ghosts in their sparsely-furnished apartments and spending their lives in a morass of loneliness and what-ifs. I've known ex-wives who refused to date until the kids were launched—cutting off their mate-search during the years when they're most likely to find a happy union, and struggling with more work, more stress, and less time with the kids even if the mom has primary custody[6].

Losing the relationship that was a foundation for your adult life rocks your world, even if you yearned for the separation. Scientists have routinely found that divorce is much harder on adults than they anticipated[7]. It's the death of many dreams, too often combined with harsh realities. As Amy put it of her ex's hurtful behavior, "When you get married, of course no one ever thinks about how bad it would feel for someone you loved enough to marry to treat you that way. It's its own special kind of pain."

I'm guessing this also applies to people who didn't marry, but who lived together and had children together before breaking up.

Yet some people do successfully recover and move forward. No matter what your ex is like, reintegrating is a choice, and one I hope you'll make.

*Because if you give up, your ex doesn't get only your past, but your entire future, too.*

## End Negative Intimacy And Become All Business

Remember when you first met your ex? I do. My best friend had stage-4 cancer. She was in a wellness-meditation group, and one of the members had asked her out. She wasn't interested, but as she talked about him, I was; so we arranged that I would drop into the group and see whether he noticed me. Shazam! The attraction was mutual, and we spent months getting to know everything we could about one another. We couldn't wait to meet each other's friends and families, and to begin the journey of planning a life together. I remember the first time he took me, a sixth-generation Texan, snow-sledding near his family home in Massachusetts. We were deeply in love. For a couple of years following our marriage, we were very happy.

And then, we weren't. Shortly after our baby's birth, I found out that my ex's drug and alcohol addictions weren't in the past; they were very much present, and he couldn't stop. Eventually, we reached a crisis and I made the difficult choice to end the marriage. But ending the relationship—at least, the parts that weren't about parenting—was a different matter.

When you first met your ex, chances are, you went from knowing very little about one another, to bonding like soul mates. It may be painful to recall it now—it took me years to begin this book, because I didn't want to remember!—but it's likely your intimacy grew as you shared more and more about yourselves. You not only fell in love, you probably grew to trust and like each other. For those of us who got pregnant on purpose, many chose to have a child with this specific person because we thought the world of them. You had a lot of positive intimacy, until you didn't.

Some people end a relationship because of abuse, but others— about 2/3 of us, from divorce stats[8]—chose a basically good partner and still have conflicting feelings about them. Either way, most people remain enmeshed post-separation rather than letting go and establishing healthy boundaries. By hanging on, we're living in limbo.

This continued emotional attachment to your ex is called **negative intimacy**, and it keeps us stuck[9]. As Joan Norton, a family and child welfare lawyer, puts it, "Like an invisible lasso, anger, bitterness, the desire for revenge, or unfounded hopes that the former spouse will return can tie a divorced couple together just as surely as their love once did[10]."

That's right, negative intimacy holds you back from fully living your life, finding a healthy new love—and raising happy children. *The top source of suffering, stress, and maladjustment in kids of divorce is the ongoing conflict between their parents*[11]. Your marriage may have come and gone, but parenthood is forever—and you deserve a happy future not just for your kids, but for yourself, too!

If I had to sum up all the science on relationships in just one sentence, that sentence would be: if you can find someone kind and respectful, and be kind and respectful yourself, your relationship will go well; and if you can't, it won't. This also rings true for divorce or separation.

So let's make your divorce work even if your marriage didn't. And that means letting go of negative intimacy, and replacing it with a new, businesslike relationship with your ex.

The trick is un-hooking—turning our previously intimate relationship with our former mate into one where we're respectfully focused on the joint enterprise of raising our children, and we don't interact about anything else. Otherwise, your ex has continual power to ruin your day, undermine your present, and wreck your future. That's too much power to give anyone!

# TAKE FIVE STEPS TO ESTABLISH A BUSINESSLIKE RELATIONSHIP WITH YOUR EX:

### ▶ FIRST: EXPECT CHALLENGES:

People will work harder and persist longer in making changes if they expect those changes to be difficult rather than easy[12]. An important first step to mastering the business-relationship mindset is acknowledging that this is hard, and that your feelings will reflect that for many months. For most of us, best-case, it takes a full year-and-a-half to reach the point where we aren't triggered anytime we see or hear our ex[13].

If exes nurse a grudge, it can take far longer. I once went on a date with a guy who was still seething with resentment against his ex a full decade post-divorce! The marriage he had ended was still ruining his life, because he was still letting it. Don't let that be you.

### ▶ SECOND: ACT AS IF:

*Next, make a contract with yourself to treat your former partner with emotional detachment, regardless of your feelings.*

This requires you to do the opposite of what most of us do, which is to act the way we feel. Most mornings, for instance, I don't feel like getting out of bed, and I hit the snooze button a time or three. And when we feel angry, we often blow up at our exes.

But the reverse is also true: we can act ourselves into a way of feeling[14]. Once I get out of bed, I feel like being up (well, usually). Science shows that acting-as-if eventually creates the emotions we're faking[15]. When we act like we're not emotionally engaged with our exes, our feelings tend to follow suit. More immediately, acting-as-if lessens drama for you and your kids, and opens you up to a new and happier life elsewhere.

For instance, let's say your ex criticizes you for putting the children in after-school care, although your ex offloads nearly all childcare to their own parents. You may feel justifiably angry, but save your outrage for a video chat with your friends later; don't show your irritation to your ex. Instead, just as you would redirect an off-topic remark in a business discussion, choose behaviors and words that show self-restraint, distant politeness, and a firm commitment to staying on-topic: "I called to discuss Jimmy's grades, and I'd like to return to that. I'm open to talking about childcare routines at another time, though."

### ▸ THIRD: LIMIT TOPICS AND TONE:

Speaking of Jimmy's exams, it's vital that you engage only on topics that directly relate to your children. The kids' health, grades, educational choices, and the parenting calendar? Check. Your/ex's dating life, your/ex's past mistakes, and attacks on your/ex's character? Nope.

Similarly, if an ex's comment is mean-spirited towards yourself, it's disallowed! *You* never *need to accept rude, unkind, inappropriate, or abusive behavior from your ex again. That is the joy of divorce. Claim it!*

Throughout this book, you'll find Exercises meant to help you apply the concepts so you succeed on every level. I myself am guilty of skipping over these in many books, reading through the whole book first and only later returning to those activities that make sense for me. If that's your preference, I understand; but you'll get more benefit by doing the relevant Exercises at any point, than skipping them altogether.

That said, please take out your downloaded Notebook (available for free from my website at www.LoveFactually.co for you to either print out, or to fill in electronically), or your own journal—and let's get started!

···

# EXERCISE 1: ◖▬▬▷

## *The no-drama deal:*

To become skilled at creating and enforcing boundaries, it is paramount to establish boundaries within yourself. Make an internal deal that you will shut down behavior or speech from your ex that is outside these limits. Put this message to yourself in positive language, such as this script:

> *"I will redirect or end any conversation with my ex unless our discussion is respectful and entirely about things that directly impact our kids."*

Write that script in your Notebook, sign it, and keep it with your phone and/or computer. We are likelier to follow through on commitments we've written out and signed[16].

There's no need to inform your ex of your new standards, especially if that in itself would create drama. He or she will learn your boundaries anyway, because you're going to reward respectful, on-topic conversations by giving them your full attention!

We know from experiments in behaviorism that mammals learn best as a result of rewards following action[17]. For instance, without being told the rules ahead of time, Shamu the whale learns that if he swims to the trainers at the platform, he gets a fish. That makes him likelier to swim to the platform again and again.

Now, you may think your ex is reptilian, but I assure you that they're mammalian like Shamu, and they learn in this very same way. Instead of working for fish, exes fish for attention. Ever notice your ex trying to get into fights with you just to keep a discussion going? That's how powerful attention is: many exes would rather argue with their former mate than have no contact at all.

Turn this to your and your kids' advantage. *Give your ex polite, positive interaction when they're observing your boundaries, and withhold attention when they're breaking them.*

Simply stop or redirect the conversation any time you feel the emotional temperature rising between the two of you, or the topic is out-of-bounds. Be respectful, firm, brief, and clear: "I'm going to hang up now. Let's pick up the talk about Cammie's summer camp when we're both feeling calmer."

Whatever form your interaction is taking, end it when your boundaries are crossed. Don't initiate or return texts or emails until you think calm has returned. You give attention to your ex only when they're abiding by your appropriate, if unspoken, rules!

### ▸ FOURTH: PUT IT IN WRITING:

Increasingly, courts require warring exes to limit their communication to writing[18]. Most people maintain a cooler head and choose more appropriate words when it's documented. Plus, a written record is proof, and courts may wish to monitor who says what, especially if abuse is in the mix.

**Abuse** is any method used to systematically control you—such as weaponizing your kids by making them spy on you, neglecting or hurting the children to punish you, etc. We are going to discuss abusers and how to avoid them in detail in Chapter 4. For now, though, it's important to know that abusers abuse regardless of their (ex-) partner's behavior[19]. Expecting polite, reasonable behavior from an abuser is like going to the hardware store and demanding steak. They don't have it, and insisting will just frustrate and hurt you. You won't be able to politely get them to be reasonable in undocumented talks.

However, studies show that court-imposed consequences do tend to curb abusive behavior[20], and sticking to writing is one way to tacitly remind abusers that all their words are on the record and can bring about those consequences. Additionally, many abusers are lethally dangerous for up to two years after you leave them[21]. So no matter what type of abuse you were subjected to, make the effort never to be in their presence. Apologies to Shamu, but don't try to train the abusive killer whale on the phone or in person—avoid it instead.

The upshot? Refuse to engage except in writing. Never answer the phone, but do save all your ex's voicemails. Keep a record of everything they email and text you, in case it's needed later. If they show up unannounced, call the police, and use your phone to record your ex, preferably from behind a door while you say, "I am recording this[22]."

Writing everything down can be helpful in sticking to kids-only topics even without court orders or abuse in the mix. This letter from Barb exemplifies why:

*"I find a weakness sometimes where I feel obligated to vomit my life on him. I will write an email like we haven't talked in years...and I tell him EVERYTHING.... This has bitten me several times. Then I am beating myself up over it and swear I will never do it again, and then next week, 'Here goes motor mouth'"* ...

*"However, I have figured out a way to control it. I copy my current husband on the conversation, so I can get myself to edit my letter before sending. If it seems inappropriate or not in reference to our child only, I delete it. So by the time the 2-page email is ready to go out, it's only like 5 sentences, sometimes less. We only communicate in writing, so EVERYTHING is documented, with good reason, and face-to-face contact is only if it is unavoidable. And I still have to be so very careful not to fall into his trap of giving up too much ORAL information. Especially when I don't have the time to respond appropriately."*

### ▸ FIFTH: DON'T PICK UP THE ROPE/DO FOSTER GOODWILL:

What's the most recent argument you and your ex had? Chances are, it was like tug-of-war, where one person jerked the rope and the other reacted. In fact, in science we know exactly how this goes, and in this order: the first person criticizes; the other defends themselves; the first person shows contempt for the other; and the other eventually stonewalls, refusing to engage at all[23].

In long-term marriage research, this pattern is the single biggest predictor of divorce[24]. Afterwards, it keeps you stuck holding onto a filthy rope on the muddiest day of the year, with not a hope of winning.

So don't pick up the rope. If you can see through the dynamics and leave that rope lying in the muck, you and your children will be much better off.

In longitudinal science and in case studies, we know that happy couples tend not to construe their relationship as a power struggle[25]. By being consistently kind and understanding and treating one another as they would a cherished friend, they create goodwill that sustains them during arguments and makes it likelier that they will make some headway on their issues[26]. Their relationships don't feel like a tug-of-war, but a team[27].

Unless you have sole custody, you and your ex are still on Team Parenthood. *Fortunately, barring an abusive ex, it takes only one person to start growing* **goodwill** [28]. In my observation, post-divorce goodwill extends to being as polite, respectful, and open to your ex's wishes as you can be, all of the time—only picking up the rope when your ex breaches a firm boundary.

For instance, when our child was little, I said yes to my ex anytime I could safely do so about parenting matters. He worried that I would shut him out of our child's life, so I went out of my way to include my former spouse. He and our son had time together at my house, and my ex received invitations to every possible event our child was involved in, offers from me to drive our son to meet him at restaurants and parks, offers to deliver and stay with our child at his parents' home in another state, invitations to all family holidays, etc. When Vic and I married, Vic welcomed my ex to our home at least two full evenings every week; sometimes, my ex stayed at our home overnight so he could have breakfast with our son and walk him to school the next day.

But when my ex wanted to drive our kiddo around, travel alone with him, or keep him overnight where I couldn't monitor medical care, that desire threatened a firm boundary of mine. His possible insobriety plus our child's certain medical needs equaled a risk I was unwilling to take. The law didn't support me on that, by the way; my ex could have shown the custody agreement to police officers to enforce on the spot. But he didn't, and I think it was at least partly because of our basic goodwill towards each other.

Goodwill between non-abusive people tends to breed further goodwill[29]. My ex said yes to me whenever possible, too, from small matters to large. Our decree stated that both of us had to continue living in the same county where we'd divorced, until our child reached the end of high school. When Vic and I got engaged, my ex allowed me to move to another county to live with my new husband. And my ex moved there, too—renting an apartment on the edge of our neighborhood so he could be as available to and involved with our child as possible. Vic is amazing for having welcomed my ex into our home; and my ex also deserves credit for coming over, even though seeing his former wife happily wed to another man, a man who spent a lot more time near his son than he got to, might not have been the easiest thing in the world.

Just as I had uncrossable boundaries, so did my ex. When I crossed a major boundary of his by suing for full custody, he said no, and won.

Which brings me to another point: *custody issues are the most frequent reason ex-couples return to court*[30]. Remember Amy, whose ex objected when she slept in a tent with her then-fiancé and her kids? Many single parents have echoed her sentiment that "Our court system is very broken. Not picking up the rope is critical. Like you said, you can only control your responses, and don't think the court has your back, either!"

You can save big money and heartache by being respectful, yes-oriented, and drawing boundaries only where you must, because that may help you avoid legal battles. You don't want your and your kids' fate to hang on the decisions of strangers if you can get what you need for free simply by using diplomacy!

True, these five steps require you to gain perspective and to exercise a high level of self-control. But those two qualities are generally needed for a happy, successful life with your someday-partner anyway. Plus, it's good modeling for your kids, who will one day need their own roadmap to a satisfying relationship.

The more you can follow these steps, the better your parenting relationship will be, and the better your children and you will feel. *Yet you don't have to be perfect.* Think of it like a batting average, where you try to hit a home run every time, but usually don't. Thankfully, good enough really is good enough.

...

# *EXERCISE 2:* ▭▬▬▶

## *The camping tent:*

Imagine that your ex, like Amy's, has just angrily voiced their view of your sleeping arrangement in the tent. What diplomatic response could you make, one that would avoid picking up the rope, use detached behavior, and focus only on the direct, best interests of the children? Take a moment to consider your answers; write them in your Notebook, and then I'll provide some possibilities.

........................................

## Ready? Here are some recommendations.

▸ **FIRST:** do not take the oh-so-tempting bait and point out your ex's hypocrisy—in Amy's case, that he himself had a series of girlfriends sleeping over when his and Amy's kids were also staying there. That's a guaranteed fight, no matter how right you are. Pick a mantra and repeat it to yourself: "I can be right or happy, and I choose happy," "Put down the rope, pick up peace," or, simply, "Detach."

▸ **SECOND:** if the ex's complaint or criticism is in writing, save it but don't reply. Give your ex attention solely when they approach with something that is directly about the children.

▸ **THIRD:** if the ex's remarks are in person or on the phone, firmly but politely redirect to the topic at hand: "Let's get back to discussing what time I'm picking the kids up for the weekend."

▸ **FOURTH:** it's likely that the first few times you redirect an inter-action like this, your ex won't give up easily. So you'll need to have contingencies in mind:

· If your ex insists on bringing the topic back to your time in the tent with your new partner, say, "We probably aren't going to agree about this. Let's get back to discussing what time I'm picking the kids up for the weekend."

· If your ex persists or becomes disrespectful, you can say, "I'm going to hang up (or leave) now. Let's discuss pick-up times when we're calmer." Then, hang up (or leave). Give your ex more at-tention solely when he or she approaches with something that is directly about the children.

▸ **FIFTH:** let's say your ex tries to reframe your dating arrangement as being about the kids' interests. Unless you are endangering your children, your dating life is legally and in all other regards no longer your ex's business. And you are moving this relationship towards a more detached, businesslike relationship, whether or not your ex agrees. Don't tell them that; just know it within yourself.

▸ **FINALLY:** what you write or say aloud to the ex needs to re-establish your boundaries in a firm and polite way:

> *"Our children will learn from each of us. We may not always see things the same way, but we are both good parents who love our kids. Let's get back to the topic at hand. What time works for me to pick up the kids this weekend?"*

...

# *EXERCISE 3:* ✏️
## *The go-to argument:*

Every couple, whether together or apart, has hot-button issues. Please take a moment to think of a recurring argument between you and your ex. Write your responses to the following in your Notebook or journal. What's your usual reaction? What's the result? Knowing what you know now, what could you do instead to stick to kid-centric topics in a respectful, detached way while holding onto your firm boundaries?

## KEEP YOUR KIDS OUT OF THE MIDDLE

It's no accident that this chapter's first example involves former mates arguing about one another's new partners. When I was planning this book, about two-thirds of my survey's respondents said they wanted more information on this specific issue. A second major area of interest for respondents was keeping the former couple's kids from being in the middle of parental disagreements.

We've already done an Exercise about handling your ex's direct questions and criticisms. But sometimes, the questions are indirect—as in, your ex asking the kids about your love life.

It's only natural for a parent to be curious about someone their child might be spending a lot of time around. It's also normal for parents to ask children what went on anytime they're away from their kids— whether at the end of the school day, or after a weekend or holiday where the child was with the other parent. And all good parents want to know that their children are safe. It can be nerve-wracking to wonder about the ex's new partner, knowing you have no say in whether they're a good person for your kids to spend time with.

As a single mom in her 30s wrote," What questions are okay to ask your children about who the other parent is dating? My favorite to ask my kids is: 'Is she kind to you when you're alone together?'"

Folks, that's just about the only question I can think of that is appropriate to ask your children about the other parent's romantic relationships. Otherwise, although it's natural to wonder, don't ask the kids. Put their well-being above your curiosity, and keep your questions to yourself. Kids need to not be asked to spy or carry messages; being in the middle is stressful and that stress is harmful to them[31].

I'm so serious about this, I'd recommend hiring a private detective to investigate your ex's new partner before I'd recommend quizzing the kids. Google is our friend. Police reports are our friend. *There are predators in the world, and if you believe your ex could be dating one, investigate. Just don't do it through your children.*

What if it's your ex putting the kids on the spot about your dates, though? Avoid discussing your ex's questions with the kids. If they're very young and lack deception skills, your children might innocently say something like, "Mommy wants to know how many women spend the night here with us."

In that event, tell your child,

*"That's something parents talk about. Your mom and I will discuss it."*

And change the subject.

And, tempting as it is—and I do know how tempting it is!—don't pry to see what your ex has been asking. Instead, mustering all your politeness and detachment, you might email something like the following script:

*"You've probably heard that I'm dating. Nobody can take your place in the kids' lives, and I speak well of you to them. I'm being careful not to ask the kids about your dating life, and I wondered if we could both agree on that as a family policy, so the kids aren't in the middle."*

As we'll see in Chapter 9, non-abusive people are more able to respond positively to polite, respectful, non-accusatory, reasonable requests that indicate faith in their goodness, than to direct or implied attacks[32]. This script is polite and detached, which keeps you from getting sucked into drama, and it's healthy for your family too. All our children need to see what self-control, respectful behavior, and good boundaries look like, and that's doubly true if the other parent behaves inappropriately. Your adult example is a huge gift, and will serve them well later in their own adult relationships[33].

More generally, your children are statistically likely to be healthier, happier, and do better in school and with their friendships if you can reduce their stress by keeping them from dealing with tensions between you and your ex, whether the issue is about dating, exchanging the kids, skipping important activities, religious differences, trash-talking, or anything else[34].

For instance, Tim, a single dad in his 50s who was raised by a single mom, faced a common problem:

> *"My ex kept trash-talking me continuously with our kids, to the point that one of my daughters got so furious with me about everything that she refused to talk to me for months and would skip much of my visitation time with her. I refused to engage in the same kind of behavior because I thought it was destructive. It's also one of the things that I most respected about my single mom, who refused to throw my dad under the bus even though an objective observer might think it justified. It did eventually resolve itself years later as my daughter started to see through it. But I really don't think I handled it that well and I think suggestions in this area would be helpful."*

I don't have any suggestions for Tim for a simple reason: I think he did a great job. He didn't have the option to change his ex or her behavior, but he did have the choice not to worsen the situation by behaving the same way. One of the hardest life lessons for me has been that we cannot raise another adult. They've already been raised, and if they're set on doing destructive things, we can't control them.

We can, however, raise our children to be kind and respectful, and in that process keep from increasing the damage. Trash-talking the ex in front of the kids is harmful for many reasons[35], including that

*Chapter 1: Put The Past—And Your Ex—Behind You* · 45

the child is half-them and by extension may also feel worthless. Kids feel they're at war with themselves when they are directly or indirectly called to side with one parent over the other[36]. And as Tim found, kids may eventually learn the truth and resent the parent who disrupted the ex's relationship with them.

Tim didn't pick up the rope. He was supremely adult: self-controlled and loving even when it hurt. I don't know whether he sought counseling for his daughter, or whether his ex would have allowed it if he had; giving a child a safe space to talk to a therapist can be helpful. But he gave his daughter the gift of not having to take sides, and of not having to defend her mom or the half of herself that comes from her. I applaud him.

...

# EXERCISE 4: ▱➤

## The respectful request:

What if Tim had chosen to say something to his ex? Given what you now know, what do you think is a healthy response? I'll include a possible answer just below, but please take a moment to think about it first, and record your ideas in your journal or Notebook.

...........................................................

### HERE ARE MY THOUGHTS:

Tim could have written to his ex and said something like,

*"I respect you and the job you're doing with parenting our daughter. Sometimes you and I disagree, but I want you to know that even if we parent differently sometimes, I speak well of you in front of our child,*

*and I am hoping we can both agree to say only good things about the other, for her benefit. Thank you if you're willing to do this."*

Like an earlier example, this speech avoids making accusations, and keeps the tone and request polite, reasonable, detached, and respectful. It also gives his ex the chance to soften up, by avoiding commands and by including praise[37]. Tim's ex may have continued with the trash-talking even with this message, but it's worth a shot, don't you think?

...

# *EXERCISE 5:*

## *The kids as messengers:*

Let's say that your ex is sending messages to you through the kids, rather than speaking with you directly. This is classic putting-kids-in-the-middle, and very stressful for children. Given the information you have now, what do you think is a healthy response? Please write your answers in your Notebook or journal, and then I'll share mine.

### HERE'S MY IDEA:

One possibility is a written note from you to your ex that says something like:

*"André asked me if you can have him at Spring Break. I'm open to discussing it. I want to ask you a favor, though. I'm trying to make all my requests directly to you, so he has less to remember. I respect you and your parenting, and I'd like us to agree to write to one another directly, rather than asking any of the kids to make requests for us. What do you think?"*

You might not get what you want. Not every polite, reasonable, respectful, and detached request will be met with similar adult behavior from the other parent. But you will have avoided making things worse, and will have said what you could.

Unfortunately, sometimes it's not only your ex who may put the kids in the middle, but the extended family and maybe your ex's new partner. As Hannah remembers from her childhood following her parents' divorce,

> *"At my father's house, I wasn't allowed to have photos up of my mother, or even mention her name. My stepmom involved herself by saying ugly things about my mom, and that damaged our relationship permanently. I have also seen friends and family members involve their children in their negative feelings about their other parent, and that is awful."*

It is. Again, we can't raise other adults or make them do what we want. But we can reduce the damage, build some goodwill, show our kids a healthy example, and exhibit self-respect by behaving in a controlled, polite, and detached way.

• • •

# *EXERCISE 6:* ✏️

## *Frontiers of diplomacy: Your ex's new partner:*

It's tempting to advise Hannah on what she could have said to her dad and stepmom, but she was a child and needed the adults to step up for her. And unless Hannah's mom has a close relationship with her stepmom (unlikely, per Hannah's description), there's really no way for the mom to talk to or about her: the dad is likely to dig in and become harder in his position if he feels that his new wife is under attack. Given all this, what do you think Hannah's mother could have said to Hannah's father? Please take a moment to record your own answer in your Notebook or journal before reading my suggestion.

...................................................

## My thoughts:

Hannah's mom could have written something like this to her dad:

> "Hannah has asked to keep photos of you in her room here, and I agreed and she now has a few. I know things have been rocky between you and me for a long time, but I respect your parenting and want her to have a good relationship with you, which includes being free to love and mention you when she is at my house. I think Hannah wants to keep some pictures of me at your house, too. Of course, that's your call. Just thought I'd mention it, in case you're open to it. Jennifer might rather not see my photos, and I understand that."

In this example, the mom is giving the dad a chance to reevaluate his position, and to have a talk of his own with his new wife. Hannah's mom's message is self-controlled, respectful, polite, detached, and non-accusatory, keeping the focus on Hannah's needs. She is giving Hannah's dad the benefit of the doubt, regardless of what she might know to the contrary, allowing him to save face and rise to his best self if he so chooses. She's reminding him of their shared business of raising a healthy, happy, loving child, and she's avoiding forceful language—a real plus, since demands tend to produce a reassertion of freedom called reactance, the exact opposite of what we want[38]. She's also avoiding critical statements about Jennifer the stepmom, which could be highly triggering and result in the dad closing down rather than opening up. Acknowledging Jennifer's position is likely to have the ironic effect of softening the dad's stance[39].

As a longtime school counselor told me, "Kids need their divorced parents to love them more than they hate each other." Yes. It's not easy; little about parenthood or divorce or repartnering is. But your kids and your future are counting on it.

## Set Boundaries Around Your Ex's Bad Behavior

Sometimes, the limit you need isn't so much about the kids being put in the middle, as about your ex's inappropriate behavior towards them or you. I'm not talking about abuse—which needs to be reported to authorities, and for which your children and you need counseling. Instead, I'm talking about things your ex might be doing, whether consciously or not, that are hurtful to the children's and/or your feelings, and that disrupt your ability to provide a healthy and regulated family life.

...

## *EXERCISE 7:* ✏️

### *The late pick-up:*

For instance, Brent was justifiably upset at his ex for repeatedly failing to pick up the kids for her time with them. She would often show up very late, or not at all, and then expect Brent to deal with the fallout. This inconvenienced and angered him, and it harmed the children's trust in their mother's word and love, and hence their worthiness.

If you were in Brent's shoes—and given how common this scenario is, you may have been—what do you think would be the most effective thing to say to the ex about late/non-pickups? Refer to the communication strategies at the beginning of this chapter if you like, and write out your response. I'll follow with an option.

...................................................................................

## HERE ARE SOME POSSIBILITIES:

Brent could say or email something like,

> *"You are the most important woman in our children's lives, and they are hurting because they wanted to see you this afternoon. I am respectfully requesting that we return to letting the kids know at least a day before-hand if a pickup is going to be late or can't happen. This gives them a chance to plan something else and avoid disappointment at not getting to be with you. What do you think?"*

As with other examples in this chapter, this message focuses on the kids' needs rather than the angered person's feelings or the ex's character flaws. It's polite, clear, respectful, reminds the ex of how important she is to the children, and avoids a commanding tone.

But what about boundaries? The fact is, the single best indicator of what anyone is likely to do is what they have already done in a similar circumstance; it's one of very few laws in psychology[40]. And the more often and more recently they've transgressed, the more likely they are to repeat their bad behavior. Meaning, Brent should start with a note like the one above—and then, be prepared with a boundary to back it up.

*Let's continue this Exercise. What do you think would be some reasonable boundaries Brent could set? Take a moment to record them in your Notebook.*

Here are some I can think of. Without threatening or warning his ex, which likely would trigger negative intimacy, Brent could:

- Take the kids out to do something once 45 minutes have passed since pickup time.

- Let the kids go to a friend's or to an activity once the 45 minutes have passed.

- Allow the kids to take a weekend trip to Grandma's once the 45 minutes have passed.

If your ex shows up later or calls, don't answer the door and don't pick up the phone. Be somewhere else, the first time or two. You may receive an angry message. You can then email later on that evening with something like this script:

> *"I waited for 45 minutes and it didn't seem like you were coming, so I took the kids to another activity. If you can let me know if you'll be more than a few minutes late, that will help with planning."*

Regardless of their response, leave it at that.

Don't shame, lecture, or argue. This is part of having a businesslike and detached relationship with your ex: you set reasonable and firm boundaries when needed, and you don't explain, warn, or beg. You probably won't need to say this very often before your ex figures out that if they want time with your child, they need to be reasonably on-time.

...

# EXERCISE 8: ✏️

## Bogus call to Child Protective Services:

Other times, your ex may behave outrageously in a manner that targets you. A common, egregious example: when exes call CPS regarding a former spouse who is in fact parenting the children effectively. That's what happened to Caroline, who wrote me about it:

> "My ex was an alcoholic and when I began dating after the divorce, he had a conniption fit and got drunk and called Child Protective Services to charge me with child abuse. Imagine my surprise when the guy at the door was not pizza delivery, but the CPS case worker."

Admittedly, this is a very tough situation, almost guaranteed to make any parent lose their cool. But that is the ex's goal: to draw you back into negative intimacy, dashing the businesslike relationship you've worked to create.

Using the tools in this chapter, what would you advise Caroline to say to her ex? How can she act rather than react--handling this situation so that the businesslike relationship will be maintained, and she isn't sucked into his drama? I'll share Caroline's brilliant solution after you've had a moment to record your answers.

Caroline's response:

> "I did not call my ex and yell at him for bringing a false charge. I mastered myself and when my ex eventually sobered up and called me, I was calm and polite and said, 'Oh, by the way, CPS was here last night.' And then the phone got real quiet. He admitted he had called them, and I said, 'Oh, well, that's a relief, I couldn't imagine who had done it.'

*"The charges were all dropped because CPS said it was clearly a false call. But I promise you, if I had had a fit or shown I was upset, my ex would have called CPS anytime he felt like it. He has never called them again. We get along well, because I don't pick up the rope or get over-heated about things, and now he's trained not to even head in that direction.*

*"So you can see why I'm not thrilled when men tell me they cannot find a way to tolerate their ex. If I could do it with an alcoholic who called CPS, I figure it is possible for these guys, too. I have told a couple of them I thought so, and they seemed to think about it."*

Good point. Everyone in this chapter has an ex who could hamper our search for love—yet most of us found a great partner, or are on the way.

Amy, whose ex was furious when she and her then-fiancé Paul slept in a camping tent together with Amy's kids, is strong proof of that. Despite her hard history with her ex, she set boundaries, avoided negative intimacy, and their relationship is now calmer and more productive.

Yet enforcing boundaries is only part of leaving your pain and your ex behind. To create a wonderful future with a new partner, you'll need to forgive at least two people, too. Let's get to that and more on loving yourself in Chapter 2.

# CHAPTER 2:

# Forgive Your Ex And Yourself

You've heard it before: to love someone else, we must first love ourselves. But is it true?

Much of our self-love is related to our upbringing[1]; the voices we have internalized were typically installed at or near the parental factory, in the form of parents and peers. Those who experienced kindness and reliable, predictable, consistent care have an easier time loving ourselves and returning the love of others[2]. Modeling matters. In this sense, the old adage is true: people who love themselves generally have more emotional bandwidth to devote to loving others, and less fear blocking that love; and they usually have more success in their relationships as a result[3].

Yet exceptions abound. Can you think of friends with crushingly low self-worth who are nonetheless loving towards others? In my observation, those with little self-love often know how to give it; they just have a hard time accepting it or believing they deserve it[4].

Which brings us to another adage supported by science: we tend to get the love we believe we deserve[5]. In my work with clients, this is spot-on. How many of us have known, or been, a good person who settles for bad treatment? Loving ourselves is crucial to believing we're worthy of a partner who adores rather than hurts us, nurturing faith that those people exist—and holding out for them[6].

Plus, life is a lot more rewarding when we enjoy the one person we're always with.

The trouble is, even if you had the ideal upbringing in a community that treasured you, divorce can be hard on your feelings of basic worthiness. As I said in the introduction, leaving my ex was the lowest point of my life, bar none. Before, my identity and much of my self-worth were tied up in loving him, loving our intact family, feeling rooted in my successful work life, and building a shared home and community. I already knew much of the research on what divorce does to children, and I felt like a supreme failure for not being able to give my child a life with both parents in one house. I overheard members of my extended family speaking of me as a loser when it came to men—and I agreed with them. At several points over the next two years, I felt suicidal. In the 20/20 hindsight of this life I am now grateful for, this seems melodramatic—but at the time, I couldn't see my future, and my present was miserable[7].

My self-love was definitely underwater.

Yet knowing you need to love yourself more does nothing for you if you're struggling with that; it's like giving a depressed person a symptoms checklist and thinking they'll recover. Insight alone is not enough. *We don't need to know we're distressed, nor even why, so much as how to heal.*

The good news is, healing really is possible, a scientifically verified phenomenon[8]. I've done it, and I've seen many others do it, too.

And a first step, counterintuitive as it may seem, is to forgive your ex.

# FORGIVE YOUR EX & FORGE YOUR FUTURE

I wanted to begin this book with forgiveness, but then I remembered how much emotional turmoil I was in when I left my ex. Forgive?! Not likely! The first things I needed were the Chapter 1 boundaries that put my intimacy with him in the past, pronto.

But eventually, forgiving my ex became absolutely necessary. Remember Amy, whose story opened the first chapter? When I asked about her path to forgiving her ex, she said:

> *"I needed to forgive him for cheating on me, and for choosing the other woman over me in the end. This was a very tough journey. It did not happen immediately. In the beginning, I did not think it was ever remotely possible to be where I am today. I do think I have mostly forgiven him. I am actually not sure forgiveness is really a destination but think it could be more like grief. It comes and goes in waves. Over time, I have gotten very close to 100% forgiveness. Sometimes, I am not certain 100% forgiveness is truly possible. Other times, I think I am there. I guess I need to forgive him most of all for how his behaviors have and will continue to affect our children. I still have a lot of forgiving to do. I'm trying. Sometimes."*

Amy's wisdom and experiences are powerful. And science shows that the struggle to forgive is worth it[9]. In the Stanford Forgiveness Project, people who attended an in-depth forgiveness workshop were later compared to a similar group that didn't get the classes. Forgiving literally caused the attendees to become happier, less stressed, less angry, more optimistic, and physically healthier. That's a lot of benefit from a nine-hour program! This was an experiment and, as you may recall from your own science classes, experiments show cause-effect. So, forgiveness wasn't merely associated with these positive outcomes; forgiveness caused these benefits[10].

The upshot? If you're going to have a happy relationship with yourself and a new partner in the future, it's helpful to forgive those who have hurt you[11]—especially your ex.

Yet why do so many of us resist it? I believe that's for three reasons: not knowing what forgiveness isn't, not realizing what it is, and not knowing how to do it.

## ▶ WHAT FORGIVENESS ISN'T:

In my long teaching career, I regularly asked college students to brainstorm why they might not have forgiven someone who hurt them. Nearly every semester, the class list looked like this:

- Forgiving means saying, "It's no big deal," but it was a big deal to me.

- Forgiving condones and excuses the wrongdoer's actions; it lets them off too easy.

- Forgiving opens the door to them doing the same thing to me again.

- Forgiving means I have to let the person who hurt me come back into my life.

- If I forgive them, I have to tell them so, and that leaves me too vulnerable.

- I want the other person to suffer for what they did, and if I forgive them, they get a good life while I'm still hurting; it's not fair.

- The person who hurt me doesn't deserve forgiveness; what they did is unforgivable[12].

*How many of these common ideas are right? None of them!*

## ▸ WHAT FORGIVENESS IS:

Now that we've seen what forgiveness isn't, let's see what science says it is. Please keep in mind that I'm coming at this from the perspective of research, not religion. It might not align with your religious tradition, if you have one. But it works[13].

...

# *EXERCISE 1:* ▭▭▭▶
## *Barriers to forgiveness:*

Let's begin with an activity my students did. Envision someone who has hurt you deeply. In the context of this book, it could be your ex, but it could also be someone else. Chances are, it's someone who was or is in your inner circle; other people don't occupy so much of our headspace. If you haven't forgiven them, what are your reasons? Please write them out in your Notebook or journal. Do yours differ from the ones my students gave?

Whatever this person did to hurt you is a big deal. Needing to contemplate whether to forgive someone means that whatever happened was a real betrayal[14]. And you're not being asked to excuse or condone this other person's actions, tell them you forgave them, or let them back into your life. Their behavior may have been inexcusable, and it would be foolhardy of you not to protect yourself. But refusing to forgive because it lets the offender off too easily reminds me of that famous quote about drinking poison in the hopes that the other person will die[15]: holding a grudge hurts you, not them. And while you may be right that this person does not deserve your forgiveness, here's the big secret:

*Forgiving isn't about them and their well-being. It's about you and yours!*

Simply put, *forgiveness is letting go of anger and the desire for revenge. It's a gift we give ourselves, regardless of whether the other person deserves or even knows about our forgiveness.*

That's it. It's about you—not your ex. It's about your feelings—not theirs. It's for your benefit—whether or not it helps others.

**Your ex may not deserve your forgiveness, but you deserve freedom.** You have lived with this pain for months, years, or decades. How much more of your time and emotional space does your ex get? Let it go. Live and love again. Here's how.


▶ **HOW TO FORGIVE:**

Here are the tasks needed for successful forgiveness[16], distilled into five steps:

## FIRST: FEEL WHAT YOU FEEL.

Sometimes my students said, "I haven't forgiven because I'm justifiably angry and I want to get back at them." In other words, they're just not ready. Anger and pain and wanting to lash out (which is different from actually doing it) are part of the deal, at first.

If betrayal is fresh, you can't force yourself to let go of anger and a powerful desire to get even. If you do, all you'll get is denial with a prettier label[17]. For instance, affairs are a common betrayal[18], and her ex's affair was the first thing Amy mentioned when telling me what was hard for her to forgive—so hard, she didn't know whether it was possible. And at first, I blamed my ex for ruining my life with his addictions. After all, from my viewpoint, his behavior had cost me nearly everything. It's not hard to see why I might have resisted forgiving for a while.

No matter what your ex did that hurt you, as we've learned, it takes about 18 months before most divorced partners can experience any level of communication from their ex without sparking bad feelings and possibly-unhelpful coping mechanisms[19]. So if you haven't had time to process what happened, go ahead and feel what you feel, keep it businesslike to the extent that you must interact, and forgive your ex...later.

•••

# *EXERCISE 2:* ▣▭▭▭▷
## *Feelings about your ex:*

In your journal or Notebook, please take a few minutes to write down what your ex did that wronged you. Be specific. Pick at least one or two especially hurtful examples where forgiveness would be a real challenge. What happened? How did/do you feel? Write it all out. We will build on this later.

How long ago were these events? As we learned in Chapter 1, acting as if we're detached eventually creates feelings of detachment. If you still feel hot under the collar when you recall your ex's more hurtful actions, and it's been less than 18 months since the separation or divorce, you might need to keep letting time pass and continue faking it 'til you make it, rather than moving to forgiveness quite yet.

## SECOND: SET BOUNDARIES.

Setting boundaries is an important part of forgiving. Otherwise, you're going to spend a lot of time dealing with fresh opportunities to forgive your ex, because chances are high that they'll do it again, whatever "it" is. The first chapter is all about how to set these boundaries so they hold.

*That said, here are a couple of important ideas to help you fortify these fences.*

You know the saying, "Forgive and forget?" Well, forget about forgetting; you need that long memory to protect you from repetitions of behaviors that injured you or your children. I no longer hold grudges against my ex, and I genuinely wish him well and happy; but forgetting his addictions and some of the resulting behavior could have led me to drop important safety boundaries regarding our child.

Forgiveness and reconciliation aren't the same thing, either. At some point, many of us yearn for the parts of our former partnership that were good, and/or our ex asks us to rekindle the relationship, claiming the past is in the past and the future will be different (see "long memory," above). It happened to me, and I often hear from people who are wondering whether they should reconcile now that they've forgiven their ex. Amy helped herself when she let go of her bitterness about her ex choosing his affair partner over her, but it would not have served her to return and let him do it again. *Remember: the best clue we have about what people will do is what they did before in similar circumstances[20]!*

## THIRD: PRACTICE EMPATHY.

When I first read about this step, I felt resentful and resistant to it. I thought this would be nearly impossible, and vastly unfair to me. See things through my ex's eyes?! Why?

Raise your hand if you relate.

*Yet science shows us that there is no forgiveness without empathy[21].* In order to free yourself, you must see things from your ex's point of view. *There is no way around this step.*

Take Tim, the man we met in Chapter 1 whose ex alienated his daughter from him. Let's say he decided to forgive his ex-wife. He'd have to practice taking her possible point of view. Maybe he'd think,

> *"Natalie's parents divorced when she was a child, too, and her mom trash-talked her dad. This was her model for being divorced, and maybe she hasn't been able to see past that. Her dad really was awful. I don't think I'm such a bad guy, but from Natalie's standpoint, maybe she feels like she's protecting our daughter by steeling her against being vulnerable to me. Maybe she believes she's saving our child pain."*

This doesn't excuse, condone, negate, or make him forget what Natalie did. Nothing short of brain injury can or should do that. And it doesn't mean he agrees with his ex's behavior, or even with her possible interpretation of it. Also, please note that absolute accuracy is not the aim; it's not Tim's job to make certain he's correct in every detail of his ex's views, but to make conjectures that help him to reach empathy.

In my own forgiveness process, I had to empathize with my ex's struggles around addictions. For him, giving up alcohol and drugs could be as frightening as my thought of giving up food; there are levels of addiction that are that deep, and that compelling. I had to envision how terrifying it would be to live without things I was absolutely reliant on, and how painful it would be to face a year or more of what would feel like the worst hangover in the world. I've occasionally had headaches that lasted for days, and I might have taken anything to stop the pain if ibuprofen hadn't worked. What would it be like to know there was something that would alleviate my suffering, and to force myself to live in agony by abstaining—not for a few hours or days, but for many months?

···

# EXERCISE 3: ▭▬▶
## Your ex's vantage point:

Please refer to what you wrote down in this chapter's first Exercise, "Feelings about your ex." Now, in the relevant Notebook space, add what you think the event(s) looked like from your ex's point of view. (Another way to handle this is to speak aloud, from their perspective.) Remember, you don't need to excuse, condone, or agree with their viewpoint. But you do need to acknowledge and fully envision it.

Having done this, how do you feel? My guess is, there's some relief there—because over the years of doing this Exercise myself, and of witnessing others do it, most of us reach a conclusion that is vastly helpful:

*The other person's actions hurt us, but they weren't about us. It wasn't personal! Their actions were about them. This insight helps us to let go.*

Natalie's trash-talking had negative effects on Tim's life, but it was about her life and concerns, not about Tim. My ex's addictions hurt me and our child, but they were about him. And even if you were with an abuser, odds are high that although the abuse affected you, it wasn't about you; this person would have abused anyone they were intimately involved with[22]!

Envisioning Natalie's viewpoint will pave Tim's path to forgiveness. Empathy towards my ex was my hard-won ticket to liberation. And seeing your ex's perspective is your get-out-of-jail pass, too.

## FOURTH: WRITE IT DOWN.

I never shared my thoughts with my ex; he might have seen them as condescending rather than empathic. Silent forgiveness, where you forgive without telling the other person, is a thing[23]; my guess is that unless the other party asks your forgiveness, it usually creates less drama to forgive without announcing it.

But I did write my thoughts and feelings in my journal, and I discussed them with friends and a therapist. Turns out, processing your thoughts, especially in writing, is helpful[24].

Here's one science-backed formula for putting the events in words so you can let go and forgive[25]. It involves four Exercises, but don't worry. You've basically done two of them already!

•••

# EXERCISE 4: ▱▬▬▷
## *A portrait of your pain:*

First off, write down that you are in pain, and specify what you're in pain about. Does that sound familiar? Yes, it's what you did above in the Exercise titled "Feelings about your ex." You can drop that language right into your Notebook again, here.

•••

# EXERCISE 5: ▱▬▬▷
## *Your ex's perspective:*

Next, jot down how your ex might see each of their actions you listed. This probably also sounds familiar; it's what you did above in the Exercise titled, "Your ex's vantage point." You can enter that language into your Notebook again at this point. *Even if you're reading most of the Exercises rather than doing them, please don't skip this step! This is the part where we see that our ex's bad behavior isn't really about us—and that's hugely helpful in regaining emotional freedom.*

...

# *EXERCISE 6:* ◰▬▬▷
## *Your fences:*

In Chapter 1, we worked on setting boundaries. Now, in the context of forgiveness, it's time to specifically write down what you will and will not tolerate, and how you'll respond. At this point, you probably know which limits your ex is likely to ignore, so as you write down the lines you're drawing in the sand, also please describe what specific action you will take if your ex breaches these boundaries anyway.

For example, Amy's boundaries included committing to getting off the phone immediately if or when her ex became verbally abusive. She forgave, but that didn't mean she compromised her dignity or let him mistreat her again.

Please refer to Chapter 1 if you need help with this Exercise.

...

# *EXERCISE 7:* ◰▬▬▷
## *Your forgiveness list:*

What, specifically, are you forgiving your ex for? The final task in writing it all down is to list the wrongs—and let them go.

For example, Amy could write:

> *"I forgive my ex for being verbally abusive towards me; for putting our kids in the middle by having them report to him about my life with Paul; for being a hypocrite by having multiple women spend the night,*

*yet calling me out for sharing a tent with my then-fiancé; and for leaving me for another woman. I relinquish my anger and desire for revenge towards him, so I can have a happy life."*

You will have your own facts and details. And if you find it helpful to burn a copy of your forgiveness list in the fireplace or bury it in the yard, go for it! The essential thing is to commit, at the end of the list, to something like this: "I relinquish my anger and desire for revenge towards my ex, so I can have a happy life."

### FIFTH: BE PERSISTENT.

Remember Amy's brilliant quote, where she said forgiveness is like waves, coming and going, rather than being a firm destination? She's not wrong!

Forgiveness is not achieved in a flash of insight, but gradually. The greater the betrayal, the truer that is. And sometimes hurt and anger will rear their snakey heads, Medusa-like, just when you thought this was done.

Additionally, Amy was right when she said, "I guess I need to forgive him most of all for how his behaviors have and will continue to affect our children." The ex we're co-parenting with is still in our lives in a very important realm. What are the odds that nothing new will emerge for us to move past?

So, forgiving your ex may represent more of a journey than a destination with a fixed endpoint. But it's a worthwhile trip to becoming fulfilled, happy, and whole. Persist!

# FORGIVE YOURSELF

I ended Chapter 1 by saying there were at least two people to forgive in order to move forward with your life and love. The first is your ex.

The second is yourself.

Single parents routinely contend with thorny issues such as feeling guilt for their divorce or separation; being less available to the kids because of now needing to work at two jobs; being too busy to attend the school play; being too tired to show joy or to have fun with the children; being short-tempered due to stress; not being able to put the kids in sports or other activities, due to limited time and money; taking time away from the children so the parent can date; involving the kids too much in their dating lives; and getting into new relationships that don't work out.

*Divorce frequently puts us in painful circumstances that we blame not only on our exes, but on ourselves.* For instance, I blamed myself for the following—and this is just a partial list!:

- choosing a mate with serious, lifelong addictions

- deciding to bring a baby into a situation that was dangerous

- giving my baby a life-threatening and chronic health condition

- depriving my child of an intact family

- losing not just my job, but my entire academic career

- losing at love (again!)

- having a bad filter when it came to picking men

- failing to protect my child from solo-custody weekends with his father when he was very young

- introducing him to men I didn't wind up with

Even as I write this, I see how unrealistic large parts of this list are. For instance, I did not knowingly choose a partner who was so ill. I did not knowingly bring a baby into a dangerous situation; the ongoing nature of the addictions became apparent only after he was born. I needed to leave in order to protect my baby, and I didn't have the freedom to live away from extended family in order to prioritize my career. It took me a while to set boundaries around ways my child could spend time safely with his dad. And my son's medical condition is genetic, so it's ridiculous to consider that as something I willingly "gave" him. Plus, my filter wasn't "bad"—my child's dad has abundant wonderful qualities and just one (really big, dealbreaking) aspect.

*The things we need to forgive ourselves for don't have to make sense! But they have power to the extent that we haven't acknowledged them.* Writing a list like this can help you to see clearly whether you're berating yourself for things that aren't plausible, so you can release their tyrannical hold.

At the same time, some of my list items were more realistic. I had a long history of choosing unwisely when it came to men—overlooking red banners (nevermind flags) because I wanted things to work out. I introduced my child to some men that, in hindsight, weren't important enough to our futures for the introduction to make sense.

My mistakes motivated me to continue learning the science of finding and keeping strong relationships, which ultimately led to my happy remarriage, blog, client practice, and books. I'll bet you know many people whose struggles turned into stepping stones to better-than-before. If you need to, borrow my faith that your hard time can become a catalyst for a life you will cherish—because it really can.

Like writing or doing math, love and parenting take practice, and we can get better at them—especially if we are kind to ourselves in the process. We need to embrace a growth mindset when it comes to love, just like we do other things[26]. Don't berate yourself for not being perfect; draw encouragement from getting better, and keep going! Making the list below can help you to see where you can improve, in addition to what to release.

...

# EXERCISE 8: ◖▤▤▤▷
## *Self-forgiveness fill-in-the-blank:*

Please take out your Notebook and add a list of things to forgive yourself for—just as you made a list like this about your ex, earlier. These are things for which you blame yourself, wholly or in part. Try not to edit or censor yourself as you write the list. Even if items seem ludicrous to you as they come to mind, write them down so you can deprive the false ones of their power over you, and create an action plan to do better for things that are based in reality.

Now, let's review the steps you used earlier to forgive your ex. *Do all the Exercises from that section—applied to yourself rather than to your ex, as follows.*

#### ▶ FIRST: EXPRESS YOUR FEELINGS ABOUT THE THINGS YOU NEED TO FORGIVE YOURSELF FOR:

Are you feeling shame, or guilt? **Shame** is a sense that something is wrong with you, whereas **guilt** is a feeling that what you did was wrong[27]. Shame keeps you stuck in self-loathing, whereas guilt allows you the freedom to change in healthy ways, so you love yourself more and your struggles become your catalyst. See if you can redirect shame to become guilt.

For instance, feeling shame about introducing my child to new men too quickly would have kept me stuck in a cycle of self-blame[28]. But feeling appropriate guilt allowed me to do better: I was making some specific mistakes, and I could stop making those. This improved how I felt about myself.

Similarly, one single mom named Mary wrote that, "I feel some sadness that I drug my children through relationships that I was attempting to have during their growing-up years." She felt regret because the changes she made came after her children reached adulthood, because she swapped time with them for time with men she didn't wind up with, and because she had perhaps involved the kids too much in her adult dating life. The word "drug" also indicates she might feel some shame. Maybe she could reframe this way: "I had relationships that didn't work out, and some of those were during my children's growing-up years. I regret the lost time with the kids, and that I let the kids get close to men who wound up not being right for us. I'd like to forgive myself for all of these things."

...

# EXERCISE 9:
## *Your feelings inventory:*

Now it's your turn. Take the list of items you need to forgive yourself for from Exercise 8, and add your feelings beneath each one. Note whether you're feeling shame, or guilt. If it's shame, can you redirect your words so you focus on what you did that was wrong, rather than feeling that you yourself are wrong?

▶ **SECOND: SET BOUNDARIES BY DESCRIBING BEHAVIORS YOU WILL AND WON'T ENGAGE IN ANY LONGER:**

Be specific! For instance, I could have written, "I will learn more about choosing good men, and will date only those who meet my Must-Haves." Additionally, I could have listed, "I will not allow men to spend time with my child unless they have met my Must-Haves (more on this in Chapter 3), we're in love, our relationship is trending towards marriage, and they've asked to meet my son—plus, my intuition says it's a good idea."

...

# EXERCISE 10:
## *Your boundaries:*

As with Exercise 6 above, write down specifically what you commit to doing differently in the future regarding each item for which you need self-forgiveness.

▸ THIRD, FOURTH, AND FIFTH: NURTURE EMPATHY
FOR YOURSELF AND YOUR MISTAKES—PUTTING THIS
IN WRITING, AND STICKING WITH IT AS LONG AS YOU
NEED TO:

Re-live the events you're forgiving yourself for, and write down your
thought process at the time, to create empathy for what you were
going through. Persist, revisiting this process as often as necessary.

...

# *EXERCISE 11:* ✏

## *Your empathy list:*

Take the self-forgiveness Exercises you've already written, and
underneath each item you're forgiving, explain your feelings and
thoughts from that time.

For instance, Mary could have written:

> *"I was lonely as a single parent, and overwhelmed. I needed time with
> another adult; I needed love and sexual attention, and I needed com-
> panionship with a man so I didn't turn my kids into inappropriate
> repositories of my adult emotions. I wanted to take the necessary time
> to find the right partner, and I could only do that by either spending
> time away from the kids, or involving the kids in time with my romantic
> partners."*

Or maybe her efforts at empathy would have looked like mine:

> *"I thought I was helping my child by introducing him to some men fairly
> quickly, because it seemed like that would give me insight into whether
> a given man might become a good stepdad. At the time, I was worried*

*about getting in deep and only then finding out whether someone was appropriate as a stepfather or was open to nurturing a stepchild."*

Then, specifically state your forgiveness for each item: "I was doing the best I could, and I forgive myself."

Generally speaking, we're all doing the best we can, all the time, given our current understanding and circumstances[29]. Just as when you forgave your ex, when you forgive yourself, hopefully you'll see that you, too, were doing your best—and that you're learning, always learning, to do better.

As a formerly single mom in her 40s wrote to me after her eventual success in finding love again, "I want to read about being kind and gentle to ourselves as we navigate dating and trying on new people. It brings lots of mistakes and the need for forgiveness."

Yes. It does.

## ENHANCE YOUR SELF-TALK

None of us is in danger of perfection when it comes to life, dating, or parenting. We can learn more and get better at making choices that are likely to lead us to success; science is about the best odds, and excels at telling us what will work for most people most of the time. That's what this book is about!

But nothing—scientific or otherwise—tells us what will work for every person every time. So even with the most rigorous approach, we'll mess up sometimes. As I tell my now-teen, "I'm not making the same mistakes with you that my parents made with me. I'm making new ones."

How do you talk to yourself when you err? A vital aspect of self-love is catching ourselves in the act when we are unkind and disrespect-ful—to ourselves.

I received the following letter from Eva, a woman known for her outstanding kindness to others:

*"My kids were both teens when we divorced. I not only was a single parent, but was a single parent of a guy with a medically complex dis-ability. You know a thing or two about that. I always related to that scene in the film 'As Good as It Gets,' where Helen Hunt was on a date, kissing on the sofa, then went to help her son who was having a coughing fit that resulted in mucus on her shirt, which repelled her date. The line that became my motto was, 'Too much reality for a Friday night.'*

*"Dating with my son Adam was tricky, although some guys found it attractive that I was such a good care provider and Adam was so charming. I was dating a man who felt that way about me, when Adam died...and then my boyfriend passed away too. What a time that was. Then I was the bereaved mother and I feel that took me out of the world of dating altogether.*

*"Now I think it is more that I am undefined by a career and without many prospects. One guy I went out with told me I had no business dating at all until I was making at least $60,000 a year. As much as I would love to find someone, I have pretty much given up hope. Dating and relationships have a code I have not cracked. I fill my life with friendships, mostly female. I am someone who has not only been rejected by men in the dating world, but my entire family of origin spurned me at the time of Adam's death. There seems to be something*

*inherently flawed in someone who cannot keep a marriage or even a family. I don't know how to be pleasing to others. I don't know what they want or need, so I just keep skippity-hopping along on my merry little path, working to make the world a better place in my flawed and goofy way. I view it as a character disability. I think I am just not cut out for being loved like that."*

Initially, this letter really threw me. Here was one of the most generous and decent people I had ever met, who had suffered tremendously through no fault of her own, being so unkind to herself! Here is part of my response:

*"I am wondering what you would say to someone who said these words to someone you loved: 'There seems to be something inherently flawed in someone who cannot keep a marriage or even a family. You don't know how to be pleasing to others. You don't know what they want or need, so you just keep skippity-hopping along on your merry little path, working to make the world a better place in your flawed and goofy way. I view it as a character disability. I think you are just not cut out for being loved like that.'*

*"Would you be hurt, shocked, and angry if someone spoke to your beloveds that way? Would you want to defend them, and help them see their worth?*

*"Please be as kind to yourself as you would to others. Be careful how you talk to yourself, because you are listening. And you are priceless."*

Here's the problem, though: unlike when others openly disrespect us, we're often not aware of our self-talk. It flies under the radar, which gives it power to tear down our self-love.

So take these two research-proven steps to combat negative self-talk:

**Notice** when you are speaking to yourself in unloving ways, and **redirect** to align with reality[30].

It's well-known in research on cognitive behavioral therapy that the first step to change is catching ourselves when we have distressing thoughts; that's half the battle[31]. Once we're able to notice these thoughts, we can then shift our attention to ask whether there's any evidence to support them—or whether we've simply internalized terrible things others may have said to us. And then, it's a matter of continuing the notice-redirect cycle as needed.

It's simple—but not easy.

For instance, Eva had internalized many of the criticisms thrown at her by her family and even by men she barely knew, for circumstances that were beyond her control. In redirecting her thinking to align with reality, she could say:

> *"Taking care of my child who had a serious illness and disability meant my options for making money were very limited. It's amazing that I was able to hold down a job of any kind. I was on my own, and I provided as well as I could for my son and myself. I was heroic and sacrificed myself in ways that most people can't imagine—and I would do it again. I'm a good person and I deserve love."*

Eva is a superhero in disguise, and her resilience and strength are to be celebrated!

...

# EXERCISE 12: ▭▭▷

## Catch and challenge your self-talk:

Here's some good news: we're almost always talking to ourselves, so we're constantly gaining options to switch off the cruise control and listen carefully instead. Your mission, should you choose to accept it, is to:

- catch yourself in negative self-talk at least three times a day;

- write down your thoughts; and

- align them with reality.

Here's a way to catch yourself that worked for me: *Notice when you're saying something to yourself that would offend you if someone said it to one of your kids.* I don't know about you, but I've accepted lots of unfair treatment for and from myself that I would never countenance if it were applied to my child!

If your self-talk is accurate, that can indicate a concrete area for improvement. For example, maybe you catch yourself thinking, "I'm a horrible parent. Look at me, taking out my bad day on the kids by yelling at them." The first part of this statement is patently untrue: we all lose our temper with our kids sometimes, and that doesn't make us horrible parents. But if it's true that your bad day is leaking out in your treatment of your children, you can apologize to the kids, and do better next time.

If it's negative self-talk that doesn't reflect what's going on around you, then it's time to realign your thinking with your reality:

> *"I'm thinking I'm not a good parent. I've had a hard day and my self-esteem isn't where it needs to be. When I feel bad, sometimes I feel like I'm bad rather than that it's just one of those days. In reality, though, I made everyone dinner, listened attentively about the kids' day, and planned a date for the one night they're with the sitter. I'm doing a great job—all the more impressive because it's hard, and I don't feel good."*

You might be able to eventually jump straight to legitimately patting yourself on the back, like this single mom:

*"Once I became a single parent, everything suddenly was in my hands. All the where's, how's, and when's are all up to me and me alone! That's made me stronger! I've done whatever needs to be done, which included working three jobs at one point. Single parenting has made me realize I can do whatever I set my mind to and do it with more confidence."*

My hat's off to her!

The upshot? *To love yourself more, talk to yourself as if you were someone you loved.* Treat yourself like a treasured friend, because you are the one friend who is always with you. You can take responsibility for areas of improvement—just not at the cost of disliking yourself.

## TAKE CARE OF YOURSELF

One of my favorite things about being married is that I'm not the only one taking care of me anymore. I also appreciate not being the only one taking care of the house, the kiddo, the pets, the car, the bills, the repairs, the stress, making dinner, going to the store, filing taxes, taking out the trash, unclogging the sinks and toilets—everything. The first day I was ever in Vic's presence, he noticed something broken in my house and leaped to fix it, and he's been fixing and tending and helping ever since. I love him for a lot of things, including how he lifts so many burdens from my shoulders. Adulting can be hard, and it's so much easier with two! The first couple of years that we were married, I marveled constantly at how easy it is to be with an equal who pulls his weight, where we're each looking out for the other.

What a contrast to my life as a single parent. When we're single-parenting, it's easy to put ourselves dead last on the list, as almost every minute is consumed by have-to's. Self-love requires that we engage in at least some self-care.

Plus, I'm of the view that life is a gift to be enjoyed. It can't be all work, work, work. Or it can be—but that's not a joyful way to live, nor the example I want to show my child.

Many of you may have a shared-custody arrangement where a percentage of your time is sans children. For you, much of your self-care might be scheduled for those times. Others of us have full custody; whether or not it's decreed, the parenting falls to us full-time. Either way, our quality of life requires us to carve out some time to take care of ourselves.

Let's do another Exercise. You go first, and then I'll make some suggestions.

...

# EXERCISE 13: ▱▬▬▷
## Single-parent self-care:

This one's in three parts.

### ▶ FIRST: WHAT DO YOU DO TO CARE FOR YOUR FAMILY?

List everything you can think of that falls under this heading. For instance: your daily commute, your job, housework, paying bills, making medical appointments, driving people places, packing lunches, reminding kids to do stuff (their homework, their bath, their teeth, their hair, their share of the chores).

▶ **SECOND:** list everything you do for self-care each day.

(You are doing some stuff, right?)

▶ **THIRD:** list what you want to be doing for self-care (and can realistically do).

...............................................................................

## MY THOUGHTS:

The steps you take towards self-care need not be dramatic, nor require much time. "Small stuff often" is the key.

For instance, we know with certainty that daily exercise—especially if it's outdoors—is enormously beneficial. In rafts of studies, just half an hour of daily moderate-paced walking causes improvements in nearly every aspect of physical health, and it has the same benefit for most people as taking antidepressants[32]. It also improves sexual health and performance for women and men. And you don't need to do your walking all at once: three breaks of 10 minutes each are as helpful as walking the whole half-hour at one go.

Here's a menu of other "small stuff" possibilities to add to your list, and you are probably thinking up others I haven't mentioned:

- Eat chocolate for breakfast. It stimulates the reward centers of your brain[33]. Okay, confession: this is something I do, to bribe myself to get up in the mornings. (It works.)

- Listen to your favorite music during your commute.

- Look around you. Do you own any stuff you really like? Take a moment to enjoy it. I happen to really like the feel of the keyboard I'm typing on right now (nerdy, I know).

- Thank someone, preferably in writing. Gratitude creates joy[34].

- Take a real break at lunch and turn off all electronics for just a few minutes (your kids can call your work if there's an emergency).

- Ask a friend to join you for a walk around the block in the evenings. You'll get an endorphin-release twofer, from the exercise and the company.

- Engage in a little escapism. Watch a show that makes you laugh out loud. Pop popcorn.

- Throw the ball for your dog, or your cat if it's one that fetches.

- Get a cat or dog if you don't have one. It's good for you[35]!

- Re-read something you know like the back of your hand, where the words themselves are a pleasure and there's zero pressure to keep reading to figure out what happens next. (For me, this is *Pride & Prejudice*. Mr. Darcy, take me away...)

- Liberate yourself from chores, as your children's abilities allow. My favorite was the year I graduated from doing my child's laundry. Now, he makes dinner on Friday nights, underscoring that Friday is the best day of the week.

- Eat something delectable and take the time to savor every bite.

- Call—don't merely text—a friend who knows you well and loves you just the way you are.

- Take a hot shower and lock the bathroom door.

- Take your kids and volunteer someplace for a few hours a month. For my kiddo and me, it was an animal shelter first; now, we volunteer separately. There's solid science behind volunteering as a pathway to meaning, and thus to self-worth and happiness[36].

- Build community. This could be with fellow worshippers, fellow volunteers, your colleagues, or your neighbors. When I was a single mom, I invited neighbors over for Christmas carols, Valentine's parties, a housewarming, movie nights, and for no reason at all. Loneliness is a health risk for single people[37], and the friends you make are a hedge against that—plus, having friends is fun.

- Write three things that went well for you today, and your role in them. In experiments, doing this for as little as six weeks causes people to be happier for months[38].

- Meditate for five to 15 minutes daily. Research proves it truly improves our mental health and coping skills[39]. Some meditation is better than none, so do it when it works for you—such as on that phone-free lunch break.

- Oh, and here's one more thing: get into a good relationship.

**The single most important thing I ever did to recover my self-love, self-worth, self-care, and enjoyment of my daily life, was to persistently engage in the search that resulted in meeting, dating, and marrying Vic.**

If that sounds over the top, it's not. E. Mavis Hetherington's research followed dozens of divorced couples for over 20 years. During that time, she conducted extensive yearly interviews with not only the formerly married couple, but their children and any new partners or spouses. That's a lot of data[40].

And what she found directly counters the old saw that we have to be happy by ourselves before we can be happy with someone else. That's simply not so. Our issues arise in the context of relationships, and it is in the context of relationships that we are healed.

Hetherington looked for every predictor she could think of that might be smoothing adults' pathways to recovering their sense of whole-ness and happiness after divorce. My self-care recommendations are empirically good for well-being, but they weren't enough to create the total reintegration and satisfaction that Hetherington looked for in her participants. What was enough? A good intimate relationship. It was the one and only thing that brought about wholeness for the adults she studied[41].

Conventional wisdom holds that many people get happy alone, and then find a good relationship. The reverse is true. People find a good relationship, and then become much happier. So, think of everything you've ever been told to do in order to be happy on your own—and know that while those things help, they're usually not enough.

Two single dads who responded to my single-parents survey gave very different advice on post-divorce healing. The first, Ben, said, "Learn to be okay by yourself before trying to be someone's 'other half.'"

But science backs this input from Alex instead: "I would encourage all single parents to go out and date, and find a good partner. Life is fantastic when shared with a great partner, and your kids will be better off with a happy and healthy parent."

Yes. Your self-love will be vastly enhanced by getting into a healthy, solid, loving relationship. You don't need to "fix" everything about yourself to begin! Amy met Paul while still dealing with her abusive ex; I certainly wasn't done with my travails when Vic and I met; and Hetherington's research shows that is how it is for most people most of the time.

It's a both/and world. You can work on healing your past while you move towards getting into a new and better relationship. You can forgive your ex, and forgive yourself, and enhance your self-talk, and begin your mate search—all at once.

But what about the what-ifs? Dating can be risky, all the more with kids in tow. Facing your fears and figuring out who's right for you are coming right up in Chapter 3.

# CHAPTER 3:

# Face Your Fears And Fix Your Picker

**W**e ended the second chapter with a strong statement: getting into a loving, lasting relationship is the one thing that makes men and women feel whole and happy after divorce[1].

Yet although many of us would treasure a great relationship, most also have a tremendous amount of fear that it can't happen for us. After all, nearly everyone is in love when they wed[2]—but divorce can occur anyway, and single parents know that better than anyone.

Our losses frequently lead to a loss of faith—in ourselves, in others, in relationships. When I led *Love Factually* seminars for adults in my community, most of them wondered some variant of, "Is it even possible to get what I want and need in a partner?"

These fears may be especially common for single parents. One of them echoed the voice of many:

> *"I feel defeated about dating. I don't have time to put into a relationship, nor the emotional energy. I also feel damaged and exhausted by the trauma of my ex's deception, and unable to have faith in myself or others to have a successful relationship. UGH!! Thanks for letting me get that out!"*

(You're welcome.)

*But airing fears is not the same thing as giving in to them.* Again, love is literally what saves most people's emotional—and even physical—lives[3]. Chronic loneliness, something singles are likely to face if they do not marry well, is riskier for most folks than a pack-a-day cigarette habit[4]. So let's make a plan and move past the fear.

## FACE YOUR FEARS

Almost every reader of this book is someone who wants love. And almost every one of us is afraid. What to do?

### ▶ FIRST, IDENTIFY YOUR MONSTERS:

Most of us have hidden ambivalence—simultaneous fear of and yearning for love. Unnamed and unaddressed fears can stop us from making or following any plan at all, and the word for those who don't make and follow a solid plan is "single." Single is fine if that's what you want to be!

But since you're looking for love…to de-fang these little monsters, drag them out into the cold light of day.

Here's my own list of everything that I worried was keeping me from finding love when I was single. *Note that the point was not whether I was correct—but what I thought:*

**I'm afraid I won't find love because:**

- I'm too needy/depressed.

- I'm too old (at 35!).

- I'm too afraid of another failed marriage.

- I don't trust my judgment to pick a good partner.

- I don't want anyone else to have a say in raising my child.

- I like being boss and having latitude to make all my own choices.

- I fear a child predator/the Wrong Stepdad.

Attendees of my *Love Factually* seminars came up with everything on my list, plus these items:

### I'm afraid I won't find love because:

- My life is too serious because of my parenting responsibilities.

- Nobody will want a partner with kids.

- I'm afraid of exposing my kids to emotional risk and needing to get out after I'm deeply involved.

- I'm not over my ex.

- I'm still hurting from my ex/divorce.

- I've got body image/sexual performance issues.

- I'm fearful of dating and of how to balance my kids and a new relationship.

...

# EXERCISE 1: ✎▭▭▭▷

## The monster mash:

Whether or not it might make sense or be realistic, use your Notebook to write down every fear you can think of that, in your opinion, is getting in the way of your search for love.

*"I'm afraid I won't find love because:"*

Does your list resemble my students' and mine? Do you have unique items that are specific to your circumstances?

▶ **SECOND: ACKNOWLEDGE THAT MANY OF YOUR FEARS MAY BE REALISTIC—AND THAT YOU CAN FIND LOVE ANYWAY:**

I'm not asking you to call BS on your fears. That would be naïve of both of us.

Some or even most of your monsters are reality-based, and all the more daunting for being so. For instance: although we're older and perhaps wiser, divorce rates increase for each subsequent remarriage[5]—more so when kids are in the mix. There really are predators who harm stepkids[6]—and in the next chapter we'll learn how to avoid them. Custodial parents are indeed less likely to remarry even when they want to, largely because potential mates tend to consider other people's kids—whom they don't yet know or love—to be costs, not rewards[7]. This is why we'll cover when and how to introduce children to a new love. Around the world, heterosexual men tend to prefer women who are younger than themselves, and childless[8]; we'll explore overcoming those odds as well. And do we really need science to show us that our schedules are now fuller and it's harder to find time to date?

*I found lasting love while facing all of these challenges—and you can, too!* Just because something is hard doesn't make it insurmountable, and just because we're afraid doesn't justify giving up on our need for intimacy. Yes, a lot of your worries are likely to be real. Yes, you have more challenges than Before Children, and many of them are about serious issues. *That's exactly why I wrote this book—so you can use best-practice science to overcome these barriers rather than being defeated by them. Name your fears—and face them anyway.*

### ▶ THIRD: SOURCE YOUR ANXIETY:

In addition to some worries that come from a place of reality when dating After Children, our orientation towards relationships in general plays a role.

...

# EXERCISE 2: ▭▬▶

## *The attachment match:*

Before we go further, please take out your Notebook and give the answer (A, B, C, or D) that best reflects you and your feelings during intimate relationships. *You may be a combination of two or even all of them, but please pick the one that you think fits you most closely[9]:*

**A: I find it relatively easy to get close to others and am comfortable depending on them and having them depend on me.** I don't often worry about being abandoned or about someone getting too close to me.

**B: I find that others are reluctant to get as close as I would like.** I often worry that my partner doesn't really love me or won't want to stay with me. I want to merge completely with another person, and this desire sometimes scares people away.

**C: I am uncomfortable getting close to others.** I want emotionally close relationships, but I find it difficult to trust others completely or to depend on them. I worry that I will be hurt if I allow myself to become too close to others.

**D: I am comfortable without close emotional relationships.** It is very important to me to feel independent and self-sufficient, and I prefer not to depend on others or have others depend on me.

Picked one? Your **attachment style** is your habitual way of being, acting, and feeling in close relationships[10]. We have attachments all of our lives, from the deep bond we feel as toddlers with our mothers, to the romantic relationships we have as adults[11]. Interestingly, we tend to have the same attachment style across time--and across all of these relationships[12].

*Your attachment style affects your relationships and your search for relationships in profound ways.* So let's learn about it, to give you more insight into possible fears, and to help you succeed at love this next time around.

About two-thirds of people seem to have the same attachment style into their early 20s that they had as toddlers, and most of us have the same type our mom had[13]—partly due to biology, and partly because parenting styles tend to carry down through the generations[14].

Babies who are parented with a high level of responsiveness—being rocked, held, fed, changed, and paid attention to consistently on the baby's timetable rather than the adults', tend to become **Securely attached (A)**. As adults, they cherish their partner, expect to love and to be loved, and think of the sex as only getting better over the long haul. When they disagree, Secure partners keep problems in perspective, and argue in a way that protects the relationship. They agree that part of their romantic job description is "taking care of my partner," and place a high value on mutual care and interdependence[15].

Sound co-dependent? Think again: these folks have the highest satisfaction with their relationships, and tend to have very long-lasting marriages. If a relationship ends, they process their grief, and then usually move on into another solid relationship. And the good news is, they are in the majority, with about 60-70% of adults in the Secure category[16].

My husband is Secure. He is totally emotionally available to me, and thinks of it as teamwork rather than demeaning to check in before making plans. He includes me in decisions, and is my biggest supporter. Loving me is, for him, a huge part of his job description in life. Ten years into our marriage, he spontaneously asked if I was happy, and then said, "Good. You are my world, and everything I do is to make you happy." He feels safe loving me, and being loved by me. It's not a constant surprise to him that our life together goes well, nor that we've grown closer: that fits his map of how the world is supposed to run.

Then, there are the rest of us—and I include myself here!—who fall under the other two major categories: **Anxious (B)**, and **Avoidant (C and D)**. Just like Secure folks, we seek relationships, but our map of l'amour is a bit different.

Anxious and Secure people are similar in that both are sure they want a lasting relationship, and they're willing to invest themselves fully to get it. Both types value interdependence and want a partner to share deeply with. Metaphorically speaking, if they were atoms, Secure and Anxious types would want their partners right there in the nucleus with them, not orbiting in the electron cloud.

But where Secure people remain relatively unruffled by the inevitable hard times in love, we Anxious folks tend to worry that the whole relationship is up for grabs whenever a disagreement occurs, to take things personally that aren't, and to feel, well, anxious. We often overreact to perceived signs that our partner might be hedging towards abandoning us, for instance, or wonder whether that smile our partner gave the waiter was really an attempt at flirting[17].

A big tip-off that you might be Anxious is if you catch yourself thinking you love your partner more than they love you, and/or that they don't really want to be with you, despite solid evidence to the contrary[18]. You also might break up with the same person, repeatedly, or even go so far as to line up a "backup mate" in case this relationship ends—ironically increasing the odds of a breakup[19]. Anxious folks tend to think they're likely to get dumped or cheated on, even when their partner's behavior doesn't support that conclusion; it makes sense that they're more likely to be jealous than the other types[20]. And women are more likely to be Anxious than men[21].

98

Here are two notes sent to me by women in their 30s who score as Anxiously attached. Having been Anxious for most of my adult life, I can relate:

> *"I think the problem with me lately is that although I'm not just settling or looking for just anything, I also want it too much; I want to be with someone, I want to fall in love, I eventually would love to get married, etc. I know that's the desire of a lot of people, but because I want it so badly, and I admit that, it does weigh heavily on my mind often, daily even."*

> *"There are few things harder for me than when my partner says, 'I just need 5-10 minutes to decompress by myself,' without me jumping, literally, on them and asking, 'WHY?? WHAT DID I DO? WHAT'S GOING ON IN THERE? WANT ME TO MAKE YOU A PIE?? IS YOUR FAVORITE FLAVOR STILL BLUEBERRY?? WHEN WILL YOU HOLD ME AGAIN?'"*

(By the way, she's relaxed more since then, and yes, his fave is still blueberry.)

Speaking of flavors, **Avoidant** people come in two varieties: **Fearful (C)**, and **Dismissive (D)**. Although the term implies staying away from relationships, that's not the case. These folks do want partnerships—they're just not comfortable with ongoing, soul-baring emotional intimacy. What feels safe and comfortable to them is *closeness at arm's length*. To continue the atom metaphor, if they were in the nucleus, they would much prefer for their partner to be in the electron cloud—knowing where their partner is, but also knowing that the partner isn't going to encroach. As one Avoidant-type man said of a former girlfriend, "My favorite time was when she would go take a bath while I was home. I felt loved and secure and safe, because I knew she was right there, and at the same time, nothing would be asked of me."

As that example shows, Avoidant-Fearful types are worried that the other person will need them too much, and/or that they can't live up to their partner's needs—and vice versa. They yearn for, and simultaneously fear, intimacy, and usually prefer it only in small doses or brief, intense bursts they then pull away from.

Avoidant-Dismissive people aren't afraid of closeness, so much as really independent; they don't get why others want intimacy, and they value their autonomy much more than sustained relationships.

If you're Avoidant, you might find yourself creating distance with a partner just when things are going really well. Maybe you've noticed that partners seem to be asking for more contact and closeness than you want to or can give. A huge tip-off is if you find yourself feeling that every relationship is a power struggle between you and a partner who seems like a bottomless pit of need, constantly demanding that you put more into them and your connection. Another clue is the idealized ex you still dream of being with, even though they had the same complaints about your emotional unavailability that you're hearing from others, and even though you also wanted to run away from them when things got too close[22].

Avoidant men I've worked with—and scientifically, most Avoidant folks are male[23]—tend to nitpick their prospective mates, looking for a safety valve that gives them an excuse for leaving the relationship emotionally if not outright[24]. That way, it's every partner's fault when relationships end, not a matter of working things out or changing oneself; and the illusion is maintained that a perfect partner is out there--they just haven't found him or her yet. In my experience, this does not come from poor character or a mean plan: they usually aren't aware that they're doing this, or why.

*In a moment, when we get to your standards for a mate, we'll return to attachment styles and cover who should date whom—that's how important your style is.* For now, though, know this: if you look back across your relationships and notice a pattern of worry related to needing either more closeness or less of it, there are things you can do to change. We are covering them in this chapter. And knowing your fears are in part coming from your attachment style is a big first step.

## ▸ FOURTH: TAKE ACTION ANYWAY, NOTICING WHEN YOUR THOUGHTS ARE RUNNING AMOK:

This taps into a concept we covered in Chapter 1: **acting as if**. Faking it 'til you make it is a legit way to change your emotions. Instead of waiting to feel comfortable before you begin dating, take action: go ahead and look for love even though you're afraid, and ironically, you'll find that your fear lessens. Apply the concepts in this book, and your confidence will increase, leading you to take even more action. *Don't let your fear rule you and prevent your search for love; seek love and rule your fear.*

To boost the power of acting as if, **notice-and-redirect**, as discussed in Chapter 2 about negative self-talk. Remove your fears' ability to control you: move them from the realm of unconscious thought and into the light where you can examine them. **Notice** when you're having fear-based thoughts, and then **redirect** them to align with the evidence around you.

I especially recommend this for those with Anxious or Avoidant attachment styles, because fears related to our style are habitual and largely unconscious unless we make the effort to examine our patterns. And our patterns have a big impact on how our relationships go.

For instance, let's imagine that a woman named Mandy—whose attachment style is Anxious—is worried that Dave, whom she met online, is losing interest in her. Her first step is simply to notice herself worrying. She needs to be gentle as she does so, rather than beating herself up over it, or else this does not work; noticing gently is the key. Then, she needs to redirect by looking at the evidence: "Dave sent me a long email today and asked lots of questions about me; maybe he has not yet asked me out, but it doesn't look like he's lost interest, either." Alternatively, maybe her worries are founded in reality: "Dave hasn't said anything for a couple of weeks, and when I go back over his messages, they were all about him. He never showed much interest in me."

Or imagine a man named John, whose Avoidant-Fearful attachment style often leads him to feel like partners are controlling him. His first step is to notice when he's thinking something along the lines of, "Karen is being so controlling, expecting me to call her every night." It's vital for him to gently notice; guilt-inducing judgments keep people stuck, and the goal here is forward momentum. Then, John can redirect by examining his evidence: "Is that really controlling? Or could it be that she just loves hearing from me? My friends seem to think that communicating with a girlfriend every day is pretty normal." Or, maybe Karen really is controlling: "She also tells me what to wear every day, who to talk to, what to eat, and how to do even the simplest task. This is too much."

*The point isn't to deny reality, but to stop unconsciously accepting the internal dialog we all have as hard fact, until after we've examined it.*

Although some of my clients have a Secure attachment style, most of them don't. And most of the letters I get from Wise Readers also seem to be from people who have non-Secure styles. I know from research, clients, and living in my own skin that being non-Secure comes with a big set of perceptual challenges.

That's why *noticing* when we're having non-Secure thoughts, and *redirecting* those thoughts to align with reality, is important to your dating success.

...

# EXERCISE 3: ◼▬▶
## *The mind police:*

Please catch yourself, three times today, thinking something non-Secure—and then, compare your thought against reality. Record all three instances in your Notebook, so you begin to get the hang of doing this.

**My Thought:**
_____

**Reality:**
_____

**My Thought:**
_____

**Reality:**
_____

**My Thought:**
_____

**Reality:**
_____

Lather, rinse, and repeat, doing this exercise as often as you find helpful.

Over time, you'll get good at it, and your fears won't have as much power over you. Your attachment style may even become more Secure[25].

## Fix Your Picker

When I was dating, my No. 1 problem was seeing what I wanted to see in prospective partners instead of what was there, and spotting potential that was more imagined than real. A friend of mine calls this "having a broken picker," and mine was flat busted.

I got serious about fixing it after my child was born, though, because I deserved success the next time around, and I refused to expose my little one to a series of failed marriages or move-ins; he'd already been through one of those, and that was more than enough.

Decades-long studies show that kids can reintegrate after one divorce—but that most divorced parents subsequently repartner again and again, with men likelier to have a string of remarriages, and women more likely to have a series of live-in partners[26]. This means the parents are repeatedly unhappy, life is much less stable, and the kids absorb the impact. Factually, it's a lot harder for children to thrive under those circumstances. Says Dr. Judith Wallerstein, who studied over 6,000 children of divorce across thirty-plus years, "More people come and go, and life is different and harder to adjust to for the child of divorce, not only at the time of the breakup but all through[27]."

*Let's set things up so that neither you nor your kids need to adjust to another upheaval—not by avoiding relationships altogether, but by getting into the right one.* This is largely under your control if you fix your picker, because to a great extent, the choosing phase is where future success resides. You can find the intimacy and support you need to be a happy adult and an effective parent who comes from a place of contentment, peace, and security. You can choose wisely this next time around, and here's how.

### ▶ SET YOUR STANDARDS:

Here's some good advice from one single mom: "Figure out what you want in a partner and don't settle. People are who they are. See them for that; don't change them or hope they will change."

In my first book, I go into detail about the following steps. Here, I'm going to list them—and then go into new details about the specifics you as a single parent should be requiring.

···

# *EXERCISE 4:* ▱▬▬▶

## *Build-a-mate:*

▶ **STEP 1:** Brainstorm a List of everything you want and need in a partner, and avoid self-censoring:

Your List should be as detailed as possible. Even if you think "enjoys being a stepparent" or "would go with me to my kid's t-ball games" is pie in the sky, put it on the List! A good way to brainstorm this is to think of all the stuff you loved and hated about former partners, and qualities you yearned for but never got.

▶ **STEP 2:** Review your List and put everything in positive language of what you do want, rather than what you're hoping to avoid:

Our brains process what we give them and seem to ignore the word "not," so unless you want a polar bear, don't say "is not a polar bear." Instead, say what you do want: "is a brown or black bear." Put into dating terms, you'd avoid the language, "not an alcoholic," or, "not a drama queen," and instead say, "drinks socially and responsibly," or, "is stable and calm even in a crisis."

▶ **STEP 3:** Make a third pass, separating the items on your List into two categories: Must-Haves, and Wants:

Must-Haves are qualities that are so essential, you would need to stop dating anyone who was otherwise perfect—but lacked just this one (deal-breaking) thing.

▶ **STEP 4:** Reread the entire List, putting a check mark next to every item that basically describes you:

If you want someone who values time together and that's what you value? Check. If you want someone who wants (or does not want) to adopt or make more babies, and that's how you feel, too? Check. If you want someone who likes exotic small mammals and you have several ferrets? Check.

How did you do? Did you go for as much detail as possible? Are all your Must-Haves truly things you can't live without? Remember, the things you prefer but can compromise on go in the Wants bucket, even if they're very strong desires!

When I do this Exercise with clients, they tell me it's one of the most important things we work on. For one thing, it makes you aware of good prospective mates you might have met already, or who turn up. I have letters from men and women alike who literally would not have approached their spouse had they not made their List!

The List also helps keep you honest with yourself by clarifying your needs and boundaries. And it will become the basis for your internet ad—meaning, *we're going to be taking this List out and using it in other chapters, so even if you've skipped other Exercises, please make your List now if you haven't already. This is a foundation document for your success.*

## ▶ WHAT DOESN'T MATTER:

Just before starting this part of the chapter, I ate a chocolate bar. My ancestors would have loved it in all its densely caloric, sugary, fatty glory—which is precisely why I do. It would have helped them to survive in a calorie-scarce environment, and I'm the repository of all the desires that helped them. In my case as a modern person surrounded by grocery stores and restaurants, of course, gorging on fatty, high-calorie candy isn't helping at all. It's doing the opposite! But my genetic evolution, like everyone else's, moves too slowly to catch up to the modern world.

Our desires for partners are like that too. We all inherited our "You're Hot" buttons from our ancient ancestors—people who were alive before there was language, religion, or art[28]. Any quality that helped them survive or reproduce eventually spread through our entire species.

The trouble is, many reasons people inherited these mating urges are now a moot point—just like my lust for chocolate bars—yet our psychology goes right on snarfing up snacks and wielding a rather sexist club. Our brains consciously register conveniences (like grocery stores) that can address some of our ancestors' challenges. But at the unconscious level, we're still cave-dwellers who want what the ancient cave-people wanted, even when it makes no sense, or goes against our modern best interests.

Because so many of our inherited preferences focus on appearance, resources like money, and other surface qualities, I call them "shallow drives." They come from deep needs to procreate—so I don't mean to dismiss them as meaningless, because they aren't. *Just remember that, given our evolutionary heritage and the way the world has changed, there are times when what we want is not actually what we need. Shallow drives are not excuses for being shallow people!*

So take a look at your entire List, noticing items that are more focused on appearance, money, status, education, youth, or other demographics than they are on similarity between you and the beloved you seek. These surface items can keep you single, especially if you don't match with what you're asking for!

If you want to pursue these ancient inclinations, realize that if you cannot match or offset these preferences with qualities of your own, you may be in for disappointment. Putting this in terms of your List, most men prefer a partner who is young and beautiful. This is a true human universal, found literally everywhere from hunter-gatherer tribes to fully developed nations, and even among the blind[29]. Guys, if you're gorgeous yourself, that's fine—it's a match. Or if you have a lot of ka-ching to offset the trade, that works too. But if not, shooting for Those Who Are Out of Your League is likely to get you dumped, cheated on, or both[30].

Ditto for women who want a partner with far greater wealth, status, education, and other markers of resources than they possess: unless these women are young and beautiful enough to trade up financially, insisting on this is the royal road to getting ignored[31]. Although it still makes sense for many women to desire a partner who can help out economically and provide for children, asking for great wealth is very limiting if a woman can't trade it for youth and beauty; the richest partners typically can and do get what they want in the looks department[32].

Also in women's ideal world, about 80% list that they Must Have a partner who is six feet tall or taller[33]. Height criteria likely made sense to our ancestral mothers, who relied heavily on a big man to protect them from other men[34]. And it still makes sense in some hunter-gatherer tribes. But it's not really serving those of us in the developed world now: the average height for American men is 5'9"— five-and-a-half inches taller than the average for American women, but three inches shorter than most women demand[35]. By insisting on the tallest of the tall, women are seeking something that can only be available to a small percentage—leaving millions single if they truly won't bend on this.

The upshot? It's not pretty and I don't like it, but at the start, before you know or love someone, mating is a market—and smart people aim to achieve a match rather than an ideal[36]. *Demanding what you yourself can't provide or trade for leaves you vulnerable to remaining alone, or getting into relationships you are unlikely to keep.*

...

# EXERCISE 5: ✏

## *The cross-out stage:*

With the above in mind, delete every item on your List that reflects someone you aren't, or emphasizes money, appearance, height, and other demographics that you don't match or can't trade for.

### ▸ WHAT MATTERS A LOT:

Just this morning, a man sent me this note: "Over my morning coffee I was thinking about my List of Must-Haves and Wants, and wondering if there is any research on attributes that contribute to a happier or longer marriage?"

I'm so glad you asked.

Ever been told your standards are too high? Well, except for stuff like money, height, and hotness, you won't hear it from me. *That's because in my experience, many folks' standards are actually too low on the really important things.* Some things matter a lot—and they belong on everyone's List.

### KILL: STICK WITH INTERNATIONAL TRAITS FOR A MATE.

Globally, men and women alike say that the following four (okay, five) qualities are so important, they're indispensable or nearly so in a potential mate[37]. As one of my students pointed out, the helpful acronym is KILL:

- Kindness and respect

- Intelligence

- Love

- Loyalty

## Kindness:

Kindness refers to someone who seeks the best in you and believes the best about you, even when you're at odds or they're having a bad day. Kind people speak well of others when they can, and avoid hateful statements even when they dislike someone (such as their ex). They are not boundaryless doormats, and they can be fierce in the service of justice and the greater good—but they are courteous with those who can do nothing for them, such as kids, animals, and strangers. And okay, nobody is kind all of the time—but when kind people mess up, they own their errors, and they are motivated to make things right.

Here's how this remarried mom describes her husband's kindness:

> *"He inspires me on a daily basis with his warmth and genuine care for not just me, not just our children, but for his co-workers, his clients, telemarketers, car mechanics... you name it! He is patient, committed, and is willing to look at himself when he does make a mistake. I can trust that he will take time to think about things and to come back to me with clarity and insight once he's thought things through. In past relationships, it was much more surface, and I was much more on guard because I chose relationships with men I didn't really trust*

*to be kind. My husband and I share a depth of relationship that I feel secure in. It's wonderful."*

## Respect:

Respect is Kindness' sibling: it takes you seriously, listens deeply, and cares about your opinions and desires. Respect pays attention and tries to find a way, incorporating your needs and feedback even when the two of you disagree; it calls you when it's going to be late, and it asks you before it makes plans. Respect considers you, the life partner, in all it does, because that's a good thing to do—not because they're "whipped" or fear a consequence. The opposite includes using sarcasm, belittling, undermining, overriding, and ignoring you and your input.

This morning on Facebook, I asked single parents: "Looking back, what's a quality you wish you had insisted on having in your past partners? What's something you wish you had NOT accepted?" Almost every response mapped onto Kindness and Respect. Here's a sampling of deeply wise responses:

*"I never thought to look for a man who would be kind to others, so long as he was kind to me. Those men who were only kind to me [and not others] in the beginning, were unkind to me eventually. I'm with a man now who goes out of his way to help people, the kind of guy who gives his co-worker - who was robbed just days before Christmas last year—all the presents in the trunk of his car. We had to go Christmas shopping twice! And it was totally worth it. His kindness is consistent, to me and everyone."*

*"Seems so obvious now: don't overlook disrespect, ever. If they're casually disrespectful of people, especially a parent, they'll certainly be disre-*

*spectful of you. In fact, the worst way they treat other people is how they will eventually treat you. Never think that their love of you would prevent them from doing what they do to others, to you."*

*"Wish I had insisted on kindness and a generous heart. Wish I had not accepted mere entertainment. That includes their being good-looking or sexually attractive, which led me to put up with a lot."*

The simple rule of thumb is this: if they're not treating you with the kindness and respect you need during courtship, that won't improve over time, and it's not worth risking your and your kids' stability and happiness. *There is literally no way to be happy in a marriage without kindness and respect from both of you, consistently[38]! So don't date anyone who shows a lack of these qualifiers.*

## Intelligence:

Intelligence doesn't mean everyone wants an Einstein, but you'll do best if you partner with someone on your intellectual par. They might have more, or fewer, degrees than you do; some lifelong learners become well-educated at the public library, where others achieve education more formally. Regardless, you should each feel that you're dealing with a peer when you speak.

I also suspect that many of us lump **emotional intelligence** into the general concept. Women and men alike have written me to say, in one person's words, that they want a partner who "knows their emotions and wants to know mine," and has "the ability to talk about anything with me in a constructive way, especially about things they expect, want, and need from me to help us have a healthy relation-ship." One man specified needing "someone who actually talks about their feelings and listens when I talk about mine." Another woman was to-the-point: "I should NOT have accepted selfishness and a lack of sensitivity." And a man summarized, "I would bolt at the first sign of meanness." Words to love by.

## Love and loyalty:

Speaking of which, everywhere in the world people want and even demand mates who not only feel but show love to them through actions, and who will be faithful to them in all senses of the word[39]. The love and loyalty they seek are personal—as in, they want to know that their partner fully chooses and commits to them specifically, cutting off their other sexual, romantic, and emotional options[40].

Many people seem to consider **mental stability**, **emotional maturity**, and **honesty** to be components of these qualities. In fact, lacking any of these will eventually undermine the foundation of nearly any relationship. Emotionally unstable men are especially concerning, because they're about four times likelier to physically abuse their partners than are men in good mental and emotional health[41].

Honesty includes not only speaking the truth, but living it. *When you see a mismatch between a partner's words and actions, ignore the words and believe the actions.* This quote from one of my Facebook respondents explains it perfectly:

> *"Someone who states that they believe in being a certain way, and then not being that way, is an issue. For example, saying it's really important to have peaceful relationships, but then all they have is drama, or valuing reliability when they're not reliable, or wanting something but not taking any action towards achieving it. Big red flags."*

Yes. In my experience, liars lie early and often. If you catch them in something small at the start of your relationship where telling the truth would have made just as much sense, they'll probably lie about things that are big. This single mom learned that the hardest way: "Little lies turn into a lifetime of nothingness and no reality to depend on. It started with his age, then his willingness to be a partner, and next thing you know, I've wasted 30 years of my life for nothing."

**Teamwork** is another important aspect of loyalty that my Facebook respondents correctly identified. One happily remarried woman wrote, "Looking back, I'd most seek a teamwork mentality that uses more 'we,' 'us,' and 'ours' language instead of 'me,' 'mine,' and 'I.'" Science agrees[42].

The upshot? You'll search far and wide before you find any tribe or nation where most people want marriage with immature, mean-spirited, self-centered, emotionally clueless, abusive, cheating mates. Despite shallow drives emphasizing qualities that don't last, this truth is much deeper and enduring:

*Good character counts. Make sure you count it very heavily in your Must-Haves.*

## PERSONALITY: SEEK AGREEABLENESS AND MORE.

Do you know the five scientifically validated, global personality traits? They are summarized by the word OCEAN: your range of fit on Openness to experience, Conscientiousness, Extraversion (introversion's opposite), Agreeableness, and Neuroticism. Online, you can find free, valid tests that give you your result on each factor and help you to understand them[43].

In research, personality differences are at the root of more marital arguments than anything else[44]. Yet happy marriages are possible even with a personality mismatch, unless it includes having either partner at the very low end of Agreeableness[45]. Disagreeable people make bad partners because they do things that cause the mate to have to clean up their financial, social, metaphorical, and actual messes. As we'll see in the next chapter, they also humiliate, irritate, disregard, or even abuse their partners.

Being disagreeable is such an effective way to ruin a relationship that some married people become disagreeable specifically to get their partner to leave them[46]. It's the opposite of kindness and respect. Just say No.

## SIMILARITY: FLOCK WITH BIRDS OF A FEATHER.

Earlier, when you put check-marks on your List for every quality you're seeking which you yourself also possess, you were testing for a very important Must-Have: similarity.

For several decades now, research has indicated that you Must Have someone whose values match yours[47]. What do you care about so deeply that it defines the way you view the world, and the action you take in it? That's a value, and if you pick someone who doesn't match you, it's a bad risk.

People tend to be most drawn to others who are similar in many other regards as well, from appearance to what kind of movies they like[48]. Similarity is so important that when one dating site led people to falsely believe they were a good match, that untrue belief was enough to inspire them to communicate longer than mismatches who weren't told the fib. An actual match was even better: people communicated the longest if the similarity was real[49].

Similarity increasingly maps onto politics, especially as they have become more polarized[50]. My clients specify political similarity even more often than similarity of religious affiliation as a Must-Have. Whatever is vital to you, make sure it makes your Must-Haves, too.

## THEIR PAST: HEED THE CRYSTAL BALL.

When it comes to dating, we're all gamblers, betting that the good times we've got now will last into the future with this new partner. Gambling is about odds, just like science is. But science is better, because it enables prediction—meaning, you're not playing a game of pure chance.

So to recap the science: your prospective partner is almost guaranteed to do again what they've done before. You have a crystal ball into the future, and it's this person's past! If you find out about or witness a behavior you can't live with, you can make excuses for this person; you can ignore the issue and hope it goes away. But it's much safer for you and your kids' stability for you to stop the relationship now.

## ATTACHMENT: FILL YOUR EMOTIONAL GAS TANK.

Earlier in this chapter, we explored attachment style, and how to deal with yours if it's not Secure. I pointed out that noticing and redirecting your thoughts can be a valid pathway to change. *But the simplest way to become or remain Secure is to be in a committed relationship with someone Secure*[51]. In studies, people whose attachment styles changed usually did so as a result of a partner's style[52]—and Secure partners are sustaining for all who wish for Security.

Your emotional life will also be far smoother if you pick the partner whose style meshes with your own. This does not necessarily mean choosing someone of the same style, but someone who brings out your best.

*To do that, think of your intimacy needs as a gas tank.*

Let's say Secure people have a 14-gallon tank, whereas Anxious folks' tanks may be closer to 20 gallons, and Avoidant tanks are full at six gallons. If you're Secure, other Secure individuals and Anxious people will naturally fill your tank; you may need to work a bit harder to fill the Anxious partner's tank, but that's okay with Secure folks, because taking care of your beloved is part of what you love to do.

If you're Anxious, an Avoidant partner doesn't think it's their job to fill your tank: theirs is quickly full, and the fact that yours isn't may strike them as threatening, needy, or judgmental of their efforts as a partner. You'll feel even more insecure as your tank is not only at a constant low, but you're told there's something wrong with you for needing more than six gallons of fuel.

And if you're Avoidant, a Secure or Anxious partner's needs are in such excess of yours, you may be made miserable, angry, and annoyed by their chronic efforts to over-fill your tank—and to get you to fill theirs.

The short, factual way to say that is: Secure people belong with other Secure people, and can also do well with Anxious people. Anxious people need someone Secure—period. It belongs on your Must-Haves. These matches work because they both want a deep bond, and both will work to get it. And if someone Avoidant wants to change and embrace deeper intimacy, they need someone Secure; otherwise, they need a partner who is also Avoidant[53].

You might think people naturally gravitate towards this system. But people who frequently cycle back into and out of the mating market are usually Avoidant or Anxious[54]. That's because, despite the much higher percentage of Secure people in the world, they tend to stay in workable relationships once there, and their partners usually remain with them. As a single parent, you might have higher odds of meeting people with non-Secure styles than you did earlier in your life, because Secure partners probably partnered around the same time you did, and most are still in those relationships.

Additionally, for reasons that aren't yet clear, Anxious and Avoidant people tend to be strongly and tragically attracted to each other[55]. I suspect that's because, at first, these two types seem to offer what the other seeks. At the start of a relationship, Anxious people yearn for instant bonding and deep sharing so they feel safe; they feel most excited if someone seems to get them right away. Avoidants want a partner they get intense feelings from, who they can then have in the background of their lives; they unconsciously understand that to bond, they must provide some of the trappings of intimacy (such as deep sharing and intense sexual bonding). But since they can't sustain those behaviors, Avoidant folks offer them in abundance up-front...and then create emotional distance.

Whether or not I'm right about the reasons, the fact remains that this dynamic is at first seductive, and then very painful. If Anxious and Avoidant people marry, a top cause of divorce is the **pursuer-distancer pattern**[56], where the Anxious partner continually seeks more intimacy than the Avoidant partner is comfortable giving or receiving. This results in a painful cycle where the Avoidant partner pulls away in order to get the emotional distance that feels safe to them, causing the Anxious partner to feel rejected and to cling even more tightly, which elicits still greater distancing from the Avoidant partner. Think *Men Are from Mars, Women Are from Venus*[57]—a bestseller about this whose lasting impact hints at just how common this pairing is. Its terminology differs, and it focuses on gender rather than on the attachment styles themselves, but that book strikes a nerve for a reason.

At heart, people have different capacities and needs for genuine closeness. There is a therapy that can help about two in three couples with the Anxious-Avoidant mismatch[58]—but *I urge you to choose a Secure partner from the outset, or someone who prefers low intimacy if that's what you're after.* Reread the description of Secure people earlier in the chapter. Learn more about Secure attachment so you can recognize it[59], or work with a therapist or coach with expertise in this area. *Cease dating anyone who does not fit your needs.* And stop wasting months and years of your life with those who can't or won't give you what you want, whether that is distance or closeness.

# *EXERCISE 6:* ▭▭▷
## *The life you seek:*

Please take a moment to envision and then to write down a description of the ideal relationship for you. This is different from writing down your List of Must-Haves and Wants, because this list isn't about the individual traits of your mate, so much as how you want your life with them to run. How much time do you spend together? Is it okay, or even preferable, if they have friends and activities that are separate from yours? When you vacation, is it always together? Is there a lot of emotional sharing, or does that term make you shudder? Do they snuggle with you in bed, or do you prefer that they stick to their own side (or live in a separate house altogether)? Are they clear about wanting the same level of commitment you need, or do they say they're unsure of whether they'll ever marry again—and you're crystal-clear that another marriage is a goal for you?

Now, go back to your earlier List, and put the results of this Exercise on your Must-Haves. *Intimacy mismatches create huge and ongoing amounts of conflict and pain for both partners.* Don't settle for someone who will chronically over- or under-fill your gas tank, someone who lacks a shared vision for the future, or someone who hasn't bothered to figure out what they want, when you could pick someone similar from the outset!

## DESIRE: PICK SOMEONE WHO PICKS YOU!

Women, I'm speaking mostly to you here. So often, I hear from women who go to extremes to interpret any signal as a commitment sign, or who pursue a man, hoping he will choose her in return.

In heterosexual relationships, it's still very much men who are the pursuers: if they're not making moves towards commitment that are so obvious anyone could read them, they have a reason, and that reason amounts to, "I'm not the one for you[60]." In Chapter 6, I'll present why, but for now, know this: men can sometimes pursue and win a woman, but the reverse is rarely true[61]—and a bad bet for busy single moms.

For instance, Joy wrote to me about a man she'd befriended and seen over the period of a year, whose one sign that he might feel romantically towards her was when he asked if she'd like to meet his sister. But he never asked her on official dates, he didn't attempt to kiss her or have sex with her in all that time, he never said he loved her, and he often told her he liked her as a friend. To help me understand more, at my request she shared her vision for her future:

*"Short term, I want to enjoy each day of his friendship knowing I have a true friend who understands me and my quirks. Long term, I want to*

*hear him say 'I love you,' then have that conversation of managing a long-distance relationship. 5+ years? Marriage. He'd make a wonderful husband. I've had a 'list' since my divorce! LOL. This man matches the Must-Haves more than anyone I've met."*

He was such a good match, she was wondering about moving her career to another state to be closer to him.

*But perfect partners who do not choose us are not perfect. And not being fully chosen should be a deal-breaker.* "Fully chooses me" is a Must-Have.

What Joy had settled for was unrequited love with a man who wasn't putting forth the effort to be in more than a friendship with her. I reluctantly responded,

> *"You can have a conversation about what you want. But men know how to ask women out. They know how to say, 'I love you,' and how to pursue a sexual relationship. They know how to ask women to be their girlfriends, and wives. Stan is over 40, has known you over a year, and has not done these things. It's not because he is ignorant. He is making a choice. A conversation does not change the information his inaction is already declaring, loud and clear. You're in this relationship alone right now, and the price you're paying is steep: you aren't looking for anyone else, which means that time is going by and all the right doors are remaining closed. Your investment in a man who isn't investing in you means you are losing out on the chance of being really happy with someone who fully, completely, without reservation wants and loves you. That needs to be a two-way street."*

Shortly after, Stan sent Joy a note that cleared it all up: he wanted friendship, and friendship only. Joy is a kind, pleasant, fun person who was putting her hopes into a man who was perfect...except that he didn't love her.

Heterosexual women, I leave you with this final Must-Have that I hope you will all add to your list:

*This person fully chooses me, pursues me, and asks me for an exclusive relationship—without my saying so.*

...

# EXERCISE 7: ◖▬▬▷

## *More Must-Haves:*

Please go back through each of the six sections above, adding each item to your Must-Haves. These go far in fine-tuning even the best picker.

### ▸ STICK TO YOUR STANDARDS:

Now that you've updated your Must-Haves, it's got to be said:

*Your List can't help you if you won't stick to it.*

Many of us have ignored known deal-breakers from the outset. When I asked *Love Factually* seminar attendees to list their reasons for doing this, the results included the following:

- trying to be "nice," avoid another breakup, or cut the other person some slack even though there was a deal-breaker from Date 1

- fearing I would not find anyone else

- fearing I would not find someone better

- being tired of looking

- just wanting a relationship to work, already

- feeling beyond ready to be in a relationship

- fearing how I or they will react to a breakup

- telling myself we should be more relaxed or shouldn't scrutinize so much so early in a relationship: "Chill out, it's only one date."

- giving in to peer pressure, following bad advice and examples from friends

- not recognizing unacceptable behavior, having poor boundaries

- thinking a bad relationship will improve on its own

- believing, "I can change them."

- believing, "Maybe I'm making too much out of this and being too picky."

- telling myself, "But" ("But she's beautiful." "But he has great kids." But, but, but.)

- telling myself, "Their good points outweigh the bad."

- feeling lonely

- not wanting to be judgmental

- lacking confidence or trust in my own perceptions, boundaries, and needs

- not recognizing a deal-breaker for what it is

• • •

# EXERCISE 8:

## My "but" list:

Now it's your turn. Please take out your journal or Notebook and write down every reason you can think of for why you ignored known deal-breakers in the past:

The truth? No matter what your rationale was for living in denial of deal-breakers before, none of those reasons are good enough now if you're going to put your life together with a great partner. It's time to abide your Must-Haves.

Your Must-Haves can help you protect yourself—and your kids.

Abuse is a top killer of women and children around the world, and odds are high that at least a third of you have been abused before[62], which unfortunately can put you at risk of being targeted by abusers again[63]. The stakes are higher than ever once you're a parent. But you can learn to see the signs before abuse happens, and in Chapter 4, we'll learn more about that.

# CHAPTER 4:

# Protect Your Kids And Yourself

There's no way around it: reading about abuse is tough, and this chapter is about preventing, avoiding, and if needed, escaping abuse.

So let's start with the good news. Of the many people who generously shared their painful past in this chapter, one is happily single, and the others are all happily wed to someone who cherishes and adores them. All escaped abusive marriages. And neither they nor their children are abused anymore.

## THE CHILD ABUSE MYSTERY

As parents, we know our children are our most sacred trust. Around the world, mothers and fathers are expected to protect and nurture their children. And it's an expectation that's usually met.

Unfortunately, child abuse also exists in every society. Where does it come from? Over a period of seven years, when I asked my college students to guess at the top contributor to severe physical and sexual abuse and murder of children, not one got the right answer (which we'll get to in a moment).

My students believed that abuses the parents endured in childhood caused those parents to later abuse their own children. And that's a big contributor to men abusing their girlfriends and wives[1]. Still, most formerly abused moms and dads do not take it out on their kids[2].

Evolution has selected against abusing our own children: to the extent that abused children have not survived long enough to reproduce, or have not raised thriving offspring themselves, the eventual winners of the biological struggle for life—our ancestors who primed the human psyche—are parents who raised their children with kindness[3].

To understand one of child abuse's probable origins, consider lions. Evolution favored thick manes, loud roars, huge paws—and a psychology that says, "Kill unrelated lions' cubs." There may have been kind, gentle lions in the ancient past who waited to mate with the lionesses until the cubs from the other guy were raised, but their genes didn't hold sway. Simply put, a new lion king does not have the time to wait around: lionesses don't go into estrus until the cubs are weaned, and lions have a short window of fitness before they're toppled by a younger and stronger male. Waiting might mean never passing his genes forward at all. Even if he did breed in that time, the cubs would be in danger from the next guy unless they were of age to flee or to be sexually available to the conqueror. Any trait that favors survival and reproduction eventually passes to the entire species. That's how evolution works: not only through physical adaptations, but through largely unconscious psychological adaptations that get individuals to do what it takes to perpetuate their genes[4].

This example does not mean that evolution is moral, fair, or pleasant—nor that it is invariably evil, unjust, and painful. Lions also protect, nurture, and play with their cubs, and participate in an impressive social network. But it does show that evolution is highly rule-driven: across time, whatever passes more genes in a given species spreads, and whatever doesn't, ends.

Back to us. *Although most people will never injure others' children, there are human predators too. The No. 1 threat to children's survival and physical safety is not their own parents, but the wrong stepdad*[5]. In Canadian studies, serious violence, sexual abuse, and murder of children was 40 to 100 times more likely to occur if there was any man living in the home who was not genetically related to the kids[6]. No other factor—including whether biological parents were abused in childhood—even came close to explaining the risks. And this is probably global. Consider: all cultures have stories of lustful stepfathers[7].

So it's not surprising to me that a single mom in her thirties sent me this note: "Dating as a single parent is hard! You're looking for someone that accepts both you and your child and who is good for your child. I worry about trusting men around my daughter."

Of course, the wrong stepmom is also a risk. Women rarely become violent with other people's children, but every culture has lore of wicked stepmothers who show a cruel, open preference for their own offspring, and who employ psychological torment against the stepchildren[8]. Cinderella, anyone? In some tribes, it's been observed that stepmothers feed their own children more than their stepkids—which results in better health and greater survival odds for their biological children[9].

Additionally, even if no abuse ever happens, parents nearly always like and love their own children more than other people's[10]. Preference for one's own genes and for those who carry them forward is global and exists in many species[11].

Note that evolution is not an excuse for being cruel or criminal—nor is biology destiny in human beings. Humans do not have instincts that must be obeyed; that's for the birds. Instead, we have inherited strong preferences which we have some freedom to override. Plus, social order and hierarchy are part of the universal human psychology that has evolved—meaning that humans everywhere have evolved morality, laws, religions, and customs that seek to guide us beyond our most base urges.

But the inherited preference for our own descendants partly explains why step-parenting is usually experienced as more frustrating than parenting; why we are so careful about who can adopt, but not regarding who can have their own children; and why we need high standards for who we let into our kids' lives.

So, a major question single parents need to ask is, "Are you good for my kids?" Child abuse is an age-old threat that remains a reality today.

## JEALOUSY'S DARK SIDE

There is a second big question in the area of abuse: "Are you safe for me, too?" Because in every part of the world, the top danger to women's physical safety is a jealous male partner[12]. It's the top reason women in every country and culture are injured during women's reproductive lifetime[13]. And this male sexual jealousy is literally lethal for many women.

Jealousy isn't always a bad thing. In fact, it's been likened to a smoke alarm that tells all of us when our mateship might be in danger from an outside threat[14]. Sexual jealousy saves many unions by alerting us to others who might like to lure our partner away from us; and men's usual and most effective response is to step up their love and attention towards their mate[15].

Women and men alike feel jealousy, of course. Women's is usually aimed at the threats ancestral women more commonly faced, which involved our cave-dude running off with another cave-woman and leaving the wife and kids relatively undefended[16]. That loss threatened ancestral moms' and children's survival. Women today hate a male partner's potential emotional affair even more than the idea of his sexual affair; literally, their heart-rate spikes more in response to the emotional threat[17], and for good reason: men abandon their wives more over falling in love with the other woman than just over a sexual liaison[18]. Even so, it's rare for a woman's jealousy to result in her physical violence towards a male partner—nevermind an ongoing plan of cruelty aimed at controlling his sexual behavior[19].

But men's sexual jealousy can have a dark side characterized by sustained and violent efforts at control, and that's where the abuse comes in. This response to jealousy stems from a time-immemorial problem called **paternity assurance**—namely, the need to make sure all the kids are genetically his rather than some other cave-dude's[20].

The mating mind is selfish: just as lions are trying to pass their own genes forward rather than the genes of all lionkind, humans are seeking to replicate their specific genes. For a woman, a child is always a genetic slam-dunk. No woman looks down at the infant she has just delivered and wonders, "Is it really mine?" But until recently, men could never be sure: women's ovulation is hidden, preventing men's knowledge of the right time to have sex for procreation. If his wife had just one dalliance while he was away hunting, Mr. Cave

Husband could wind up putting his resources into some other troglo-dyte's offspring. As we've seen, evolution has no off-switch, and our mating psychology comes from antiquity, not from recent times—so even though paternity tests are now a thing, the male mating mind retains its focus on ancient problems and solutions[21].

So, men's sexual jealousy is one evolutionary solution to the uniquely male problem of paternity assurance. It can go horribly awry, resulting in domestic abuse against women that peaks during their most fertile years, waning only when women's ability to become pregnant tapers off[22].

Cultural expressions often mimic this mating psychology. Think chastity belts in the Middle Ages—or, today, laws that punish women (but almost never men) for infidelity. Think entire cultures that strictly regulate how much skin women can show, if any; whether they're allowed any personal freedom to travel; and whether they can ever be alone with a man they're not related to. Which gender has historically been considered property? Not men! If you look around the world even now, some cultures give women a lot of physical and sexual freedom, but almost never as much freedom as males; and in some cases, entire cultures make enormous attempts to control female sexual behavior while turning a blind eye to men's escapades.

I don't like any of this, but I do think we know where it all comes from: paternity assurance. It's no excuse for misogyny, systematic oppression of women and girls, or domestic abuse. But it's one heck of a well-supported hypothesis.

And so, while most men don't abuse a partner, nearly everyone who abuses a partner to the point of injury or terror for their lives is male. Plus, heterosexual men seldom choose a mate who is physi-cally capable of controlling them[23].

# PRACTICE SAFE DATING

Given these threats, how do you safeguard your and your kids' welfare? There are several ways, and one is to listen to your hunches.

## ▶ TRUST YOUR GUT:

Tonya, a single mom who is the daughter of a single mom, had this to say about what she wished she'd known: "My parents were alcoholics. I needed to know that emotions are valid indicators of knowing right from wrong, appropriate and inappropriate behavior."

In that brief statement, she's hit on something profound: if you were raised by people or in situations that did not allow you to act on your emotions, you must begin tuning in to your feelings now.

Listen to your gut, your knowing-without-proof, your unconscious wisdom, your Spidey-senses: in short, your intuition. Because if that's a no-go, no amount of logic, evidence, or seeming niceness in the world should be enough to override it. ***For any ancient threat, there is an ancient protector: intuition.*** *It's a lot smarter than you, or I, or anyone else. Ignore it at your very real peril.*

Tonya was also right about how we know our truth and save our bacon: intuition uses our emotions as guides. Intuition resides in the right, non-conscious and nonverbal half of the brain, which is part of what gives us our "gut" feelings[24].

This is not to be confused with attachment style, which can come with fears that should be examined against evidence; intuition is

about the unconscious knowing evolution has gifted us with. Intuition isn't something to notice-and-redirect away from, but something to hear and heed. Most of our mental processes are non-conscious, and even if they lack words to tell us what's up, they more
than make up for it with gut-level emotions that serve to warn us.

Unfortunately, some of us were forced to ignore our intuition-
inspired emotions. Like Tonya, maybe we were raised in bad
situations where we were too young, vulnerable, and powerless
to protect ourselves; we had to emotionally check out and make
it through those years any way we could. If that's you, be gentle
with yourself. Remember that you did the best you could, and your
old coping skills got you to this point of survival, even if they need
updating now.

Others of us were raised with kindness and consistency, but we got
babies, got divorced, and got lonely. Loneliness can create such a
sheer desire for closeness that we might ignore what our intuition is
telling us in the hopes that it's wrong, engage in extensive searches
for evidence to override our gut, and will ourselves to believe that
the right partner has finally appeared. This was me to a tee—until I
finally realized the cost that not only I, but my child, might pay for it.

Still others believe in fairness, and it seems unfair to stop dating
someone when you don't know with certainty that they'd be cruel to
you and your children. If that's you, turn off the mindset that says,
"I have to give this person a chance until it's crystal-clear they're
dangerous." Nope. Actually, you don't, and you shouldn't.

Flip it around: *"I'm under no obligation to trust anyone until they've
proven they're safe. Trust is earned based on behavior, not given
based on faith."* The only entity to trust *"just because"* is your intu-

*ition!* Heed it—your gut is literally there to save you. It's your right and your responsibility to exclude people simply because you feel like something is off about them.

While you're checking in with your intuition, check your kids', too. The biggest threat to babies' survival in the ancient past was violence at the hands of non-relatives[25]; by the age of eight months, nearly all babies fear strangers, an adaptation that keeps them close to those most likely to offer protection[26]. It makes zero sense to assume that kids wouldn't develop intuition regarding their safety as they grow! As another single parent said, "If your children don't like someone you're dating, listen to them. Perhaps they are seeing red flags intuitively that you can't."

If your kids tell you your new partner is hurting them, or describe touches in the bathing-suit region, believe them. Do not assume your children are overreacting. You may be aware of research that shows that eyewitness testimony is often inaccurate, and that kids are even worse than adults at identifying a perpetrator they don't know[27]. And that's true. But just like you, kids are very good at identifying whether they have been touched or injured by someone they know; more than 99% of sexual and other assaults children experience happen at the hands of someone they know well[28].

### ▶ TRUST THE WEB:

It was one of the saddest days of my teaching career: a woman who had been a single parent realized in class that her little girl had been telling the truth about a boyfriend who had offered to babysit. She sobbed as she told the class that her relationship with her now-grown daughter had been permanently damaged and that she, the mom, hadn't thought the child could have understood or accurately related what was happening. Because of that, the mom had left the child with the boyfriend a few more times.

The mom is a good person with good intentions. She was working hard to make a living, and she needed help—and here was someone who seemed safe, offering it. It makes me sick to my stomach to put myself in her shoes. I can't help but wonder whether, if she'd had this information sooner, the whole thing might have been avoided.

*Please do your homework on all prospective dates.*

In Chapter 1, I mentioned Google and private investigators as options. While telling you exactly how to engage the help of search engines and professional detectives is beyond the scope of this book, I urge you to do an extensive internet search on everyone you date, as soon as possible. It's amazing what's online if you have the person's full name, date of birth, and current address—or even just some of that information. You can always hire an investigator if the relationship is further along and you want more details or confirmation of something you unearthed.

Using online search tools, a single dad I was assisting found out that the woman he was planning to date had been arrested for drunk driving the year before. He canceled the meeting, knowing that the best predictor of what's going to happen is what the person already did; that the police rarely catch someone the only time they drive under the influence; and that he was not okay with exposing his kids to someone whose judgment lapsed that much. And I've known women who safeguarded themselves and their families by canceling dates after discovering online that their would-be Romeo had done time for crimes against women or children.

## ▸ TRUST THEIR EX:

Here's a note I received from a thirty-year-old abuse survivor: "My ex's girlfriend just filed criminal charges against him for beating her. She used to call me a 'lying bitch' for saying he'd done the same to me. Wish she had listened when I tried to help."

Me, too.

Yet the new girlfriend's refusal to believe the ex is the rule—as is the subsequent, preventable abuse. Be the exception: check in with the prospective partner's ex and others who know them well!

*Exes are an underutilized gold mine of information.* "If your ex were here right now, what would they say went wrong in the relation-ship?" is a question I have all my clients ask everyone they date, because it's a fast-track to figuring out whether there are notable flaws. And if you have kids, actually talking with the ex should be a requirement of yours before making any serious commitments.

Does your prospective partner refuse to give you the ex's name or contact information? Duly noted. In the wise words of another single mom who survived abuse, "Beware the man who is not trans-parent! You don't know his friends, the names of at least one of his exes, and his family members. This is a guy who is hiding some-thing or is afraid to commit! Run the other way!"

*People with nothing to hide will hide nothing.* If the person you're considering won't yield details, in my view that's enough evidence never to see them again. If you still want to date them, though, find one of the exes on your own (see Google, above). Then, ask that person for names of the other exes, and contact them, too. In the personal protection biz, these are *"developed sources[29]."* They are valid precisely because the person you're seeing did not name them. And they will tell any tales that need telling.

## ▶ TRUST THE SCIENCE AND AVOID P.A.I.N.:

*As we've seen, your partner's absence of kindness and respect towards anyone is reason enough to end a dating relation-ship.* **Please don't settle for not-quite-abusive. Go for a pro-actively healthy relationship.** Selecting for these qualities is the single best way to avoid abusers[30], because they can't maintain the façade of basic decency for long.

Unfortunately, it's also true that many divorced people may not know what kind, respectful behavior looks like—after all, abuse is a common reason that divorces occur[31]. If this is you, you might not recognize early warnings of the sustained cruelty and control that constitute abuse. Maybe you were raised in situations of abuse, married or partnered into them after that, and escaped without ever having had close personal experience with someone worth commit-ting to. If so, abuse may have become so normalized, the red flags don't register.

Which is why I'm providing this list so you can recognize and avoid P.A.I.N.: pre-abuse indicators.

Based on in-depth scientific sources, these are known red flags for impending abuse. Some of these indicators almost guarantee that you and your children will be abused by this person if you stick around, while others are dangerous in combination with other factors. The more indicators you spot, the more certain it is that abuse will happen.

In the following list, I use masculine pronouns for abusers for the simple reason that life-threatening levels of violence are almost always meted out by men, towards women and children. It's possible for women to abuse, but it's improbable. This is not my opinion, but the finding of the best scientists in this field—almost all of whom are men[32]. Your mileage may vary, so as with all other aspects of this book, take what fits and leave the rest.

...

# EXERCISE 1: 

## P.A.I.N.s you have known:

Before reading the extensive list of pre-abuse indicators below, take a moment to guess at what these indicators might be, and also which ones you might have encountered. If you were ever in an abusive relationship, or if you later found out that you had broken up with someone who had abused others (but not you, yet), or if you've known someone who escaped an abuser—looking back, what were the early warning signs? Write your hunches and memories down in your Notebook or journal. We'll compare your list to the one below, towards the chapter's end.

Now, let's explore twenty-five scientifically proven pre-abuse indicators[33].

### YOU'RE VULNERABLE IN SOME WAY.

Abuse is about control and power; vulnerable people are, from the abuser's standpoint, a trove of helplessness to be exploited[34].

This means you, single moms—every one of you. Abusers are looking for you, particularly if you're parenting preschoolers, because that status makes you vulnerable to abusers' charm and financial and physical power[35].

Other vulnerabilities that abusers may try to exploit include: your poverty, your relative youth (you are 15 and he is 18, or you are 20 and he is 40), any financial setbacks you've had lately (you lost your job, your car has been totaled), your or your child's chronic illness or other physical vulnerability, or your history of abuse from partners or parents. *Because you are vulnerable, and abusers are seeking that, it's safer to scrutinize potential partners with extra care and an extra-long time frame before you commit.*

One woman who had escaped two abusive men wrote me that, "I was bullied as a child, and my home life was less than perfect. I coped by being a people pleaser. It took a lot of healing work on myself to recognize that I did have needs, it was okay to have needs, and reasonable to expect a partner to want to meet some of them." The man she is now happily married to cherishes her kindness rather than viewing it as one more vulnerability to exploit.

## YOU HAVE INTUITIVE FEELINGS THAT SOMETHING IS WRONG, OR THAT THIS PERSON COULD BE VIOLENT, ABUSIVE OR DANGEROUS.

It bears repeating: this one factor overrules all other information. Do not pass Go, do not collect $200, and do not date this individual ever again. Period.

## HE SHOWS HIS JEALOUSY IN HIS BEHAVIORS, NOT JUST IN HIS ATTITUDES.

Any man can feel jealous, but the abuser feels he must do something about it. And that something is to intimidate you into closing down your world until he is perhaps the only one left. If he isolates you, makes you account for your time, tracks your car, turns on settings that remotely tell him where your phone is, goes through your things, or follows you, you can either roll out the "Welcome, Abuser" mat, or you can move on.

As one woman said of her now-ex abuser: "I wish I had not accepted that, when we first started dating, he regularly searched for and read my private journal to see how I felt about him...I thought it was a quirk, but it was in fact a huge red flag in so many ways."

Possessiveness is an aspect of jealous behavior. Said another respondent when I asked my Facebook audience what they wished they had not accepted in past partners:

*"I wish I had not overlooked having a partner who was possessive. He didn't allow me to have an identity separate from being a couple. The smallest of signs warn of the larger troubles ahead, such as his being upset you're going to happy hour after work instead of coming home and spending your time with him. When your friends are over while your partner is home, he should give you space unless invited in. A partner that has to insert themselves into everything is way too overbearing and possessive. Maintaining your identity as an individual as well as a partner is important."*

In response, I asked whether he had ever abused her, and the answer was yes:

*"It was a sign of things to come for sure. When I was in it, I thought the more that time passed and love grew, the better it would get. I thought he'd learn to trust me and be ok with me maintaining my independence without thinking it somehow was a measure of my love for him. But it was possession turned aggression before I knew it. It took a while for me to get out, but I eventually realized it wasn't a relationship at all; it was ownership. I'm so fortunate now that I have a husband who allows me to still feel like I'm my own person. We show one another respect and give each other space to have more than just each other in our lives."*

## HE SPEAKS DISRESPECTFULLY OF HIS EX OR OF WOMEN GENERALLY; HIS ATTITUDES ARE SEXIST, HE BUYS INTO MALE PRIVILEGE, AND/OR HE BELIEVES MEN SHOULD BE THE HEAD OF THE HOUSEHOLD.

Disrespect should be a deal-breaker anyway, but pay special attention to this pattern. Male abusers share an ill opinion of the women they've been involved with in particular and a sense of male superiority over women in general. This is easily picked up in stereotypical sex role expectations and contemptuous, degrading speech that goes beyond mere anger about their past partners. If he speaks of his ex as less than human, or denigrates women as a group and expects your servitude and his superiority, consider yourself warned.

As abuse expert Mr. Lundy Bancroft put it so well, "If you are a woman, why be involved with someone who sees women as inferior, stupid, conniving, or only good for sex? He isn't going to forget for long that you're a woman[36]."

## HE'S DISRESPECTFUL TOWARDS YOU.

Abuse always begins with disrespect. This may entail put-downs of you and your opinions, rudeness to you in front of others, or sarcasm and mockery of you. Of course, nobody is perfect, and everyone is rude on occasion, but abusers place the blame on you when you ask for better treatment: suddenly, you're "too sensitive," or don't understand that "I was only joking; have a sense of humor." A non-abuser takes responsibility for having behaved badly, apologizes, and behaves more appropriately in the future.

What if you're convinced this treatment isn't really that bad? In that case, he's still a disrespectful, mean-spirited person you should have zero involvement with unless misery is Goal 1.

## HE'S VERBALLY ABUSIVE TO YOU–OR TO ANYONE.

Verbal abuse goes past disrespect. If you feel scared or controlled, you don't need an abuse thesaurus and you don't need to go to lengths to explain away what's right in front of you. You just need to listen to you, and act on what you know.

## HE'S NOT TO BLAME FOR ANYTHING THAT WENT WRONG IN HIS RELATIONSHIPS.

Abused people sometimes go to stunning lengths to find examples of their own relationship errors, taking responsibility for abuse they did not cause and could not prevent. A woman once told me she was partly to blame for having been abused, because she had tried to shove her husband away when he was pinning her to a wall and crushing her head. That's not abuse, it's self-defense.

But an actual abuser found no fault in himself when his wife hit him in his testicles—to try to get away from him as he launched a life-threatening beating.

A woman who'd been with a string of abusive men told me they "rarely if ever took responsibility for their part in relationship challenges. Moreover, they also tried and succeeded in making me think and feel like I was not capable of accurately assessing reality. With a lot of work, I got my 'picker' sorted out. And I've been married for twelve years to a fabulous person!!"

Also be wary of anyone who doesn't accept their role in negative outcomes in other areas of their lives. The man or woman who won't admit to failings in life will make a bad partner for anyone, *but the man who can't find anything wrong in himself is potentially dangerous.*

## HE SAYS HE WAS FALSELY ACCUSED OF BEATING ANY FORMER PARTNER, OR HE CLAIMS THAT HE WAS THE ABUSED PARTNER IN HIS FORMER RELATIONSHIP WITH A WOMAN.

Just from the stats, *it's likely that men who claim they were abused are actually abusers looking for their next mark*—an appallingly common practice.

Neil Jacobson, a leading researcher in this field and not one given to over-generalizing, bluntly warned formerly abused women who were seeking to repartner that "any man who tells you that he was a 'battered husband'…is lying[37]." Women do sometimes attempt systematic control, which is indeed abuse. But the woman who uses physical intimidation and beatings over an extended period of time to control a man is so rare that precisely zero of these researchers and abuse experts whose work I consulted had ever seen even one.

## HE CLAIMS WOMEN OVER-REPORT, EXAGGERATE, OR ABUSE JUST AS MUCH AS MEN.

The opposite is true: only 1 in 15 abused women reports any abuse to authorities, and only 1 in 10,000—yes, *ten thousand!*—acts of abuse against women results in the abuser's fine or jail time[38]. Real formerly abused men do not villainize or castigate women as a group; they identify with other victims, supporting all the abused as people who have shared a common albeit horrific experience.

## HE HAS HIT ANY PRIOR PARTNER, NO MATTER HOW HE JUSTIFIES IT.

He's a poor risk no matter why it occurred, and no matter how sweetly he's behaving with you. He may tell you a story about how he had no other choice, or she deserved it. But a man always has choices besides hitting his partner.

## HE USES DRUGS OR ALCOHOL WITH NEGATIVE RESULTS (ILLEGAL ACTIVITY, CRUELTY, AGGRES- SION, MEMORY LOSS), AND/OR HE EXCUSES THE BEHAVIORS HE ENGAGED IN WHEN HE WAS UNDER THE INFLUENCE.

Don't be fooled: it's not "the booze talking," it's them, and the booze is one more problem[39].

## HE USES INTIMIDATION, BULLYING, OR SYMBOLIC VIOLENCE TO RESOLVE CONFLICTS WITH YOU OR ANYONE ELSE.

One reason more women don't get out in time to save their lives is the common belief that the guy will lessen the intimidation and the honeymoon will return[40]. And abusers are known for great honeymoons. But as a rule, intimidation escalates to abuse.

For instance, he is a high abuse risk if: he drives too fast when he's angry; he raises a fist to you or grabs you when mad; he responds to reasonable requests from you by doing the offending behavior even more ("You don't like it when I read all the texts from your guy friends? Well, I guess I'll just have to text them before they can text you."); or he damages property such as walls, doors or photographs. In the unlikely event these behaviors don't worsen, you will not make him a kind, respectful person. Give up The Dream[41] and see reality: he will make you miserable.

## HE USES THREATS TO CONTROL ANYONE.

For example, if he tries to limit anyone's freedom by embarrassment, extortion, secret-telling, or threatening to kill himself, or if he threatens physical or any other harm to any person or to a person's animals, he's a high risk of abuse, and a certainty for unhappiness.

## HE USES OR HAS USED MONEY TO CONTROL YOU OR A FORMER PARTNER.

Although economic abuse on its own does occur, it's usually paired with eventual verbal and physical assault[42]. Plus, you're a grown-up who should not have to beg for money, which equals begging for freedom. If, on the other hand, your relationship has degraded to the point that you must have a separate account lest your man keep you broke and broken—you're already in an abusive relationship, and you're protecting yourself by keeping your own separate funds.

## HE'S CONTROLLING, EVEN WITHOUT THREATS.

If this person, male or female, feels free to tell you how to dress, whom to associate with, what to eat, and where to work, you've got a control freak on your hands. Which is so not-fun. What could be worse? Abuse could be worse, and abuse is all about control, so guess what…

## HE HAS A HISTORY OF CRIMES, INCLUDING BUT NOT LIMITED TO CRIMES AGAINST WOMEN.

It all counts: injury to animals; sexual harassment or stalking; assault, theft, vandalism, drug dealing; having come to the attention of authorities for anything sleazy or mean. Keep in mind that anyone with a criminal record has probably committed many, many more crimes than were detected. Additionally, abuse is so rarely prosecuted, a guy could have a long history of partner violence with no record at all—so any record is damning, or should be. Again, you don't have to "prove" he might abuse you someday. Just wanting to associate with non-criminals is enough.

Two women told me they'd left abusive marriages, and regretted overlooking the men's relevant past actions. Said one, "I shouldn't have accepted it when he said that how he was in the past (violent, dismissive, demeaning, living off his mother's Social

Security) was not how he wanted to be." The other added, "The quality I should have made SURE about was no criminal record. I can understand traffic violations or something else minor, but a record shows a pattern of pathology and rebellion towards legal matters as well as authorities."

It does. Next!

## HE WAS ABUSED AS A CHILD, OR WITNESSED ABUSE TOWARDS HIS MOTHER OR SIBLINGS AS A CHILD.

As personal protection expert and child-abuse survivor Mr. Gavin De Becker aptly says, "Children learn most from modeling, and as a mother accepts the blows, so likely will her daughter. As a father delivers the blows, so likely will his son[43]."

Again, the abuse is most likely to be dealt to non-relatives: you and your kids.

De Becker's point was corroborated by Dr. Neil Jacobson and Dr. John Gottman's research: more than half of all the male abusers in their five-year abuse study had witnessed abuse and/or been abused as children[44]. You can't fix that, and it's sad. And certainly, there is tremendous cause for compassion, plus an understanding that many abused men do not go on to become perpetrators. But an abuse history isn't a strong recommendation for picking a partner, most especially if you are a parent to children who aren't his. *If you choose an abused man, hunker down for the lengthy, eyes-wide-open court-ship that tells whether he's going to pay hell forward.*

## HE THINKS PEOPLE IN GENERAL SUCK AND HAS LOW REGARD FOR LIFE.

This includes glorifying violence, thinking violence is valid to solve many problems, and/or identifying closely with violent main characters in any form of media[45].

## HE HAS A LOW REGARD FOR HIS OWN LIFE.

This may show itself in suicidal threats/thoughts, or large mood swings with sullenness, anger and depression. Remember, a lot of abusers were themselves abused; understandably, they might not feel great about other people, the value of any life, or themselves. *You aren't going to change that for or about him, no matter how loving you are*[46].

## HE HAS A SPECIAL RELATIONSHIP WITH WEAPONS.

Abusers often indicate that weapons are for revenge, power and control; they might have quite the identity as weapon owners, and they like to collect guns, especially[47]. Are there gun collectors who aren't abusers? Yes. But when you're a single mom, it's not the way to bet. Watch the way he expresses his relationship to the weapons, not just the fact that he owns them.

## HE WON'T TOLERATE REJECTION, AND APPARENTLY BELIEVES YOU HAVE NO RIGHT TO DECIDE WHO IS IN YOUR LIFE.

If you break up, he may try to persuade others in your life to urge you return to him, or he may respond to your bluntly stated wish for no contact with…more contact! Don't let him back into your life, but do consider whether to get a restraining order and learn more about dealing with stalkers[48].


## HE WON'T TAKE NO FOR AN ANSWER WITH SEX.

Some research indicates that the very worst, most violent and murderous abusers are also the most sexually forceful[49]. If he wakes you at night and literally won't let you go back to sleep until you've given him sex of any kind, you should see red flags flapping on the ceiling tiles.


## HE TREATS YOU BETTER IN PUBLIC THAN IN PRIVATE.

Non-abusers may treat you the same, or even better, in private. But abusers are keenly attuned to putting on a show and charming the audience, when there is one[50].


## HE TALKS ABOUT COMMITMENT, COHABITING, OR MARRIAGE MUCH TOO SOON FOR YOU.

There are two kinds of men who do this: abusers, and men who really are madly in love with you. But it happens really often with men who want to own and control another person, possibly due to their having a tough time maintaining the nice-guy façade for more than a couple of months. See this in light of the overall pattern of the other risk factors, and take the time you need rather than the time he pressures you on. The good partner will wait!

## HE BUYS THINGS FOR YOU AND DOES FAVORS YOU DON'T WANT OR DIDN'T ASK FOR, SO HE CAN GUILT YOU INTO HIS CONTROL LATER.

This is a classic technique known as "loan sharking[51]." If your gut says, "Toooo much," and your mouth says the same, and he keeps at it, that's not generosity. It's control.

One single mom recalled,

> *"I wish I had ignored the guy who made overly large gestures of affection. He would sometimes make a HUGE scene. At Disneyworld, when I was about 6-months pregnant, he told every poor passerby, 'I put a baby in THAT!' He would send gorgeous bouquets of flowers to work and eventually made a very grand proposal with a very large ring. Turns out, he was probably just compensating for all the guilt he felt about cheating with my sister. And he was eventually physically abusive. Wish I had known these things. At least now I can teach others, especially my kids!"*

...

# *EXERCISE 2:* ✏️

## *P.A.I.N. list 2.0:*

Revisit your pre-abuse indicators list, and compare it to the list in this chapter. How many signs did you already know about? Had you overlooked any of the signs from your past? What do you want to add now? Please take a moment to beef up your list so you can protect yourself in the future.

## ▶ TRUST YOURSELF:

"Dear Duana," Denise began,

> "Sean is emotionally and physically abusive, especially when he drinks. He slaps, shoves, and pins me down, taunts me that I have no friends, and screams into my face. He says he has to hit me because I don't express my anger. I don't know if I can forgive him or let him touch me again after the last time, but I would rather fix my relationship if possible. I'm writing because you know science and you give good advice to help relationships."

Denise was past the P.A.I.N. list: she was already living in hell. And because some of you either have been or are right there with her, or may know others in that situation, it's important to learn more about abusers themselves—and how you can learn to trust yourself to do the right thing.

She ended with the three questions that are at the top of nearly every abused woman's mind:

- **"Will the violence stop on its own?"**

- **"Can I do anything to stop the abuse?"**

- **"What should I do?"**

The answers are not easy, but they're clear.

- **No, the violence will not stop on its own.**

- **No, you can't do anything to stop it.**

Abuse is violence with a purpose: to control another person through fear and intimidation[52].

Control is partly established through the partner's unpredictability and seeming irrationality. Things you do with no consequence one day can lead to battery the next. The violence is not about you—it's about them, their characteristics and beliefs, and their perceived needs.

Consequently, nothing you do or don't do in your relationship will predict or prevent your partner's violence[53].

An abysmally small 7% of violent men eventually stop hitting their partners[54]. But they don't end the abuse.

Instead, they learn to maintain dominance solely through verbal abuse[55]. These abusers learn that words alone can remind their partner of the abuser's ability to do physical harm, saving the abuser from jail time while giving them what they want: a slave, not a mate.

And per the science, most women find verbal abuse even more degrading than physical battery[56].

In the many sources I read for this chapter, and in all the abusive relationships I have professionally observed, one man stopped abusing his wife. One.

And his mindset was opposite an abuser's. He felt to his core that there can never be a good reason for a man to hit or verbally abuse a woman, and that he—not she—deserved all the punishment and blame for his actions.

Sean has the right to help Denise feel safe to express anger, to ask her to go to therapy about that, or simply to accept that Denise doesn't feel safe expressing anger. He even has the right to exit their relationship altogether.

But nothing Denise could say or do, or not say or do, would ever be a valid reason for hitting or verbally abusing her. *These acts can never be the abusee's fault, because by definition, the abuser always has options besides behaving abusively.*

Sean disagrees. He thinks Denise causes his abusiveness. That mindset is a hallmark of abusers who never stop.

### "WHAT SHOULD I DO?"

*In brief, what you should do is prepare to leave, and then actually leave.*

It's true that I often advise on how to keep relationships together. For most couples, one person's increased kindness and respect will turn around even a very unhappy relationship, because it changes their whole underlying dynamic[57].

But abuse of any sort is a huge exception. That's because abusers actively oppose anything that requires relinquishing their utter control...such as kindness and respect.

By human right and right of law, we all have the right to be safe and unharmed. Heck, we have the right to pursue a happy, healthy relationship even if we aren't being abused! Achieving these things will eventually involve leaving—safely, but surely and permanently walking out the door.

The problem, of course, is that leaving a relationship is difficult. To leave means uprooting yourself, your kids, and your life as you know it. It looks very much like failure, and it inarguably is an end. It may make you ashamed and prompt others to criticize you. But the only alternative is staying—and staying is worse.

Among the many, many obstacles to leaving, two are especially hard.

## Obstacle 1: The Dream:

I referred to this in the P.A.I.N. list. We know from Jacobson and Gottman's five-year study that women with no plans to leave their abuser are enamored of his potential[58]. They feel that their man is special, misunderstood, an undiscovered genius—a guy who is loving, deep (very deep) down; a man who could be a great soulmate or husband and father if only she could love him enough, or if only his tragic childhood could be overcome.

This Dream is the top factor that prevents women from leaving[59].

Although stereotypes abound that most women choose to stay with abusers forever, that's untrue. The reality is that in any given two years, about 2% of non-abusing couples split up; but among abused wives, nineteen times more (38%) leave in that same period[60]!

Abused women leave in droves—after they give up The Dream.

## Obstacle 2: Further violence:

Stats show it, experts know it, and I'll bet your gut tells you, too: men usually become more violent as or after women leave[61]. If they're also facing his threats against children, pets, and finances, it's no wonder that abusees are scared about leaving and need to plan their departures with great caution.

All abusers are much likelier than average to hold misogynistic attitudes, use drugs and alcohol, and to have been raised in abusive families. But otherwise, there are two distinct abuser profiles[62]. Knowing which type your partner is can help you plan a safe exit.

## Pit Bulls: Pathologically jealous:

Your partner is a Pit Bull if: he's clingy and fearful of losing you; he checks your email, monitors your phone calls, puts a trace on your cellphone, reads the odometer; he controls the money, and "needs" to know where, when, how, and with whom you've been; he rewrites history, denies abuse has even taken place, or says you're the batterer; he has abused you for being looked at by other men, or makes ludicrous and baseless accusations that you're having an affair. In short, a Pit Bull is a bottomless pit of insecurity and jealousy[63].

Named thus by researchers because of these men's tendency to cling tenaciously to you once they've sunk their teeth in, Pits use violence to keep tabs on you, and they usually aren't violent outside the family[64].

They may let you leave without much fuss. But in the long run, they may be the most dangerous, because Pits often believe life isn't worth living without you—or more accurately, that your life is not worth living if you leave. And they can remain lethally dangerous for up to two years after you escape[65].

## Cobras: Antisocially pathological:

Your abuser is a Cobra if: he is independent, angry that you won't let him alone, and only wants you around when he needs some-thing; he feels entitled to get exactly what he wants, exactly when he wants it; he has a history of crimes or violence going back to adolescence, often including violence against animals or non-family members; he uses people as means to an end and thinks that people in general suck, or has a low regard for life; he usually admits the violence but sees nothing wrong with it[66].

Called Cobras because their heart rates slow and their bodies calm down just before they strike, these men are violent for the purpose of getting their way—not only with their partners, but often with other people, too[67]. Their partners usually (and justifiably) are terrified of them.

Cobras can be very dangerous at the moment you're departing, and for a short time thereafter. But they may be far easier to leave safely in the long-term than Pits, because Cobras are too interested in what's in front of them to bother hunting you down. It's too inconvenient.

# THE PATH OUT:
## INTUITION + TIMING + PLAN

The most accurate assessor of your partner's likely violence, and thus the best resource as you plan for leaving, is scientifically established to be you[68].

Only you know when you're ready and it's safe to leave; nobody can pick the time better than you can. When it comes to your partner, nobody else is the expert on what he's likely to do. For this reason, the women who escape and stay safe are the ones who rely on their own intuition, intimate knowledge of their partner, and ingenuity to make their plan.

*But they almost never plan alone. The top piece of advice that scientists and abuse specialists agree on is that you need help to develop a safety plan for before, during and after your escape[69].*

You can get that help free from an abuse specialist at a shelter, the books listed in the references for this chapter, over the phone, and by text, without giving away who you are. In the USA and Canada, you can reach the National Domestic Violence Hotline at **1-800-799-SAFE (7233). Or text the word "*CONNECT*" to 741741**.

● ● ●

# EXERCISE 3: ▭▬▬▷
## *Your escape plan:*

Even if Denise's severe problems of abuse are familiar to you, you may also not yet be ready to leave. But when you are ready, it is important to plan very carefully. Your assignment is to revisit this chapter at that time, and use the resources here and in the references to begin planning your escape. The women throughout this chapter did it, and they eventually found love, too.

Now that we've covered your safety, it's finally time to specifically prepare to date. How long has it been for you? Some things have changed; others haven't. We'll start on those in Chapter 5.

# PART II:

# Mastering The Mechanics Of Dating

# CHAPTER 5:

# Balance Your Life And Your Dating

⚖

When I was single-parenting, I was lucky to have the love and support of my mother and stepdad. I bought a house just around the corner from them, and Mom often got my son to and from daycare, or even spent the night at my place so I could sleep through. Meanwhile, my stepdad routinely cooked gourmet dinners; all I had to do was show up and say thank you. Many times, I arrived at their door to find a happy child, a warm meal, a loving family, and a relaxed atmosphere. I will always be grateful to them.

But even then, I often felt alone with my parenting. There's some-thing isolating about not having another adult in the house day-in and day-out, and something fearful about knowing that the finances, healthcare, scheduling, and parenting of this precious child fall mainly on you. There's something vulnerable about trying to meet your child's needs given an ex who has serious issues and partial custody—and not having a partner in the house to process it with. And there's something bordering on desperation about feeling like you're not good enough compared to the other parents who are somehow getting their kids to all the extracurriculars, while you're trying to content yourself that everyone's still alive. I'd had enough of not being enough! I was exhausted, depressed, lonely, and scared.

It wasn't my sexiest moment. These weren't the years I felt most appealing or alluring. I wouldn't have picked this as the optimal time for dating. But that's exactly why it was time to launch my search: finding my right partner would help me be a better parent and a better me, while hopefully improving my new mate's life, too.

What's more, like all of you, I was an adult—and I had not taken a vow of celibacy! I needed and wanted emotional and sexual intimacy. And I also believed that if I had a great partner, I would be much, much happier—something research agrees with[1].

So the case for a mate search was compelling, from all angles. The catch for a super-busy single parent, even one with a supportive family, was time.

You might recognize parts of your own story in mine—or maybe in these observations from other single parents who wrote me about their concerns with balancing time:

> *"Sometimes it's easy to devote your life to your children. I feel like I have done everything for my daughter and have forgotten to live life for myself as well. We need to find a healthy balance for ourselves as individuals and not just as mothers."*

And:

> *"You really have to be a strong and independent person who isn't looking for your children's replacement parent. [At the same time, you need to] balance that with the fact that your children should see you happy, and that a healthy relationship is a very positive thing. It's not easy or for the squeamish!"*

It's certainly not.

Yes, balancing your life and your dating is a big issue. I wasn't sure I was up for it. Even more, though, I knew I wasn't up for permanent single parenthood. Yet it seemed unlikely that Mr. Right would stride purposefully to my door, knock three times, and announce: "My fair one! 'Tis I, your future true love, come to save you from loneliness, sex with machinery, and the gnawing sense that you are screwing up your child! I mean, of course you're making major mistakes that will require years of therapy; that's a given. But you don't have to do it alone anymore!"

Nope. I was going to have to actually plan, strategize, and search. And, yes, that was going to take time. But even though it felt over-whelming, I did it. I found my balance, hit my stride, and, after a string of dating Mr. Wrongs and Mr. Almost-Rights, finally met my Vic.

Here are some strategies so you can balance your search for love while single parenting.

⚖️

## TRADE, BORROW, OR PAY FOR CHILDCARE

If you have an ex who is good with the kids and shares custody about evenly, count your blessings: it might have seemed awful to part with the children even briefly when you negotiated your separation, but now, you've got built-in time for dating.

*If you're a full-time single parent, finding time is much more difficult. As one single mom wrote to me:*

*"My ex is long gone. Being 100% responsible for raising my children AND rebuilding my career has left me little time to focus on building MY life. My responsibility to take care of my three children has definitely held me back. Lacking an ex to take them every other weekend is a huge problem. How do I find time for me when I have to take care of them?"*

Here's how.

Do you know someone who can provide safe, reliable care for your children while you go out? For some lucky people, it's your ex, mom, dad, or other relative who adores your kids. That was my situation.

But what if these people aren't in your life, are working too hard to be able to help, live far away, or simply aren't appropriate? Then, it's time to get creative.

•••

# EXERCISE 1: ▭▭▭▶

## The childcare brainstorm:

Please take out your Notebook and make a list of everyone you can think of who might be safe and willing to babysit your children. Write them all down—you can argue with yourself later about why so-and-so won't work out. At this moment, the task is to cast as wide a net as possible.

Next, write what you can offer in return for their babysitting services. In some cases, it might be money in a standard babysit-ting arrangement. Or maybe you can barter home repair services, cooking, or childcare swaps. Think about each person's circumstances. Does Evelyn have a full-time job and a dog? Maybe you and your child can walk the dog three afternoons a week, or take the dog to the vet for her.

The third step is to approach some of these people and see whether they're up for the arrangement. Log their responses and create your childcare database.

## TREAT DATING LIKE A PART-TIME JOB

Another strategy is to turn mate-searching into a part-time job. I did, and so do all of my single clients, whether or not they're parents. That's because, just as the word for people who don't job-hunt is usually "unemployed," the word for people who don't mate-search is usually "unpartnered."

Sometimes, of course, the right partner may simply happen along. Maybe you know a single mother of five whose handyman turned out to be the perfect husband and stepdad. She never even had to leave the house, she got her sink fixed, and love found her. It's a good story. But it's not the way to bet.

Social science improves our chances by showing us how most people will behave most of the time. Even though science can't predict what will happen to every person every time, nor answer all our questions, it's still far more useful than anecdotes. Our friend with the handyman-turned-husband is very lucky, but she's exceptional—and exceptional stories like hers don't undo science's helpfulness any more than the rare thriving lifelong smoker negates tobacco's deadliness.

*Science shows us the rule, and the rule for finding love involves planned and sustained effort.*

When you have kids, this is doubly true. It's absolutely necessary for you to identify blocks of time that you can calendar for finding a mate. It's not romantic, but in the single-parent world, romance is what happens after you do the work of finding and getting into a great relationship!

...

# EXERCISE 2: ◗▬▬▷

## *Pockets of time:*

You've heard it all your life: failing to plan is planning to fail. So plan to succeed, labeling the time you're going to devote to your search. This usually won't involve more than a handful of hours weekly.

In your Notebook, please identify the pockets of time in your life. We all have them. Perhaps yours are from 9 to 11 p.m. on Mondays, Wednesdays, and Thursdays. Or maybe you get an hour for lunch each weekday. List these times even if they seem out of step with the rest of the world. As we will see, you can make the most of the time you have, even if the hours themselves appear unlikely for meeting people.

In my single years, the best mate-search times for me were late at night—so I went online. Using dating apps and sites can happen anytime, and I was able to respond to messages no matter how late it was. Additionally, online dating can be a streamlined process that saves you time by allowing you to meet only those candidates who seem like the best fit. We'll discuss that topic more in this chapter.

Workday lunch was the other time that routinely worked for me. After all, everyone has to eat, and most first meetings don't need to last more than an hour in order to learn whether there's any point to a second date. Meeting during workday lunches also automatically limits the scope of the date. If it's bad, you haven't lost much time, and if it's good, the delicious thrill of anticipation is there to build on.

Or combine dating activities, such as by using the internet to vet people, and then keeping the first meeting brief. Of the men who approached me, I accepted lunch or coffee dates with those who seemed to fit my Must-Haves and Wants. Occasionally I took a personal day and met men on the hour nearly every hour for a full day.

There was a particular restaurant I preferred for these series of meetings. The food was good, the service friendly, and the wait staff discreet. One day, one of the men caught on. He called me that evening and said, "I know you met at least one other guy today at that restaurant." He was hurt and angry. I'm assuming he felt a bit duped and not very special, and I felt bad about that.

But I was a single parent, with limited time, and when you're meeting people on these first dates, you're merely interviewing them. You owe them kindness and respect, the same as you owe the staff at the restaurant, bar, or coffeehouse. But you do not owe them loyalty.

When I explained this to him, the lightbulb went off. He saw that it wasn't reasonable to expect my devotion at a first meeting. His respect for me instantly increased. In fact, he asked me out again.

Note that kind, direct, and firm honesty won the day—because we'll come back to this in a couple of chapters when I talk about women, men, and differences in mating psychology that some refer to as game-playing.

## FIGURE OUT WHERE TO MEET PEOPLE

One of the most-asked questions from clients and *Love Factually* class attendees is, "Where can I meet the right partner?"

And folks, if I knew the exact location, I'd bottle that secret and be a billionaire.

Unfortunately, there is no one right place that suits everyone. And even with more information about you, nobody can predict the precise location where you will find love; there's no magical venue filled solely with people who are right for any of us, where the ick-factor is nil, the dates are always terrific, and our time is never wasted.

Instead, let's make the odds as favorable as possible. We can suss out what's likeliest to work for you, given what's worked across decades and continents, plus your specific interests.

*To start, science identifies four commonly successful ways to meet potential partners:*

- through family or friends who set you up[2];

- through your past, by re-approaching someone who was a great match but was removed from your life due to circumstances such as parents' disapproval[3];

- through places you go to repeatedly like work, school, places of worship, and interest groups[4];and

- through dating sites and apps[5], which we'll cover later in this chapter.

*Notice that these four options can be boiled down to just two: personal contacts, and online.*

Let's begin with the three personal contact methods. These strategies are effective because they maximize the odds that you and a potential mate will be at least somewhat alike, and as we saw in Chapter 3, similarity is a good foundation for a life together. Another bonus is the layer of accountability: you and your date probably know people in common, so you could be safer and endure less bad behavior than you might with a total stranger. Also, these methods exploit the impact of familiarity. We tend to feel more comfortable with someone familiar, and familiarity routinely leads to greater liking[6].

...

# EXERCISE 3:
## *Places to mix and mingle:*

Please take out your Notebook or journal and create three headings, one for each in-person method of dating:

- friends and family I trust

- people from my past

- places I go

Under each category, list everything you've already tried to find love. Then, brainstorm what you're willing to try going forward—being as specific and detailed as possible as you list them.

For "friends and family," list every person who might care about you enough to become invested in your search. In "people from my past," consider whether any of your exes were the right one at the wrong time, and put their names on your list. And for "places I go," list locations, events, and groups where you are already a regular or are willing to become one. Then, add as many new groups as can fit in your schedule. It's okay if it's a short list, but be strategic. If you are looking for a woman, consider joining groups that might appeal to the kinds of women you like, and if you're seeking a man, select groups your kind of guy might already be involved in.

A word of warning: avoid the "I already tried that" trap. Did you give each place or method a real and repeated attempt—or did you give up after a time or two? Every method relies on repeated exposure[7], so hanging in there is vital.

And methods that work for some people might not pan out for you. I couldn't tell where Vic would be hanging out, so I tried libraries, bookstores, the Unitarians, networking events, setups, and online dating on three websites. Only one of these ways brought me my beloved, but since I couldn't have known which one that would be, I needed to do it all. Ditto for you! Keep using all the methods you can. *Persistence is the most important dating strategy, because giving up is nearly guaranteed to keep you alone.*

Expecting challenge is helpful. The people who hang in there and prevail are those who know dating often sucks (just like a job search does) and realize it's going to take time (just like a job search does)[8]. Whatever you do, no method will bring you truck-loads of available and appropriate hotties: you will have some bad dates and some bad options. Remind yourself: it only takes one! Ultimately, you're seeking just one right partner. And that's doable.

The upshot? There may be just a few main methods for meeting people, but there are many ways to leverage them—and I encourage you to try as many as you can. Finding the right spouse once you have kids can be a needle-meet-haystack phenomenon, so use all the tools at your disposal, from tweezers to metal detectors!

## BE YOUR OWN DATING SERVICE

Matchmakers have a long and venerable history. Typically, they attempt to pair people with similar values, goals, and attractive-ness—things that really are important in a forming a satisfying partnership. Maybe that's a reason research has found that arranged marriages are surprisingly happy compared to chosen marriages[9]. In arranged-marriage cultures, parents usually scour their social networks, sometimes globally, to find a partner who is so similar to their child that, if the proposed pair are hot for each other, it's very likely to work out.

...

# EXERCISE 4: ▭▬▶

## *People to approach:*

You can still hire matchmakers today, of course. But it's far more affordable to DIY. Leveraging your social network is a technique social media has capitalized on. Social media is new, but social networks are ancient. Use them to your advantage.

To be your own matchmaker, revisit your Must-Haves and Wants. Now, create a version that removes sexual and other sensitive information—a version you're willing to share with trusted friends and family.

Next, review the names you put under "family and friends I trust" in the "Places to mix and mingle" Exercise, above. Take out your calendar, and commit to a day to call or email each of them to ask for a few minutes of their time. Avoid texting: serious communication deserves a method of communication that underscores your sincerity.

If you're having trouble with a script, feel free to use this one— omitting the last sentence if they answer your call:

> *"Hi, [name], I'm wondering if you can spare a few moments to talk with me next week. You're someone I trust and respect, and I'd like your input on something that's important to me. Looking forward to hearing back from you soon!"*

This is almost guaranteed to elicit a favorable response. First, most of us like to help others and we don't get asked for our input nearly often enough; second, it's true that you trust and respect this person, and that message never gets old; and third, it's a cliff-hanger: you haven't said what, exactly, you need help with.

When people respond favorably, set a time to speak with them for between 15 minutes and half an hour. You might want to meet in person over lunch, but if parenting is taking all your oxygen, this chat can be done over the phone. In-person is best if you suspect your friend is very busy, distracted, or might be hesitant: research shows that it's harder to say No when face-to-face[10].

When you meet, tell them something like,

> *"Thank you for talking with me. As you know, I've been a single parent for a while. I'm trying to balance my parenting with finding someone great for me and the kids, and it's proving challenging. I respect and admire you, and it's occurred to me that you probably know, or at least know of, people who might be right for me. I'm wondering, would you be open to helping me find someone?"*

You might find it a little embarrassing to ask for this kind of help, and I can't blame you. You're definitely making yourself vulnerable here. But think of this: we know for sure that the one life circumstance that leads most powerfully to better health, happiness, contentment, longevity, wealth, and even more frequent and more satisfying sex is a good marriage[11]. These are benefits that no job will ever give, yet we are rarely embarrassed to ask for employment references. Your mate search is more important and stands to yield better results, for far longer, than any career. Isn't it worth acknowledging feelings of awkwardness and doing it anyway?

If they say Yes, you can pull out your vetted Must-Haves and Wants and tell them you're so serious about this that you've written down the qualities you are looking for in a mate.

Then say,

> *"Here's that list, to help guide us to the kind of person I'm seeking. And of course, I'm trusting you not to share the list with others, and not to tell anyone you set me up with that I made the request!"*

What if a couple of weeks go by and you don't hear anything? In that case, it's okay to follow up with an email or phone call where you give a gentle nudge:

> *"Hi, I'm just wondering, did you happen to think of anyone who might be a good fit for me? I value your help."*

Readers of my first book may remember the story of my best friend, Bella, who followed this plan—while she had stage four cancer. Not only did her roommate happen across the tall, dark, handsome, and kindhearted man of Bella's dreams, but she made sure Bella met him. They were happily married for the rest of my friend's life. And this happened in New York City, where there was (and is) a shortage of available men compared to women[12].

## Get Your Flirt On

If you're going to max out your odds of meeting people, you'll do well to learn more about that age-old skill of flirting. Flirting was one of the things I most dreaded about post-divorce dating. I'd been off the market for most of a decade, after all. Many single parents feel the same. As one single mom plaintively asked, "Does flirting help to meet people? How do you learn to flirt?"

DUANA C. WELCH, PhD

Yes, flirting helps—so much, it's more important than how good-looking you are in getting others to come hither[13]. When employed by women, flirting creates openness that often entices a man to approach, although as we'll see, there are ways men flirt, too.

If you want to get a guy to cross a crowded room, scientists know just what gets the job done. They have observed heterosexual flirting behavior in malls, bars, and other venues[14]. This means that we have some solid answers (and also that some people will do anything for science—including bar-hopping).

One of them, researcher Monica Moore, catalogued a whopping 52 different flirting behaviors, from hair flipping to lip licking, that women use to initiate contact with men[15]. You read that correctly. Women tend to initiate the flirting, and men tend to respond to it. In public places (but not online), two-thirds of the time it's women's flirting that gets a man to approach. And we send these signals in reliable ways.

Fortunately, you don't need to recognize or employ all the signals. Focusing on just these few will do.

▶ SIGNAL #1: THE SMILE/LOOK COMBO:

Men, particularly, tend to think a woman's smile means she's sexually interested in them, especially if she also gazes into their eyes. The effect is so powerful, guys often think this even when women's interpretation is that she's merely being friendly[16]. If you're smiling at and eyeing a guy and he's not taking the bait, your work here is done: he's just not that into you, or he's not available.

The type of smile does matter, though; ditto for eye contact. The most powerful come-hither look is a genuine, eye-crinkling smile, combined with locking eyes with him for three seconds or longer—repeatedly[17]. This is especially powerful if the smile/look combo is directed at one man alone[18].

Three seconds seems like a loooong time to look a stranger straight in the eyes, and it is. But unlike Gotham, where just one signal brought out Batman, a woman hoping to be approached may need to target a specific man with the combo upwards of once every two minutes—35 times per hour[19]! The more a woman likes a man, the greater the number of times she sends out her signal.

So memorize this: a real smile plus repeated eye contact is the most reliable signal of female interest, and men easily clue in to it. If you're interested in a man, and you're only going to employ one signal, use this killer combo. And if you're interested in women, and they repeatedly smile and stare, that's a dead giveaway that you should be striding purposefully across the crowded room, carelessly throwing back your cape, and confidently introducing yourself.

▶ SIGNAL #2: THE TURN AND TOUCH:

Scientist Timothy Perper has identified, in order, what happens when an initial encounter goes well. After the woman uses her smiling eyes as a lure, couples talk, turn, and touch[20].

Again, the process isn't random. As you talk with a man, if you're interested, begin turning towards him as he turns towards you. And initiate the first touch—usually on his arm. If you're seeking a woman, as you're speaking to one another, turn towards your partner and notice whether she touches you.

▸ **SIGNAL #3: THE MIRROR:**

Watch others, and you'll see it: the I-just-met-you-and-I'm-interested folks copy one another's eye contact duration, facial expressions, voice rhythms, and body positions[21]. And the happiest long-marrieds tend to look similar in part because they've spent decades mirroring one another's expressions[22].

This does not mean you should start mimicking others like crazy. Like most human mating behavior, mirroring is unconscious, and if you draw attention to it, you might look like Weirdo Woman/Stalker Guy.

But do become aware of when a prospective partner is mirroring *you*. It means your superpowers of attraction are working.

▸ **SIGNAL #4: CLOTHING:**

People are reading your T-shirt! Seriously.

When we choose outfits, we choose messages our would-be partners then interpret. In studies, men and women alike think that anyone who wears tight, revealing clothing is probably looking for lust, not love[23]. If you want a hookup, this will attract your target audience, but if you want commitment, it can reduce your odds[24]. Dressing for success in the world of long-term mating means sending commitment signals by wearing clothes that subtly reveal your shape while leaving a lot to the imagination.

Bonus: If you want a woman, think business suit, not swimsuit, and choose clothes that look new rather than well-worn; if you want a man, show that you've got a waist, without showing your actual midriff. For reasons discussed in the next chapters, dressing as if you have a good job or high status attracts women, and emphasizing a small waist relative to your hips attracts men[25].

### ▸ SIGNAL #5: LAUGHTER:

When I ask women and men to make their list of Must-Haves and Wants, every woman puts humor on the list. I literally can't think of an exception. Research concurs: women love a man who can make them laugh, and men love women who laugh at their jokes[26]. I'm not saying to hide your humor if you're a funny woman, or to take a comedy class if you're a serious guy. We all need someone who loves us for who we are at our core, and you should be yourself. But if you're at all funny, humor definitely helps gain women's interest—and if you're at all game for a laugh, finding men humorous helps get guys.

### ▸ SIGNAL #6: RECIPROCITY:

Women are usually reluctant to lead the pursuit in courtship; even now, we tend to find the experience less than rewarding. Being hard-to-get, science has firmly proven, helps women to find out whether a man wants them for now or for forever[27]. And as we'll see in Chapter 6, when men are faced with a hard-to-get woman, it tends to make them aware of whether or not they feel any urgency about her.

But being hard-to-get is not the same as being distant, cold, or mean-spirited, and nearly everyone needs a little encourage-ment in love. *The most effective way to attract others—male or female—is in fact to show a clear liking for them[28]*. So if you want a man, enthusiastically reciprocate some of his interest. Tell him you're enjoying getting to know him, if you are; thank him for the things he's doing for you, such as planning time together and taking into consideration what you'd like; and when he kisses you, return his kiss with the ardor he shows, if you're into him.

And if you want a woman, show obvious interest in her—pay attention to what she likes and says, plan dates that show you've been listening to her, make plans well ahead of time, and initiate phone calls and not just texts. Don't wait for her to meet you halfway—but do look for some level of reciprocity in her feelings.

•••

# EXERCISE 5: ◖▬▬▷

## *Moves to use:*

Now that you know the best strategies for flirting, write down two of them that you'll commit to using (if you're seeking a man), and which flirting maneuvers you'll start responding to (if you're seeking a woman).

**Signal:**
_____

**Signal:**
_____

For the next two weeks, either send out these signals wherever you happen to be (post office, grocery store, apartment laundry facility) when someone sparks your interest, or respond to these signals by approaching someone who makes them towards you.

**Log your results here:**

_____

_____

**And then, try two more!:**

_____

_____

⚖️

## TAP INTO TECHNOLOGY

If you're not using your smartphone and computer for dating, it's time. Despite the objections some still voice, technology is your friend when it comes to finding The One. In fact, between 2005 and 2012, about a third of all married couples in the USA had met online[29]—and they were slightly happier than couples who had met through friends, family, or shared environments!

In part, this pattern may be because online dating lets you quickly clear several hurdles in the search for someone like you. This efficiency is tough to get in other circumstances. For instance, if you see someone attractive on the subway, you don't know whether a) they're single; b) they're looking for a partner; c) they find you attractive too; or d) you have anything in common other than a mode of transportation. Plus, riding the subway at the same time each day in the hopes that you'll eventually get the answers is time-consuming and could get you labeled a creepy stalker. But online, you can quickly discover whether they might be e) all of the above.

And a huge bonus for single parents is that you can not only do this with a minimum of time; you can do it at 11:00 p.m., 5:00 a.m., or any other hours that match your availability. You can sort through prospects while in your pajamas, unwashed, bleary-eyed, and fully available to your progeny. It's the ultimate in convenience, costing much less in money and time than hiring a sitter, hanging out in bars, or making eyes at your possibly-partnered colleague.

## Here are four steps to fishing with the 'net:

### ▸ STEP 1: CHOOSE THE SITES AND APPS THAT ARE RIGHT FOR YOU:

The ultimate goal is to join two or three dating sites or apps, so you can cast a wide net. But in choosing those sites and apps, it is crucial to keep in mind your specific relationship goals.

Why? Because, to put it bluntly, not all dating sites and apps are created equal. Some appeal to honest seekers of love, while others target more of a "hit it and quit it" clientele. If the letters and survey responses that led to this book are any indication, you're probably after a genuine lifelong connection.

*You're more likely to get that by choosing websites and apps that meet the following three criteria:*

- **They charge a fee for membership.** Larger fees are probably best at weeding out players. Choosing a free app or site means choosing a set of people who aren't willing to spend anything—the very ones most likely to be commitment-averse, or to already have a partner[30].

- **They include a questionnaire in order to start searching.** Sex is easily obtained using the array of sites and apps that require almost no time investment. When you use a site that requires a long questionnaire just to get started, you're instantly eliminating most of the non-serious from your search. The longer the questionnaire, the better[31].

- **They do some matching for you.** Stick with sites that either actively match you with similar others, or indicate how alike you are with people you meet on their platform. That way, the company helps you leverage similarity. This criterion is important for three reasons. First, in at least one large study, the happiest marriages were not only formed online—but on websites that did the most matching by pairing highly similar people[32]. Also, matching saves you time, something single parents nearly always need more of. And sites and apps that lack matching may attract a highly visual crowd that is mainly surfing for photos and making choices solely based on sexual attraction. While attraction is important, guess who is focused exclusively on it[33]? That's right—the commitment-averse, the sex-only seekers, and the already-married[34].

I wish I were exaggerating, but I'm not. Unless you want sex-only, apps that cost little in time, money, and personal disclosure are emotionally expensive—especially for women, who are likelier to hope that hookups will lead to relationships, whereas men usually hope hookups will lead to more hookups[35].

For example, research on the users of the pay-optional, super-easy-setup Tinder[36] app showed men routinely admitting that they used the app to get casual sex; feigned interest in commitment to score hookups; and commonly swiped right on hundreds of profiles at a go, in the hope that they'd get laid by any of them.

And nearly one-third of the men in that study told scientists they were already married[37].

It's not a stretch to guess that this mentality applies to other free sites as well. Consider the following changes that a woman made to her OkCupid profile. The profile continued for nine single-spaced pages of similar responses, and I've removed messages that were even more graphic than what you see here:

> ### HERE ARE SOME EXAMPLES OF HOW NOT TO MESSAGE ME (these are taken straight from my inbox):
>
> 2. *You have a beautiful vagina. (note: there are no pics of my vagina. Don't look for them.)*
>
> 3. *You are attractive and I haven't had sex in forever.*
>
> 4. *Do you f\*ck on the first date? Yummmy. Mmmmmmmm!!!*
>
> 6. *I would ruin you.*
>
> 7. *Do you have a nice butt?*
>
> 8. *Would it be inappropriate to ask if you enjoy nine-inch long cocks? (to anyone that may be wondering the same....Yes...it is inappropriate).*
>
> 9. *I wish I could get on my knees and lick and kiss your inner thighs.*
>
> 10. *Holy spankable cuteness, You are hot!!!*
>
> 11. *Give me an hour with your boobies.*
>
> 16. *I got some sick thoughts looking at your pics.*
>
> 17. *Wanna rate my cock?*
>
> 19. *Does penis szie (their typo) matter to you?"*

On the Facebook thread where this was posted, one of the woman's friends replied, "This is why I'm not on dating sites anymore."

To which I said, "It's not all dating sites, it's the free ones. Research-proven."

...

# EXERCISE 6: ⬛▬▬▷

## *Your dating sites:*

Please take some time to research dating sites that meet the cost, time, and matching criteria above. Think about the kind of partner you seek; there are niche sites that cater to particular lifestyles, income levels, religious affiliations, cultural backgrounds, and professions.

Next, take out your Notebook and commit to joining two or three of the places that meet the criteria I've given. Write down the names of the sites/apps, and the date on which you will launch your membership. Put the membership date on your calendar!

### ▶ STEP 2: SELECT THE RIGHT PICTURES:

One of my favorite things is helping others craft their online dating profiles, including taking, cropping, and lighting their photos. How you present yourself in pictures is very important, whether you're seeking men or women. Good character keeps partners, but good pictures attract them—opening their eyes and the door labeled "Relationship."

So look at flirting Signal #4 again: clothing. No matter your gender, if you seek a long-term relationship, wear clothes that reveal your shape, without revealing everything. Otherwise you're conveying hookup potential, which tends to be incompatible with attracting others who want a life partner.

Although this tip is good for everyone, those seeking men are especially wise to feature a profile headshot that's done in good lighting, where you're smiling in a genuine, eye-crinkling way and looking straight into the lens (see flirting Signal #1). This way, you're leveraging the top flirtation technique without ever leaving home. Additionally, having your first photo or two show a headshot will select for commitment-minded men; in research, men who want hookups are more body-focused, whereas those seeking commitment are more face-oriented[38].

Thinking of skipping pictures, or posting photos from a while back? Don't. Photos aren't really optional anymore—not if you want to get any attention. Pictures need to be from the past half-year, clear, solo (so you won't risk being compared unfavorably to others in the shot), and, after the first headshot or two, should show full-body images of you doing things you enjoy.

But not parenting. No matter who you are, your future partner needs to fall in love with you before they will willingly focus on your kids. Your profile should mention the fact that your children exist, but should not telegraph, visually or in writing, that they will always be your topmost priority (even if they will be).

For men seeking women, this means possibly having just one photo of you with your young kids. In at least one study, women were turned on by a man who was pictured nurturing a baby[39].

But for women seeking men, keep your kids out of your pictures! Not only don't they make you more appealing to guys, but posting images where you're with your children, including your teenage daughters, is a juxtaposition that can get women ignored, or targeted for their kids rather than for themselves[40].

Photos are about much more than aesthetics. I hear many complaints from men and women alike that amount to, "Where have people hidden their common sense? I'm worried about dating anyone who can't see what their choices look like to others." They point out the following blunders—mistakes I've also seen and helped folks to correct:

- posting pictures with others cropped out of the image, which makes us wonder about your past even as we're considering a future with you;

- selecting photos that are grainy, poorly lit, taken with ugly lighting from the computer camera, or shot from scary angles (such as with lighting from below), which makes us wonder whether you're a sociopath;

- posting photos with so much junk in the background, it looks like an episode of *Hoarders*;

- displaying images of yourself in overly concealing costumes, from baggy fake fur right up to a ginormous fake beard;

- relying entirely on selfies, raising suspicions that you have no friends; and

- choosing photos that no longer resemble you, which is not only a turn-off but calls your honesty into question.

The upshot? Almost nothing in online dating gives you as much bang for your buck as good photos. And they can be had nearly for free: there's an excellent chance you're carrying around a device that takes not only calls, but excellent images you can crop, rotate, and edit for color and lighting. Bribe a friend with lunch, and get them to take a few dozen pictures of you in an array of outfits, in good lighting, and with a clutter-free background that makes you look your best.

...

# EXERCISE 7: ✏️═►

## Your photo shoot:

Your mission, should you choose to accept it, is to get two dozen photos taken per the guidelines above. Avoid the blunders, and capitalize on what works! Then, show the images to friends of the gender you're seeking, and put the ones they like best into a file you'll post along with your written profile when it's done.

### ▶ STEP 3: WRITE A WINNING PROFILE:

You know how cartoon characters rub their hands together with glee when they can't wait for what's next? That's exactly how I feel about writing clients' profiles, and I'm hoping my excitement is contagious.

According to dating sites with data, if you want to attract worth-while partners, photos alone won't get you there; eye-catching content also matters[41]. And yet, the content of most profiles is utterly forgettable. They ramble on about the profile's author and ask for generic qualities and walks on the beach, rather than focusing on the prospective partner, who is the target audience.

*How can you craft a memorable, effective profile? Apply the following four techniques, which I've long used with clients:*

- **Pick the format your profile will take.** It needs to be catchy: a song that almost everyone from your target age would know, a questionnaire about your ideal mate, or a list that draws readers' interest.

- **Review your Must-Haves and Wants.** You'll be using these as a guideline for what goes into your profile. After all, in constructing that list, you thought carefully about who you need in your life. Now, you get to ask for it!

- **Fill in the content, keeping the focus on your prospective partner.** Almost everyone's favorite topic is themselves[42], which is why online quizzes are so popular. Use your Must-Haves and Wants as fodder so your profile asks all about potential mates rather than telling all about you. The major exception to this is laughter: if you're hilarious enough (and seeking a woman, especially), you can talk about yourself and how you could meet their needs, as a showcase for your sense of humor[43].

- **Post it with a clickbait title.** Write the title last, so it encapsulates the spirit of your profile.

Now, let's pull it all together with some examples.

I had a 60-year-old client for whom I'd written a profile I thought was a siren song to her future mate. But she wouldn't post it; her friends convinced her it was no good, so she put up something else and got little attention.

Here's the thing: she was not dating them! With an eye towards male psychology (see Chapters 6 and 7) and a commitment to the techniques above, I wrote another profile. For this one, I took a photo of a large world map with pins marking everywhere she'd been, and posted it alongside her main portrait. Then, in her written profile, I focused on her Must-Haves, with a large emphasis on travel. She hated fishing and lamented the number of men who posed with various denizens of the deep, so we used a humorous title: More Pins, Fewer Fish.

A week later, she found her Mr. Right. Soon to be married, they've crossed the world and crossed a lot of items off their bucket lists, including dancing the tango in Buenos Aires.

▶ **THE TAKEAWAY:** your friends might have valid insights, but then again, they might not; don't sow doubt by asking for their opinions. Instead, use science as your guide!

You might recall a portion of my own profile from my first book. Here's a stanza (out of five) that I didn't share there. I got great results from it, including Vic himself.

## (SING TO THE TUNE OF THE PIÑA COLADA SONG)

*If you don't run from challenge,*

*And you like exercise;*

*If you'll cuddle and snuggle,*

*And you relish soft thighs;*

*If you can talk but aren't a drama king,*

*And kissing's art form you make;*

*Write to me and I'll answer.*

*How much more will it take?*

▶ **THE TAKEAWAY:** use a creative format, and target your age-appropriate demographic—all while appealing to people's desire to think about things in terms of themselves.

Here's a different take a friend wrote for his profile, which he's generously allowed me to quote here. In his words, "My now-wife said that she read about three lines of it and then put it down because she knew I was what she was looking for."

Here's part of his ad:

> *"YOUR QUESTIONS ANSWERED HERE!*
>
> *Q. Can this guy cook?*
>
> *A. Yes he can. Vegan, vegetarian, and meat. And chocolate.*
>
> *Q. Does he like women who look like women or skinny girls who look like boys?*
>
> *A. He likes women who look like women. If he wanted someone that looked like a boy, he would date boys.*
>
> *Q. Is he an adult?*
>
> *A. Yes he is. He has a graduate degree, full-time dream job with benefits, his own house, and full custody of his beautiful 2 y.o. daughter, whom he protects like a grizzly bear. He does not live with his mother.*

*Q. Is he kind?*

*A. Yes. Kindness and empathy are incredibly important to him.*

*Q. Does he look like Gerard Butler?*

*A. No. But he works out, hikes a lot, and can count to 300.*

*Q. What's this about a dream job?*

*A. He's an archaeologist.*

*Q. So, he looks like Indiana Jones?*

*A. Yes, yes he does. But dorkier. And with glasses.*

*Q. I've got kids, how does he feel about that?*

*A. That grizzly bear thing? That goes for protecting your kids too."*

▶ **THE TAKEAWAY:** instead of saying you're funny, be funny. Let your writing embody the qualities you offer and seek.

And finally, here's part of an ad I recently collaborated on with a client who's given permission for this share:

*"WANTED: THE MIND OF DR. SPOCK, THE FUN OF DR. WHO*

*"In order to make things more fun I've created this short quiz. Give yourself the points for each statement you answer yes to. If you dare, send your score in a message. I promise to reply if your score tops 75."*

| PTS. | |
|------|------|
| 5 | *Give yourself 5 points if you've said some variation of, "Here, let me help you with that," at least twice this week.* |
| 5 | *Give yourself 5 points if, like Scotty from* Star Trek, *you've mastered the art of under-promising and over-delivering.* |
| 5 | *Give yourself 5 points if you have ever thought or said, "Slow and steady wins the race."* |
| 5 | *Give yourself 5 points if your reaction to the finding that liberal Boomers have more sex is, "Woohoo!"* |
| 5 | *Give yourself 5 points if you are usually the first pick for designated driver.* |
| 5 | *Give yourself 5 points if you are someone's emergency contact person.* |
| 5 | *Give yourself 5 points if you have pronoia.* |
| 5 | *Give yourself 5 points if you looked up "pronoia" and thought, "Yeah, pretty much."* |
| 5 | *Give yourself 5 points if you are the Adultier Adult people turn to for wisdom and guidance.* |

| 5 | *Give yourself 5 points if you can name the movie that inspired the above question.* |
|---|---|
| 15 | *Give yourself 15 points if you are definitively single and looking for the love of your life.* |

▸ **THE TAKEAWAY:** an interactive profile where the focus remains on the prospective partner is sure to appeal.

...

# *EXERCISE 8:* ◑▭▭▭▭▭▸

## *The advertising executive*

Now that you've seen how it's done, it's your turn. In your Notebook, please take the following steps:

▸ **FIRST,** decide whether you're going to post a questionnaire, a song, or use some other catchy format. It can help if you Google "top 40 music" for the years when your prospective matches would have been in middle- and high-school, as that's when our musical tastes tend to gel[44]. Write down the format you choose.

▸ **NEXT,** review your Must-Haves and Wants and select the qualities you want to put in your profile. Not everything on your list will wind up there; pick and choose!

▸ **WRITE A FIRST DRAFT OF YOUR PROFILE,** focusing on your future mate, and using your Must-Haves and Wants as the basis for your writing. Like the profiles above, avoid listing qualities you seek—instead, put in the behaviors that would indicate those qualities. That's far catchier.

A lot of people get very nervous at this stage because they're not writers. But here's a secret many professional writers live by: it's a lot easier to edit what's on the page than what's not. Don't worry about how terrible the first effort is. You can easily change it!

▸ **WAIT A DAY OR SO**, so your brain can do some non-conscious work on your profile while you focus on other things[45]. Then, return to your draft and refine it. Remember, "perfect" is the enemy of "done": your aim is not to craft perfect prose, because that can keep you stuck. Instead, get to good-enough.

▸ **WRITE A KILLER HEADLINE**, and post the complete profile on every site and app where you've got a membership.

## ▸ STEP 4: VET PEOPLE BEFORE YOU CONTACT OR RESPOND TO THEM:

The world is chock-full of beautiful, tempting people who have no business in your life—including, as many single parents know, our exes. Almost everyone in developed countries is in love when they wed; if love were enough, the divorce rate would be near zero[46].

Which is why it's important to vet people even before you contact or respond to them.

So here's the last bit of advice in this chapter: when you find someone online who interests you, or when someone interesting finds you, look past the pictures and compare their profile to your Must-Haves. Maybe you'll find a deal-breaker during your first reading of their profile, or maybe it will be later—or never! But if ever you do find something amiss—during your first exchange of messages, your first phone call, or your first date—end things. Don't hide the truth from yourself, and don't knowingly waste the one resource we can never replace: time.

As we've seen, balancing your life and your dating is all about time. Time saved is time spent with your children, and with your future mate rather than with people who won't contribute to your lives in a lasting and happy way.

Of course, this disciplined, goal-oriented approach is much harder to maintain than it at first appears. And that's why we're about to address common pitfalls of dating.

# CHAPTER 6:

# Watch Out, It's A Trap! Men, Women, and Games People Play

L egend has it that Charles Darwin felt sick to his stomach whenever he saw a peacock. How could that long tail help its survival or reproduction? After all, the peacock's train made it easy prey, not only because the tail is heavy, but when it's raised, the bird can't easily see or escape from predators. Its very existence seemed to mock Darwin and his theory of evolution.

And then, long after Darwin's death, evolutionary scientists made some important discoveries. First off, females mated more with the males that had longer tails and more eyespots on them (when you're a peacock, size matters)[1]. Not only that, but females' perceptions could be manipulated. If researchers snipped off some of the eyespots at the end of the tail feathers, peahens no longer wanted those guys—now, they preferred males they formerly overlooked[2]. Most interesting of all were experiments where individual peahens were put into an enclosure with just one male. Given the choice between breeding with a short-tail male or none at all, females went ahead and cast their genes forward with whoever was around...but the chicks had much higher death rates if the dad had a short train than if Daddy was well-endowed; apparently, a big train means a better immune system for the offspring, because Dad himself must be healthy to carry it off[3].

This tells us several things. Just because we don't understand something yet does not mean we won't; scientists are persistent creatures. Also, peafowl have a mating psychology that tells them who to want and how to act. Third, conscious awareness is totally unnecessary for mating psychology to function. Peahens have bird brains; it's not like they consciously think, "What a tail! I shall successfully cast my genes if I choose him!" They just know what they like. Fourth, by preferring males with big trains, peahens are choosing something that looks ridiculous to us, but is actually helpful in solving a key reproductive problem for them. And finally, beauty is much more than skin-deep. For peacocks, it literally shows their genetic fitness for babymaking.

We can reasonably expect that if birds and, as we've seen, lions have a mating psychology to help them pass their genes along, we do too. What looks like random or meaningless behavior makes sense under the inquiry of science—and it explains the apparent and largely unconscious games people play. Just as with other species, our psychology, like our bodies, evolved from what aided our ancestors to survive and reproduce.

All that said, perhaps the biggest dating pitfall ever is **mating-centrism:** the incorrect assumption that men and women share all the same mating psychology[4].

Let me be completely clear: we don't. As we saw in Chapter 3, it's true that character counts, and that's what keeps great partners around, regardless of gender. But attracting good partners requires sending out the signals they respond to, and these signals depend in part on gender[5].

These worldwide gender differences can be boiled down to two statements.

- **Men seek fertility and fidelity**—and in order to get that, they value youth, beauty, and signs that partners are likely to stay sexually faithful.

- **Women seek able and willing provision and protection**— and in order to get that, they value a partner's resources, height, and commitment signals.

My first book covered the origins of these differences, plus how men and women can understand one another, in detail. Here, I'll focus on some issues I didn't cover there, and specific challenges faced by single parents.

## THE GENDER TRAP

Unfortunately, the very idea of gender can trip us up. Although my first book has been well-received in five languages, the material on gender differences has been hard for some readers to take. And I agree; I wish the human mating ritual was fairer, more pliable, and—well, a lot less cave-personish.

But when it comes to male-female mating psychology, the evidence is overwhelming[6]. Denying the existence of gender, saying it's a purely social construct, and insisting that men and women are the same, just with different genitals and upbringings, is unrealistic. And it doesn't prepare you for our version of shaking a tail feather.

How we're raised plays a part, of course. Everywhere in the world, we are socialized for different behaviors from the moment it's announced that we're a boy or girl. But gender is bone-deep, too. Peacocks don't just have long trains—they have a psychology that says how to use them. Peahens' psychology says which tail to choose. And men and women have their very own battle of the sexes.

Gender is also far more complex than science has caught up with. There has been abundant research on cisgender men and women (that is, people who identify with the gender they are presumed to have, given their genitals at birth). This research, which includes gay and lesbian people, shows similar patterns all over the world[7]. But there is only scant research on people who identify as being transgender, transsexual, gender-fluid, or any gender that is off the male-female binary.

We do know some things about these other groups, however. We know for sure that gender orientations exist other than male-female, and that transgender people have long existed in varied cultures[8]. Even before starting hormone therapy, it's common for transpeople to report sharing psychology in common with cisgender people of their same gender identity[9]. For instance, transmen (that is, men who were incorrectly presumed female because of their genitals at birth) may have a higher sex drive on average than cisgender females do[10]—just like cisgender men all over the world. And sex drive grows or wanes in line with one's gender orientation once hormone therapy begins[11].

Regardless of your gender, you might find differences between your experiences and what's reported here. So, as with the rest of this book: whoever you are, you are welcome here. Your life is your own experiment. If you try something and it doesn't work, you can always go back to doing it another way. Take what works for you, and leave the rest.

## THE CAVE-VERSUS-CULTURE TRAP

Imagine you're on a camping trip, and you didn't bring toilet paper. In fact, you didn't bring fresh water, food, birth control, bug repellent, sleeping bags, or tents. And there are about 120 people in your group. Talk about poor planning!

Now imagine the camping trip is lifelong, in a cave. This—our ancestral past—is where our unconscious, motivating mating psychology comes from. It doesn't give a fig about enlightenment or equality. (It does want to know where you found the figs, though.) All it cares about is fight, flight, food, and the other f.

Today, most of us live in safety and luxury unimaginable to our ancestors. Culturally, we've built on one another's knowledge, and now, instead of being wowed by the wheel, we're impressed by missions to Mars. We've come a long way, baby.

If only our psychology had traveled so far. Babies still fear strangers, heights, and snakes—threats from our shared evolutionary history. But without appropriate supervision, they will hurl themselves in front of cars, point guns at their siblings, and stick forks in toasters, because those threats are too new to have become encoded on the human genome[12].

Mating psychology is like that, too. The human mating ritual is based on a genetic legacy handed down from ancestral humans, not modern culture. This is terribly inconvenient, because our genetic change is glacial, but our culture can turn on a dime. It's left us with caveman-and-woman psychologies when it comes to mating—even when it makes no sense.

For instance, in an era when both sexes make money, there is no logical reason why women shouldn't make the first moves in texting, calling, asking men on dates, paying the restaurant tab, and proposing marriage. And there's no logical reason why a man should make more money than a woman he hopes to impress, pay for the date, or be ambitious. Right?

There's your trap: caveperson mating psychology does not budge much when confronted with modern culture, no matter how logical our newer and arguably better culture may be. You can follow logic and modern culture, of course—but that caveperson is going to club you down almost every time.

Talk about baggage! Let's work our way around other dating pitfalls, then, with an eye towards understanding these sometimes-unenlightened but very persistent psychologies we're lugging around.

## PITFALL #1: THE BEAUTY BIAS

Everyone loves a pretty face. Literally, humans have an inherent bias that beautiful people are better than plainer folks: more intelligent, warm, friendly, better in bed, and superior in just about any way you could want[13]. Pretty people even get lighter prison sentences[14]! And in case you're tempted to blame the beauty industry, think again: infants gaze longer at faces adults deem beautiful than they do at plainer faces[15].

204

Apparently, like peahens, we humans unconsciously believe that beauty is much more than skin-deep. In a genetic sense, this can be true. Prettier people are more symmetrical[16], a cue that their immune systems stave off invaders; most ancestral diseases would have been disfiguring. We also become less symmetrical as we age and lose fertility. So, symmetry is a window into someone's ability to make babies at all, plus their probability of creating kids with higher odds of surviving and thriving[17]. As we've seen, our unconscious mating psychology is all over that goal.

Of course, many of you may not want to have more children—to which evolution sticks its fingers in its ears and says, "Nyah nyah nyah, I can't heeeeaaar yooouuu!" Your inherited mating psychology, being unconscious and having no off-switch, doesn't care one whit about your conscious plans to stop having babies so you can retire someday. Nope. Evolution goes right on wanting what it wants, acting as if you urgently need more offspring. That's one of the reasons I've listed the beauty bias as a pitfall: it's about procreation, but we still make decisions based on appearance long after that stops making sense.

That said, both sexes respond to beauty--but men are far more susceptible to it in courtship. The reason? Fertility. Most men make enough sperm every day to populate their own planet[18], but they can't cast their genes forward without a fertile partner. And cave-women spent most of their lives infertile – those years when they were too young, or too old, or too sick, or pregnant, or nursing[19]. So, men had to be able to discern fertile women on sight, without any advanced analysis—or be left in the evolutionary dust.

They excel at it. Today, men absolutely everywhere strongly prefer partners whose appearance and behavior suggest babymaking potential: youth, and beauty. Name nearly any quality men find sexy—an hourglass shape, smooth skin, rosy cheeks, symmetry, full lips, long shiny dark or blond hair, high energy, a bounce in your step, a fun and lighthearted attitude—and I'll show you a sign of fertility. Straight men, gay men, old men, young men, men who want children and men who've had a vasectomy, blind men, sighted men, tribal men, city men, country men: all men are bowled over by youthful hotness[20].

This is a species-wide universal—so much so, that telling guys to overlook youth and beauty is a surefire fail. You may as well order them to think sugar tastes bitter[21]. "She's got a great personality" doesn't sell men on a setup! Good character keeps the man, but attracting him requires sending signals of youth and beauty.


## ▶ APPEARANCE CUES:

Fortunately for those Wise Readers who are past peak fertility, sending the right signals to attract men is not the same thing as being a 21-year-old supermodel. Instead, ye Seekers of Men, here are some ways to put your most beautiful foot forward.

**Clearly, one thing you can do is to *look as good as you can*.** This implies dressing to show your waist without wearing overly-tight clothing; taking care of your health, skin, and hair; exercising; and getting enough sleep and water.

*But I don't advise losing weight*, unless it happens naturally as a result of healthier lifestyle changes! Not only do most men find an average-weight woman more attractive than one who is too thin[22]— but losing weight usually results in gaining it all back, and then some[23]. Men resent a bait-and-switch, just like women wouldn't like it if a guy was a doctor when they met, and then refused to work. Dress for the body you have; get rid of clothes that undermine your self-confidence; and get with a guy who likes your body as-is, no matter its size!

Plus, after age 45 or so, carrying more weight makes your face look younger[24]. As the saying goes, "After 40, you've got to choose — your face or your butt." If you want a guy who is commitment-minded, choose your face every time[25]; the guys who care more about your tush are players!

**Here's one I lived by:** if you're past your 20s, you can vastly increase your pool of partners by dating men who are around 10 years older than you. That way, you can be permanently young and hot, without doing anything to change your appearance or behavior. This strategy gives single moms many more options, without cutting off opportunities to date men your own age if they pursue you. Why is that important? Because single parents are less likely to remarry than childless people, especially if they're female and in their 30s and beyond[26]. My "10 years older" strategy gives you better odds of finding a good committed partner, because men routinely define women who are a decade younger as "young" and therefore desirable.

### ▶ BEHAVIOR CUES:

Men also infer youth and beauty from your behavior[27]. Some of the most important signals aren't the way you look, but the way you act.

**Seek your match, rather than trying to make it onto the cover of Maxim.** Biology is not destiny. Evolution handed men a strong desire for youthful hotness, not an ultimatum. In the real world, guys know who the "10s" are, yet they usually prefer approaching a partner on their same attractiveness level[28]. Next time you're in public, look around: it's not only the beautiful people who have devoted men by their sides!

- **Smile and look men in the eyes**—in your photos and in person. As we've seen, it's a vital cue of attraction, more important in getting men to approach you than your actual level of beauty.

- **While you're at it, leverage the handful of flirting techniques** in Chapter 5. I'm guessing that men read flirty behavior as not only approachable, but youthful. Whether or not I'm right, it works.

- **Act as if you're confident**, even if you're not: men construe confidence as status, and status as desirability[29].

- **Put both the word "fun" and the concept of fun in your online profile** in at least two or three places, and show images of yourself doing fun things. In studies of personals ads, men are likelier than women to ask for someone "fun"[30]—and I think that's because fun equals youthful to them. Go back over the examples of profiles in Chapter 5 for ideas.

• • •

# EXERCISE 1: ✏️

## The beauty list:

If you're seeking to date men, in your Notebook, list everything you've already done to show off your youth and beauty. The section just above can help. Can you think of other strategies? Have you used them all?

Then, list what you're committing to do going forward, and do it.

## PITFALL #2: INSTANT CHEMISTRY

What's lust got to do with it? To cavepeople, probably quite a bit. They didn't need photos, apps, or websites, because they had eyes, ears, and noses that did the mate-selection job just fine. We know, for instance, that women can sniff out the best genetic match for babymaking—and if you've ever wanted to wear a guy's t-shirt after he mows the lawn, you've had the experience, too[31].

So first, the good news: chemistry is for real. Definitely get with someone you're physically into, because it helps maintain a faithful lifetime bond[32].

But expecting chemistry instantly when we meet someone is a real pitfall. We live a lot longer and have much more complicated lives than our ancestral mothers and fathers did; the mere urge to merge can't carry us through.

You can't suss out your Must-Haves from chemistry. In fact, acting on instant attraction can blind us to whether someone's got what else we need[33]. And although men are pretty clear about whether or not they're attracted from the first moment[34], women usually aren't. We're mostly wired for sexual caution before we have a strong feeling of sexual desire for anyone who isn't an actual rock star[35].

Which means that women, especially, are bypassing partners who could make us happy, simply because we don't get butterflies at first sight.

For example, Trish had a history of requiring instant chemistry. Since women rarely get that feeling for mere mortals, she'd been going for the super-hot guys--and finding out they were cheating on her. This isn't surprising: the top predictor of whether men cheat is whether they can, and a top predictor of whether they can is how good-looking they are[36].

When we met, I encouraged her to date men who were sincerely interested in her, even when she didn't feel that immediate zing — unless her gut gave a clear No or the guy lacked a Must-Have. Here's what she wrote after a first date with a good-looking, average-height single dad named Eric:

> *"He's really nice, and I had fun at dinner. We talked for about 4 hours, so it was long. I just don't feel that interested in him physically. I don't feel repulsed, but I don't feel romantic either."*

I told her this rule of thumb for women, which I'll now share with you:

NO PHYSICAL REPULSION

+ YES ON YOUR MUST-HAVES

+ LIKING THEM

= GO OUT WITH THEM AGAIN!

And men—of course you're not going to ask out someone for whom you feel zero attraction, but don't let their presence of good looks stop you from making sure they're actually good for you!

Trish reluctantly continued following my advice. A couple weeks later, she and Eric had a six-hour dinner that flew by like minutes.

Still, she said,

> "I just don't feel physically drawn to him. I don't. I don't really want to touch or flirt with him. I don't really even like hugging him. He just feels too small. What should I do? I feel so confused because I feel like I just want him to be my friend. He's so great to me."

I wrote back,

> "'Not drawn to' and 'am repulsed by' aren't in the same league. In case you need the reminder: someone you enjoy speaking with for six hours at a stretch is someone to give a chance to. Your gut will eventually tip one way or the other, and that's when to make your decision."

She bucked her confusion and kept going out with him, and sent this to me a few weeks later:

> "Things are absolutely fantastic. Eric took me to the airport last Friday after asking me on Tuesday to be exclusive. He showed up at my house with a stack of romantic cards. One for each day of my trip. Wow. No one has ever done such a gesture like that for me before."

When she got home a week later, flowers and another card were waiting:

> "When I opened the card, it was marked with an '8' for the final day of my trip (the other cards had been numbered 1-7). Inside was a card in his own handwriting telling me how happy he was that I was home. The fact that I knew he actually went into the flower shop was huge. When I thanked him, he said that he had so much fun going into the store and talking to the florist about me."

Are we liking Eric a little more now? Trish was. A couple months later, she said,

> *"I'm very much in love with him and definitely want to be with him. As you said, sometimes the best people don't sparkle right away. I'll let you know how it goes... I've never had butterflies like this before!!!!"*

They invited me to the wedding, and I'm delighted for them as they plan their lives together.

Women, please do yourself the favor of letting a relationship develop if good things are present and dealbreakers are absent. Butterflies can happen on down the road! Your gut will push the needle towards Stay or Go, in its own time. Listen to it—but don't rush that choice.

Men, please do yourself the favor of figuring out whether prospective partners have your Must-Haves, rather than relying on chemistry and hoping for the best!

...

# EXERCISE 2: ◖▭▭▭▷

## *The patience primer:*

If you've ever rushed to judgment, either because you did or you did not feel instant chemistry, take a moment to reflect on that. In your Notebook, please write down your plan for what you will do differently going forward, given what you've learned in this section.

# Pitfall #3: Meaningless messages

*"Hi beautiful."*

*"What are you up to?"*

*"Hey there."*

*"Want to talk?"*

Pretend you're a woman seeking a man, and you're online or on-app. Now, further imagine that your inbox is brimming with messages like these.

Not very inspiring, are they? Yet this is exactly what many men are sending.

And here's my advice to recipients: ignore impersonal communication from men. Online, ignore "winks," "flirts," and other generic signals men send through the site or app. Don't reach out to men who look at your profile twenty-eleven times but don't reach out to you. Don't respond to men who repeatedly send you messages they literally could have sent, unaltered, to anybody.

These are all examples of low-cost signals—requiring nearly nothing of the sender's time, intellect, or attention and showing zero investment in the recipient. In line with the old saying, "easy come, easy go," players convey that to you through their behavior[37]. In my experience with clients, they do it from the very first wink, flirt, or generic message.

Meaningless messages are so ubiquitous, I've wondered why guys bother at all. The answer, extrapolating from a study of men on Tinder, seems to be that they work sometimes: players send these messages to perhaps dozens of women at a time, hoping even one will have sex with them[38].

These low-cost signals cater to male desires for casual sex, without meeting most single moms' desires for commitment. Women in general and single moms in particular place a huge value on commitment signals, and rightly so. In evolutionary time, they signified a mate who would protect them and their kids—something very handy back when women's life insurance policies wore animal skins and carried spears[39]. Signs that a man offers commitment remain relevant even now, particularly when you're making the big ask of a man to invest in your ex's children. Single moms need a hero—and heroes give high-cost messages!

So, all you Seekers of Men, read every low-cost message for what it is--a lure to see who takes the bait, while the fisherman casts many, many generic lines. Get rid of these players right away, simply by ignoring their messages. Respond solely to men who reach out to you with a real message that acknowledges concrete things about your profile that go beyond your appearance.

For instance, in Chapter 5 we read the profile of a woman who concocted a compatibility quiz for men to take. The questions involved such things as their liking for flea markets and their similarity to Scotty from *Star Trek*, and the woman asked men to respond to her with their score. A low-cost, generic response to this profile might be something like, "Hi there." Or even, "Nice quiz"—without taking the requested action of giving his score and some further details of why he liked her profile. In contrast, a real message might read, "Wow, you're pretty, and that's the most creative and fun profile I've ever seen. I scored an 85 and I hope that's good enough to hear back from you. I really like that you're into *Dr. Who* and *Star Trek*, and yes, I have taken out my landlady's trash (now it's my trash, since I bought a house). Pronoia is my thing, too, although I admit I had to look up the definition. I would really like to hear from you and see whether we click. Hoping you respond soon!"

Sincere Seekers of Women, you can benefit from that example, too. Write a note that references specific things you like about a woman's profile aside from her pictures, and say at least one or two things you see in her profile that could make you a good match. Also, ask her to respond to your detailed note; in my work with clients, I've found that women rarely want to respond to a message that lacks the direct request for a response, or direct questions. Above all, avoid sending anyone you actually like and want to meet a generic "Hey, how are you"—unless you want generic silence in return.

...

# *EXERCISE 3:* ◧▭▭▷

## *A better letter:*

If you're seeking men, take out your Notebook and write down the following: "I will ignore meaningless, impersonal, and cost-free messages." Sign your name. Really! When we write something down and then sign our names, we're likelier to follow through[40].

If you're seeking women, go to a dating site or app, and find someone whose profile you like. Now, in your Notebook, use the tips above and craft a personalized message as practice.

## PITFALL #4: FLAWED PURSUIT

Liz wrote,

> "After five years of being on my own as a single mother, I finally feel
> ready to take the plunge. I have now joined dating sites for three months
> and have been receiving my matches. Should I send a smile, or would
> this be considered pursuing? A friend who used eHarmony said she did
> this to encourage someone she found interesting to send her a message. I
> kind of figured if they read my profile and are paying for the service like
> me they should make the first move."

Liz is right and her friend is wrong. Much as I'd like to tell women
to go ahead and reach out to anyone they like, that's not the way
the scientific cookie crumbles. And since you're time-pressed
single parents, I can't advise you to do anything that wastes time or
emotions. Only those who can and will improve our lives need apply!

This need to save time and heartache goes for men, too. Over the
years, quite a few heterosexual guys have hired me to help them
get out of relationships they never pursued but which they were too
guilt-ridden to leave, or just to get women to stop texting, calling,
and otherwise chasing them long enough for the guy to figure out
whether he's there out of desire or guilt.

Why would men feel so guilty that they would override their own
desires and stay where they don't want to be? Why would female
pursuit confuse rather than elate men? That's a bit of a story.

Men and women have shaped one another's psychology since
we've walked upright. When cavemen preferentially bred with

fertile and faithful women, that choice eventually created a female psychology that is primed to try to give men those things. Hence the centuries-old industries to shape waists, define bottoms, and paint faces (that's the "fertile" part), and women's habit of making men wait for sex (the "faithful" part). And when cavewomen preferred mating with men who offered resources and commitment, their choice eventually resulted in a male psychology that strives to please us according to those two attributes. Historically and now, guys leverage ambition, education, money, and ardent vows to devote it all to their mate. You can see these precise behavior patterns all over the world[41].

You can also view these psychologies through the lens of lies: women may fib about having less sexual experience than they really do, just as men may hint at a shared future when they're just playing[42]. These tactics sometimes work, precisely because they activate the mating psychology of the targeted gender.

Men so want to please the right woman, they enjoy self-sacrifice in the name of their beloved. This includes the men who wait months for sex and say with no prompting, "We've got the rest of our lives to explore each other." And this desire to please continues in good marriages. Vic proactively checks the locks, waterproofs the basement, withdraws less money from his pension than he could, and goes over health insurance benefits—all to make sure I'm safe now and will be taken care of even if he dies. I've gotten letters from men and women alike quoting guys who eagerly do what it takes to win a partner's heart and trust. This is how good men behave when they love.

Plus, pursuing is one of the most effective things men can do to win a woman's heart; it's a huge neon sign flashing "commitment," not "hookup." In studies, married and single people alike rate men who go all-out to show their sincerity and interest as winners at lifetime love[43]. (Of course, the woman must be interested too. Remember, two's company, three's a crowd—and one's a stalker. When a woman says she never wants to see you again, stop pursuing. No means no!).

So my advice to men is simple: if you want a woman, don't play it cool: pursue her. Spend time with her; call and see her often, making plans at least two to three days in advance; and do the stuff in this chapter and the next. With my clients, each of these things spells out "guy I'll be seeing again," because these actions under-score that your interest goes beyond the brief(s). These signs show the willingness to provide—and that's the top signal women are looking for from you.

And guys, if she's pursuing you and you're getting confused by it, step away in order to see if you miss her. If not, find someone you feel wholehearted about!

Given all these ancestral tendencies, a major pitfall opens up when women pursue men. My answer to Liz's question about sending an electronic smile to a guy who's shown no interest in her first is a firm No! For one thing, men already assume that most women want commitment, so when women pursue men, it's unnecessary. For another thing, men perceive hard-to-get women—the opposite of women who pursue them—as high-status[44].

Men care about status in all things, including their partner[45]. To un-derstand why, consider a key difference in male-female psychology. Women live in a world of equality, where they seek connection with the next person in the grocery checkout line, but men live in a world of hierarchy, where they continually perceive themselves as one-up or one-down[46]. And men prefer to marry up. Men prize status so much that women can elevate their desirability even if they aren't especially beautiful, simply by letting the man pursue and taking time before having sex with him[47].

Still not convinced? Notwithstanding a popular dating app's recommendation for women to "make the first move," research shows that men are 6-8 times more likely to initiate contact online than women are[48]. So, women, you really don't need to do it for them. When men don't reach out, it's not because they don't know how.

In fact, women, making the first move can get you played. Some men have privately told me that they love apps where women reach out first, because they view it as easy sex: "She's already told me she's interested by contacting me, so I respond to the hottest one and set up a meeting for that night." When I've asked whether these apps really deliver sex on a platter, these men have told me yes, especially if the guy mentions possible long-term intentions—a strategy men also use to get hookups through free or low-cost apps and sites[49]. It seems that when a woman makes an obvious first move going beyond the smile-look combo in Chapter 5, it turns men on for casual sex[50], but off for commitment[51].

So even though I absolutely agree that women should have all the rights men have, I also see that if you're a heterosexual woman seeking commitment, exercising the right of pursuit does you zero favors. Instead, leverage the right of refusal: await pursuit as a power-move to avoid men who aren't really into you. Single moms, put yourself in a position to be pursued, rather than doing the pursuing. Save your time and emotional energy for someone who wants you enough to make real effort!

The upshot? Yes, heterosexual men genuinely want to win the heart of a particular woman—but if you aren't that particular woman, guys generally don't know what to do with your overt interest, other than to have sex with you and get confused about their feelings. As one liberal, educated, and successful businessman told me, "If the gazelle runs towards the lion, I kind of wonder what's wrong with the gazelle. I don't think quite enough of myself to trust women who come to me without my pursuing them." Then, when they realize they want out, some feel guilty for using you and wasting your time. In my experience, these guys didn't intend deception; they just don't know how to say No. They don't share the urgency of the female biological clock, and as a result do not focus on the passage of time. Also, they aren't primed to avoid seemingly free sex that amounts to a chance to cast their genes[52].

Whoever you're seeking, you'll need to be prepared to reply when others reach out to you online. Generic messages are not a reply problem, since you're ignoring those. As for the meaningful messages, here are two suggested responses that have worked well with my clients.

Saying No to someone who approaches you online:

*"Hi [name], thank you for reaching out to me. I really liked [X and Y] on your profile. Unfortunately, I don't think we have enough in common to talk more, but you took the time to send me a personal message, and that takes guts. Thank you."*

Saying Yes to someone who approaches you online:

*"Hi [name], how great to hear from you! I really liked [X and Y] about your profile, and I'd love to hear more about you. I wrote my profile with the right person in mind. How well do you think you fit it? Looking forward to hearing back."*

...

# *Exercise 4:*
## *The Yes and No notes:*

Please copy the above Yes and No scripts onto your desktop so you can customize them for people who reach out to you in a meaningful way.

## Pitfall #5: The texting trap

Giselle was frustrated with texting:

> *"We seemed to hit it off at the gym and he texted me that he did indeed want to grab dinner at some point. He texted me daily for two months and flirted, which showed continued interest; however, he never set concrete plans to meet outside of the gym. At some point I jokingly and accidentally blurted: 'Take me out to dinner, asshole.' He seemed rather shocked, but his response was: 'Yes, ma'am.' He texted me after that but then he just stopped. How can I prevent such a situation from repeating itself? His texts conveyed romantic interest...I honestly don't know what went wrong. Do you disagree with my approach (it had been two months though...)? I thought I should state what I wanted/take control since he wasn't, or was his lack of taking charge in itself a sign of disinterest? And if that was the case, why string me along with romantic texts?"*

I replied,

> *"Your inclination to see this man's behavior as a lack of genuine*
> *interest is the right take. He is a man, after all, and very accustomed*
> *to a world (and a psychology) that tells him—continually—that it's he*
> *who must make the move if he wants a woman. Much research shows*
> *that men who want a woman, make a plan to court that woman; men*
> *who don't, don't. They may flirt, or have a one-nighter, or a friends-*
> *with-benefits situation...but they don't pursue. If Gym Guy had a*
> *sincere romantic interest in you, you would not be left parsing out his*
> *texts to figure that out."*

We'll probably never know why this man engaged in two months of texting with nothing more. But asking him out backfired. And texting got inside her head, confused her, and wasted her time.

### ▸ WHY TEXTING IS A FAIL:

I recommend avoiding all texting with people you're newly dating. It's invaluable for requesting another loaf of bread, or asking if the car needs filling—once you're in a relationship. But it is easily mis-construed if you're not yet at a steady level of commitment[53], and here's why.

- **Texting puts everyone on an electronic leash.** People un-derstand that online messages and email might take a day or so to get to, but most of us expect a near-immediate response to texts.

- **It's not only intrusive for someone you just met to have that kind of access to you, but it kills the build-up of deli-cious anticipation in courtship.** In that way, texting upends the human mating ritual and encourages women, especially, to send signals of accessibility that men often interpret as low-status and unfavorable for long-term prospects. In my experience, when women initiate or immediately respond to texts, men become confused about whether they're into these women for anything but sex.

- **Texting enables "bread-crumbing"**—investing in one partner while sending daily texts to several others so the texter maintains numerous backup options. By encouraging meaningless, costless messages such as, "What are you doing now," or "Good morning, beautiful," or simply sending a smiley-face, texting allows some Lotharios to bread-crumb lots of people simultaneously. This might be fun for the bread-crumber, but it's very confusing to the bread-crumbees. In this way, texting is a short-term mating strategy meant for hookups, and is a total waste of time for those seeking a long-term partner.

- **As Giselle's experience shows, texting seems to draw out the actual making of a date.** I hear from women, especially, who wonder why a man is sending texts every day, without escalating the relationship to talk on the phone, meet in person, or share meaningful information. This could be bread-crumbing, or it could be something else. Whatever it is, it's not furthering the goal of making a life with someone. Refusing to text at all would get rid of these folks and save your time and energy.

- **Texting takes almost no courage.** A major reason women value pursuit is that it shows sincere commitment-mindedness, because it requires bravery as men face down possible rejection. That's precisely why phone calling is preferable: to call, men need to be courageous—to think on their feet, to figure out what to say, to figure out or ask when to call, to face the possibility that it won't go well, and to listen as well as contribute.

...............

• **Texting leaves way too much room for misinterpretation.** I've heard from a number of women who refused to go out with a guy because of how he worded his text—not that he'd said anything obviously offensive, but because the women read something into it. Keep this rule of thumb in mind: the less any of us knows about someone, the more heavily we weigh every scrap of information we have[54]. Phone calls give more information, so any one thing you say isn't weighed quite as heavily. And phone calls give you verbal cues such as tone of voice, pauses, and opportunities to explain or backtrack if you say something awkward. Texting does none of that.

...............

• **Calling allows partners to discover whether they would make a good long-term match.** Texting is fine for saying "I'm at the table nearest the bar," but it's not made for conversation, and it says almost nothing valuable about compatibility.

•••

# *EXERCISE 5:* ◖▭▭▭▭▭▷
## *The no-text script:*

If you agree with these thoughts, I hope you'll nip texting in the bud. Copy the following script and keep it where you can send it to others at the very beginning stages of interest:

If you're seeking women:

> *"I know texting is what most people do at this point, but I'd rather call you if you're okay with that. It's a better way for me to get to know you. Is there a good time for me to call you, and may I have your number?"*

If you're seeking men and someone's asked for your number or offered to text sometime:

> *"I know it's a little unusual, but I find texting isn't a good way to get to know people I'm dating. So I don't text at all with people I'm just getting to know, but I'd love to hear from you by phone. My number is _____."*

What if they text you anyway? Dating is one long social intelligence test. Frankly, the above directions are so clear, if the recipient texts you instead of calling (or answering your call), they've basically just said, "I either don't care what you want, or I'm not paying any attention to you."

That's a terrible precedent. Ignore their texts—entirely. They will eventually clue in and call/answer your calls, or they won't. Move on with your life until that occurs.

And, warning: if you send the scripts above and then answer texts anyway, you've just sent your own implied message: "You can do whatever you want, without regard to my wishes or feelings. It's okay; I don't mean what I say." You can't attract a good mate if you don't insist on one, and people usually respect you about as much as you respect yourself. Don't undermine your own boundaries!

...

# EXERCISE 6: ✏️➤
## The no-text policy:

In your Notebook, make a deal with yourself by committing in writing to a no-text policy:

> *"I will not text with people I'm dating or trying to date, and I will send them my no-texting script so my policy is clear. Instead of texting, I will call [if you're seeking women] or I will let people know they can call me [if you're seeking men]. If they text me, I will ignore it."*

Then, sign and date this, for maximum resolve.

## PITFALL #6: CONFIRMING THE DATE

This one's short but sweet: Ye who made the date, confirm the date! A full 24 hours ahead of time, reach out by phone and say something like, "Just calling to confirm; I'm looking forward to seeing you at _____ [place] at _____ [time] tomorrow!"

Why? Because it's considered rude not to, and it keeps women insecure, wondering if you're really going to show up—the opposite of the commitment signals women are looking for. And it keeps them insecure for a reason. All my female clients whose dates didn't confirm, didn't show. Yes, 100%.

A corollary is, don't go on the date if the pursuer (i.e., the guy) didn't confirm. Thou shalt not hunt him down, chase him, threaten that you're not going to show up, or otherwise pester, harangue, or cajole him into confirming.

Instead, note to yourself that you are feeling insecure and that you prefer someone who gives you confirmation so you feel secure. Then, don't be available for the date, even if all you'll be doing is watching a kid-friendly movie with your children, the dog, and enough popcorn to dig out of the couch cushions for months. Stick to this plan even if he calls at the last minute. Don't answer until the next day—you are busy! Then, if he calls again to ask why you weren't there, reply in a kind tone, "Oh, I'm sorry, I thought you'd decided against going out when I didn't hear from you, so I made other plans." Do not describe those plans—they aren't his business!

People treat us how we allow them to, and we are all constantly training one another in what will get our attention; don't train men to treat you like an option rather than a priority. Save your energy for men who make a date at least a full two days ahead of time, and who confirm a full day in advance. Pursuit and planning show commit- ment-mindedness; a lack of those tells you where you stand, too.

Of course, guys don't have the market cornered on bad behavior. Increasingly, I'm hearing from men who did everything right—only to have the woman back out of the date at the very last minute. No matter the reason, cease contact with anyone who treats you this way. I mean it: the odds that her grandmother really died that day are minuscule (and yes, I've heard of women who made that excuse and then backed out of a second meeting at the last minute, too). These women may as well hand you a card that reads, "I'm not kind or respectful, and I'm not into you. Pursuing me is the path to pain." Put your energies into women who are enthusiastic in saying yes to your appropriate date-making, and who show happi- ness in meeting you where and when it was confirmed.

## PITFALL #7: PAYING FOR DINNER

Guess who's paying for dinner? Let's get to the short answer: Seekers of Women, it's you. Yes, I realize it's the 21st century, and maybe we should all be past that. But caveperson mating psychology is tenacious, so we're not. Women value resources and commitment just as much as men value fertility and fidelity. Older women, younger women, lesbian women, straight women, rich women, poor women— all women, from Nigeria to India, and Taiwan to Colombia, prefer a partner with riches that they'll generously and permanently share[55].

In a spate of studies starting in the 1930s and continuing through today, young American women value a mate with money twice as much as men do—whether the research is from 1939, 1956, 1967, the mid-80s, the 1990s, or 2015[56]. In fact, there's not one study I've ever read or heard of showing that men value a woman's resources anywhere near as much as women value men's, just as women don't place the same value on youth and beauty that men do. Religion, continent, culture—none of them change this pattern.

So while men are busy viewing women as sex objects, women's psychology has an equivalent: eyeing men as success objects. Both of these seemingly shallow psychologies have deep evolutionary roots. Just as men desire fertility and fidelity so that their partner will bear his (and only his) children, women value ongoing, committed provision and protection of themselves and their children as a hedge against the perilous circumstances their ancestral mothers faced.

And today, an early sign of that is guys who pay for the date.

There are modern objections to this approach, though—mostly from women. One 2018 survey finds that American women typically ask to pay their half of the bill to avoid feeling like the guy expects sex later[57]. It's a realistic concern. Players sometimes offer up very expensive dinners and gifts from the start, hoping that if they drop their cash, women will read it as a commitment signal and drop their drawers[58]. Remember, when people lie, they lie in the direction of what their desired gender wants to hear!

Women, there's a way to protect yourself: don't accept an expensive date for the first meeting or three. If a guy asks you to something costly right away, tell him you'd rather meet for coffee at first. Don't explain why, just don't accept a date you'll feel sexual pressure about if he pays. He can pay for dinner later—when you know him better.

Women also worry about a sense of fairness. Some point out that they can afford their dinner, his dinner, and the dinners of people at several other tables. Why should they rely on a man to buy them food?

But paying is not about whether women can afford the date, or about who has more money; it's about sending signals that each gender responds to for making a bond. We are far from the only species that uses food gifts to begin a long-term relationship: many birds do, too[59].

When a man provides for all the expenses on dates, he's usually saying, "I'm willing to invest in you"—a possible long-term mating cue. When he asks to split the bill, he's saying something else: "I'm hoping for some free sex." Women, don't offer to pay! If you do, you don't get this very important information about his intentions, a tip that can save you time and pain. And if he asks you to pay, don't see him again.

And guys, paying is to your advantage. For one thing, it increases the chances she'll see you again. My female clients lose interest in guys who don't pay, even if these same women feel conflicted about the fairness of expecting men to pony up. An online survey I conducted on best and worst dates showed the same thing. There, women's top complaint was men's failure to pick up the tab, and their top advice for men was to "Pay the entire bill, in full and without complaint. Period[60]."

Also, as with pursuing, paying gives men important hints as to how much they care about a particular woman. If he pays for the date and he can't wait to do more for her, that's important feedback. If he pays and feels like his money could have been better spent, that's good for him to know, too. Through paying, he's learning that the pursuit of this specific woman is worth it to him, or that it isn't. He's saving time and gaining clarity.

So, men: pay for the date, with a generous and open spirit. At first, make it something simple, like meeting for coffee; flashing your cash right away probably doesn't help if you're looking for a Mrs. Right rather than a Miss Right-Now[61]. If you want someone who wants you for you, and not just your income, show interest that steadily increases, with dates to match. Later, you can take her on dates that cost more—but you don't have to be rich to win the heart of a loving woman, just as women don't have to be perfect 10s to win the heart of a loving man. The main thing is that you ask women on dates which you can and will fully fund.

Also, guys, tip well, even just for the coffee—because that shows generosity, and women everywhere despise stinginess in a man. Women care much more about a man's willingness than ability to pay[62], and generosity is a sign of willingness. How willing can you be if you won't spring for an iced mocha with whipped cream, plus a tip for the barista? The main thing is not how much you're spending, but how willingly you're spending it.

And women: let him pay, and let him feel great about it. Tell him you had a good time (if you did). Thank him, with a smile in your eyes, on your lips, and in your voice. Remember, men want to please the right woman; tell him you're pleased. That's payback enough for Mr. Right.

· · ·

# *EXERCISE 7:* ◖▭▭▶
## *The dinner bill:*

In your Notebook, write down ways you can handle the situation when the bill is presented for any aspect of a date. If you're a man, also write down some types of dates you'd be willing to pay for (coffee, picnics, a walk around the lake with a stop for sno-cones). And if you're a woman, also write down what you'd say if a man offered to take you on an expensive first date where you might feel sexually pressured; you can use the section above to guide you.

Now that we've covered common pitfalls of dating, let's move on to pitfalls in timing. Relationships have stages, and Chapter 7 is all about proceeding through those smoothly—including when to get exclusive, when and how to handle sex—and scariest of all, when to introduce your kids to your new partner.

# CHAPTER 7:

# The Parent Traps: Men, Women, and Timing Your Relationship

When it comes to (almost) everything related to timing a new relationship, the short version of the science-based take is: wait! Wait to get exclusive. Wait to introduce people to your children. And wait for sex. Deliberate pacing is the key.

You won't need to wait forever; in this chapter, we'll get to the nuts and bolts. But it's important to let each part of the relationship have its time at center stage.

Yes, timing is nearly everything. Here's how utterly crucial a waiting strategy is, and why it's central to avoiding all the following pitfalls.

## PITFALL #1: MINI-MARRIAGES

One single dad wrote to me, "If I'm dating a lot, some women think I'm a player even though I'm not having sex, but I'm just putting myself out there."

He's right: dating around early on does not, by itself, make him a player. By getting to know several people before getting in any deeper, he's avoiding what I call "mini-marriages"—situations where people get sexual, get exclusive, get emotionally attached, and only much later—sometimes after the wedding or the move-in, with kids in tow—figure out whether or not they're right for one another.

This path is strewn with lost time, bad choices, and broken hearts, because the core questions of compatibility arise so late in the process. Despite the current idea that love is a) rare, b) all you need, and c) enough to justify marriage, it's not so. My apologies to the Beatles, but research shows that love is abundant, it's likely to happen more than once in your life, and you're going to need similarity, kindness, and respect in addition to love.

The pathway to lifelong happiness moves in the opposite direction: first find out whether or not you're a good match, and only later become exclusive, fall in love, and become fully sexual[1]. Suss out your Must-Haves from the first meeting (or even before that, online—see Chapter 5). *Don't simply let time pass; use all your dates, even the first ones, to ask the difficult questions.*

### ▶ ASK THE HARD STUFF:

But, I hear you saying, isn't that off-putting and intrusive? Absolutely—to players and the highly ambivalent. But to stayers—commitment-minded men and women who know what they're after—you're speaking their language.

You can ask almost anything on a first date, as long as you're willing to:

- jettison people who aren't right for you,

- understand that players will hereby leave you alone, and

• *phrase your questions in a way that isn't about the two of you so much as it's about general life goals.*

That last part is vital. Let's say you want to know whether someone's open to step-parenting—an important qualifier, if you're a parent. Wisely, you've decided to spend minimal time on partners who aren't. But of course, it would turn off nearly anyone if you asked, "So, wanna help me and my crazy ex raise my son?" That's way too much, way too soon, and makes you look unbalanced.

However, if you broaden the question so it's about general life aims rather than about the two of you, you can find out what you need:

*"You and I are just getting to know one another, and I'm not saying I have any idea about whether we'll work out, but it would seem kind of foolish to go too far down the path with someone if we have totally different views of the future. I have a son who lives with me half the time and I'm curious: if we worked out, what would you see as your role in his life?"*

In case you think that even that softer version of the question will scare everyone away, I asked something very similar on the phone before Vic and I met in person. His answer was, "I wanted two children when I adopted my son; it would be my privilege to help you, if we work out."

Or take another big topic: commitment itself. Single moms, especially, worry they'll be living with an endless supply of Legos™, snotty noses, and loneliness if they try to discern whether a man is seeking marriage. If they blurt out, "I want to get married, do you?" that fear may well come true. Putting it bluntly creates pressure and implies desperation—and there's never yet been a perfume called Desperation.

But you can ask about general life goals around marriage. In fact, you should: men seeking a spouse place a premium on commitment, whereas men seeking a hookup are turned off by any mention of the long-term[2]. In one study, men seeking casual sex found it desirable for the sex partner to be married—to someone else[3]! When you bring up commitment in a general way, you are getting rid of the players and bringing on the stayers.

You could say,

> *"I'm wondering, what does your future ideal relationship look like—not with me, since we don't know each other yet, but in general?"* You might continue with, *"In your ideal future, are you married, or in some other arrangement? Ideally, where do you live, and who lives with you?"*

When I was dating, a few men told me they had no idea. One guy in his late 40s said, "I don't have to know that yet, do I?" Well, no—but I knew what I wanted, and I wanted to be with a man who knew he wanted marriage. There is no point to spending time with people who aren't on the same page.

Commitment-focused men do exist! Vic specifically wanted a happy marriage. Several others I dated wanted it, too. Most of my male clients hold marriage as a major goal; they hire me to help them find their Mrs. Right. And science shows that most men value and desire commitment and marriage[4]. Don't propose to the guy, but don't fail to quickly find out a date's aims around any huge goal that is a Must-Have for you! This allows you to deeply bond only with compatible partners, because similarity breeds content.

...

# EXERCISE 1:

## *The voting booth:*

Let's say that for you, politics express your value system, and similarity on this is a Must-Have. In your Notebook, please write down a general way you could figure out a new date's views on the issue. I'll wait here while you write your answer, and then I'll give a sample of my own.

.................................................

### OKAY, YOU'VE WRITTEN YOURS; HERE'S MINE:

*"In recent years, I've found myself increasingly involved in local and national politics. For the last Presidential race, I made 1,000 phone calls to voters in five states, on behalf of [name candidate]. Are you politically involved?"*

Note that this answer avoids baldly asking for their affiliation, but it puts the topic on the table and will probably elicit an answer for or against your own point of view.

## ▶ DATE AROUND:

Dating around until you've got enough evidence to merit exclusivity gives you higher odds of finding compatibility with someone, instead of wasting valuable time in dead-end relationships. It also provides helpful distraction, keeping you from focusing too intently on any one person until they've been found worthy of your laser-beam attention. That's one reason I advise using two or three dating sites or apps at once, and meeting people in real life as well. Distracting yourself with other options at first can be a good way to make sure you're not putting too much into anyone who hasn't yet shown they meet your Must-Haves.

Unfortunately, women often have a different perspective, as reflected by this statement written to me by a single mom: "I've followed your work for years, and I know you say to keep seeing others until it makes sense to get exclusive, but I've never done that and I'm not comfortable with it. I like this man and I worry about what will happen if he finds out I'm seeing other people."

Her concerns are common, and I used to share them. That's partly due to mating-centrism; because women prize commitment signs, they frequently believe that men do too, and so they give commitment signals to men from the first. Women also know that if a man tells them that he is still dating around, they would be turned off, so they assume the same is true of men.

Additionally, many single moms rightly assume they are competing against childless women. They may feel that showing strong and immediate commitment to the man they want will put them at the top of his list.

But these three assumptions are all flawed, because they wrongly presume that men and women react the same way. For a woman, overcommitting to a guy who hasn't asked for exclusivity can backfire by making her appear easy-to-get, and thus low-status and less desirable. As we learned in Chapter 6, it's the hard-to-get women that men construe as high-status. Single moms, this means you can elevate your desirability by saying you're continuing to date around--and actually doing so[5].

The upshot? Seekers of Men, there is no commitment from you until he has stated his commitment to you—sans your clingy prompting. If you're acting committed and assuming he is too, you're putting yourself in a risky position: I can't tell you how many times I've heard from women who found out "their" guy saw himself as a free agent. Assume he's dating around—and be dating around, yourself, until he has asked you point-blank to be exclusive. In fact, tell him you are seeing others!

...

# EXERCISE 2: ✏

## The dating-around speech:

Let's say you're dating multiple men, and you feel awkward, uncertain, and guilty about it—but the guy you like hasn't asked for exclusivity. What can you say that will tell the truth, without being presumptuous or clingy—and without asking him to be your boyfriend? Write your answer in your Notebook, and then I'll share mine. (If you date women, don't try this; as we saw above, that would be a mating-centric mistake that could cause women to write you off. Women respond to commitment signals, and how committed can you be if you state your intention to play the field?)

### OKAY, SEEKERS OF MEN, HERE'S MY DATING-AROUND SPEECH:

*"I know we've only been out a few times, but so often, people expect to be exclusive right away. To avoid any dishonesty, I want you to know that*

*I'm dating others and I anticipate you're doing that, too. Thank you for letting me get that off my chest."*

This short speech elevates your status by showing you have options, and by the same token, it enhances his sense of urgency if he's genuinely interested in you[6]. Several of my man-loving clients were immediately asked to be exclusive after they said this; in some cases, my clients replied that they weren't ready for exclusivity because they were still too new to one another.

And Seekers of Women, don't settle on any one woman until you feel sure she meets your Must-Haves. At that point, give her the commitment signal she's primed for by asking her for exclusivity.

## PITFALL #2: THE RELATIONSHIP RUSH

A single mom in her 40s asked, "At what pace should the relationship go, especially if you've not been in a relationship for a while?"

Good question. *Even after it makes sense to become exclusive and the pursuer has requested it, hurrying the relationship without adequate information, self-knowledge, experience, and commitment is a pitfall for men and women alike.* This includes rushing to tell too many secrets, rushing to introduce your children to your new partner, rushing to involve your partner in your kids' lives (and vice versa), and rushing to have sex.

In each of these cases, rushing is actively unhelpful for finding your Mr. or Mrs. Right, because among other things, deception feeds on hurry[7]. Short courtships may be helpful for people with something to hide, but not so much for those they hide things from. Plus, rushing can weaken rather than strengthen a bond, as we'll soon see.

What should the time frame be? For every aspect of getting together, timing is less about a given number of months and years, and more about how much you know about yourself and your partner, how old you are, and each person's commitment level.

We've covered some aspects of getting to know one another already, and will continue to do so in this chapter. Regarding age, if you're under 25 or so, brain studies hint that you might still be changing enough that it makes sense to date for a year or more. Additionally, younger people are often still figuring out what's important to them, and that takes time: you can't choose well if you don't know yourself enough to have solid Must-Haves[8]. If you're substantially older than 25, though, a shorter dating period may be adequate, because most older people are basically who they're going to be, and so their future behavior can be projected from their past history[9].

For instance, it took months, not years, for Vic and me to move forward into a happy and lasting marriage. We weren't young when we met; he was 52 and I was 38, and we'd each taken time to determine our Must-Haves. Also, he had a long history and gave me access, so I'd know he was the real deal: he had lived in the same neighborhood for 25 years, had lots of long-term friends there, and made sure I met them and all of the most important people in his life. He was sure he wanted to marry me, and told me that just a couple of months in. Although the time frame was technically short for each phase in our courtship, in reality I had a thorough knowledge of him and his intentions.

That said, let's get more specific and take each of these challenges, from secrets to sex, in turn.

## PITFALL #3: TELLING TOO SOON

All of us have secrets. For example, depression is a common side effect of single-parenting, especially for single moms[10]. One wrote me to ask, "When do I tell a new partner about my depression?"

Some well-meaning people advise laying it all on the line immediately. As one woman put it, "At that initial stage when all looks rosy and sweet, we should also be revealing the not-so-rosy parts of ourselves honestly to each other. Keeping that stuff for later is almost like a lie, and then it becomes a painful awakening. "

It's a double bind. Wait too late to tell your truths, and it looks like a lie of omission. But reveal all too soon, and Mr. or Mrs. Could-Be-Right turns into a track star. What to do?

Beware TMI—telling too much information, too fast! *Information works against you the most if it's first and worst.* People will cut you a lot more slack if they learn the good stuff about you before anything else[11]. If you're kind, honest, funny, warm, generous, sympathetic, fascinating, well-connected, and taking antidepressants, that's more attractive than having your depression be the initial thing others hear. Like your mama always said, "You never get a second chance to make a first impression." Make it a good one!

Studies on the impact of good and bad information, plus a non-representative survey I conducted on the specific subject of secret-sharing with new partners, lead to this rule of thumb: *put your best foot forward, and then reveal your secrets as it makes sense, given the level of emotional intimacy in the relationship*[12]. With that in mind, I recommend the following guidelines:

## ▸ REVEAL OBVIOUS INFORMATION IMMEDIATELY:

If you've got a physical condition or other circumstance that people can spot from a mile off, attempting to hide it just makes you look disingenuous and out-of-touch. You'll need to say something right away.

Keep your revelation light-hearted and brief, though; it's not just what you say, but how you say it. In my case, I have a neurological condition that makes my hands shake. It's noticeable, so I cut to the chase in a non-dramatic way: "I've got a lifelong tremor. It doesn't stop me from doing much, other than performing surgery."

If your date asks for more detail, keep it as light as you can. I've been asked whether my tremor means I'm getting Parkinson's, for example. My answer? "No, it mainly means I'm thankful for speech-to-text."

## ▸ MENTION YOU'RE A SINGLE PARENT EVEN BEFORE YOU MEET:

Failing to mention that you're a parent may come off as bizarre and dishonest. After all, this is basic knowledge, something you'd discuss with the bank teller—not top-secret. People expect to know that you're a parent, how many kids you have, what their genders and ages are, and whether/how much they live with you. Hiding this information isn't any more acceptable than refusing to reveal your age, height, or job.

So, tell everyone you date that you're a parent, and if possible do it even before you meet. If you're dating online, it's easy. As with other heavy information, keep the telling light. My personal ad, written to the tune of "The Piña Colada Song," had this line in it: "If you like making love at 1 p.m., when my kid takes a nap." This quickly and humorously revealed that I had one child who was still young and lived with me.

Did some prospects opt out? Probably, but I didn't know it; they simply didn't reach out to me. That's okay: you need someone who is willing to become a stepparent, not someone who is adamantly opposed. *Quickly eliminating unsuitable matches is a win!*

*But there's a difference between letting people know you're a single parent, and waxing rhapsodic, becoming dramatic, or getting overly detailed about your kids.* Give the basic information without dwelling on how you're obsessed with them, they take up all your time, you can't handle their tantrums, the weekly kid exchange with the ex has to be conducted at a police station, or that you'd rather spend every evening on the couch watching movies with them than go on one more date, etc. And don't say your kids are the love of your life, even if it's true: the person on the other end of your dating experience is looking for someone with room for them!

## ▶ REVEAL ALL OTHER SENSITIVE, NON-OBVIOUS INFORMATION IN LINE WITH THE PROGRESSION OF EMOTIONAL INTIMACY IN THE RELATIONSHIP:

The human mating ritual is no less a dance than birds' courtships. Ours involves the mutual and often gradual sharing of layers of ourselves and our experiences. One person reveals something personal; the other shares a little more; and so on. The goal is intimacy—revealing all aspects of ourselves without fearing the loss of our identity[13].

As that definition implies, intimacy is not something we can or should attain with everyone. In fact, telling new people everything right away would be foolhardy. They haven't yet earned our trust. They might exploit our secrets, use our vulnerabilities to abuse us, or blab them to the world. Until they've met our Must-Haves and an emotional bond has started on both sides, it just doesn't make sense for them to know all our stories.

Yet prior to any lasting commitment, there are big issues from your past or present that must be shared--from whether you were ever sexually abused, to whether you have been divorced (and how many times), to your criminal history, to ongoing problems your kids are having, to an ex who tries to harm you or your children, to your infidelity in past relationships, to your incurable STI.

*I've heard it all—but nobody you're dating needs to hear it until and unless they've met enough of your Must-Haves that this relationship could succeed; it's trending exclusive; and your new partner has revealed enough about themselves that it's logical and necessary for you to reveal your secrets, too.*

When you do spill your secrets, please make it clear to your partner that the issue will not derail your burgeoning relationship. The task here is to tell your truth in a drama-free manner that shows you're competently handling whatever the issue is.

For example, if your ex continues to try to create difficulties, you could say,

> *"My ex and I have a hard time communicating. We now conduct 100% of communication through writing, to keep things on an even keel."*

Or if you've got an incurable STI, you might say,

> *"In my teens, I got herpes. I've learned how to deal with it responsibly so I won't pass it on, and I take good care of myself and have not had a flare-up in the past 15 years."* For ethical and legal reasons, please reveal any ongoing STI's before you have sex!

*Finally, if your secret will raise a red flag about whether you're trustworthy, you'll need to reassure your partner on several key points*: how long it's been since the offense; your sincere regret; and your commitment to avoiding a repetition.

Here's an example of such an admission:

> *"In my marriage, I had an affair that I ended after two weeks because I felt horrible about cheating. It's not who I am, and I'd violated my own moral code. This was ten years ago, and I've been faithful ever since. I want you to know not only that I made such a mistake in the past, but that I have never been, and won't ever be, unfaithful again."*

Ultimately, we all seek a partner who lightens our load and can hear everything about us with compassion rather than judgment. Love is not just for the perfect—or none of us would find it! You can do this, one step at a time, by revealing your truths as the time is right.

•••

# EXERCISE 3: ✏️▷

## The confession:

In your Notebook, please write down how you would inform someone of a difficulty of your own, using the guidelines above. When would you tell them? What would you tell them? And how would you keep the topic as positive and detail-appropriate as possible?

## PITFALL #4: PREMATURE INTRODUCTIONS

Of all the items in the survey I gave to single parents to prepare for this book, timing the introduction of children to prospective partners generated the most varied reactions. Here are just a few of the many notes single moms and dads wrote to me:

> *"The first time I started dating after my divorce, I waited 7 months before I introduced my love interest to my children, only to find out he was horrible with kids. I felt like I wasted 7 months of my life."* (single mom in her 40s)

> *"I have gone both ways: kept my kids away from partners to protect them, and also introduced them quickly. Most recently I have decided that it's better to wait as long as possible to introduce the kids. They can get attached to partners and also feel hopeful that their parent has 'found someone' and then go through grief and disappointment when the relationship breaks down. I don't want to cause any more grief or loss for my kids—they have already been through enough. I have been married twice and have children by two marriages."* (single dad in his 40s)

> *"My mother was single from when I was 9 years old, and I didn't meet anyone she dated until I was in college. She made her mind up that she would never think to remarry until we were out of the house. It was odd, and in high school, we began figuring out she had this mysterious 'friend' we had never met and who was seeing her outside the house. My*

*takeaway as an adult was fearing how someone I was dating seriously might feel they were not worthy to meet my child. If I saw a future with them I would prioritize them interacting with the world they would be saying 'yes' to."* (single dad in his 40s)

These letters show strong arguments for waiting—and not. If you think this is a damned-if-you-do, damned-if-you-don't situation, you're in good company. Introducing kids too quickly can hurt them if it doesn't work out, and introducing them too slowly can hurt you if your prospective match sucks at step-parenting and you then must break up after a significant time investment.

What's the best answer?

There's not much research on this, so here are my opinions. There's no point in having your kids meet someone who isn't your exclusive boyfriend or girlfriend; if it's not that serious, it's not serious enough. Ditto with getting your kids involved when you're still unclear on whether this person meets other Must-Haves. The only relationships our kids need to be part of are the ones where other possible deal-breakers have already been eliminated.

*We don't have to introduce our kids to tell whether partners might or might not be kind and appropriate with them.* People advertise these qualities through how they treat those who can do little for or against them: their own kids, their own exes, service personnel, and animals. You don't have to get your kids deeply involved up-front to tell whether someone is mature enough to put their emotions aside, and treat others with kindness and respect. Look for good character, and know there will be time later on to work out details related to your children.

Some women may balk at my approach, and I remember all too well from my own single-mom days why it's so tempting to introduce someone to the kids right away. It saves on costs of babysitters, and it lets you see up-front whether your kids and this person might work well together, without sinking half a year or more into the relationship. Some women may also feel that making these introductions is more likely to gain a man's commitment. Other women are turned on by men's apparent nurturance of children, and may mistakenly think men share that mating psychology[14].

(There are tips in those ideas for you Seekers of Women, too: It never hurts for a guy to talk about good parenting choices he's made, to discuss his concern for his children, or to show photos of himself with his children. But actually involving a new partner with your kids is another matter. Be warned: I've worked with women who are wary of men who will, in their view, risk their children this way.)

As for women, despite the sound-seeming reasons listed above, rushing to introduce your kids to a man can actively derail a new relationship. I've seen many single moms who've been ditched in part because they introduced their kids too soon.

Women, most men expect that you're probably a good mom; seeing you nurturing your kids is rarely a selling point[15]. Instead, introducing your kids too soon can wave red flags of desperation, clinginess, and low-status to men. *Don't do anything that smacks of throwing your kids at a guy: quick introductions do little for your offspring, and can lose worthwhile men.*

*A much better strategy is for women to treat meeting their children as a prize that the worthy must work to win.* If a good man has not requested meeting your kids without your first hinting at it, don't offer. Even then, follow the other guidelines above regarding exclusivity and Must-Haves—and heed your intuition.

Yes, this will result in fewer possible outings at the start, because you might not be able to get a sitter every weekend. That's okay. *Men love who and what they work to have. This is the barrier method: putting up a roadblock (such as not spending time together when your kids are home, and making it a privilege to meet the children), and then awaiting someone worthy enough that he will work to overcome it[16].* Casual partners will reject you over this, which is good because it saves you time wasted on guys who were never committing anyway. Barriers block the players and bring the stayers[17].

I also recommend this cautious approach for including your kids in the relationship (including the relationship with your new partner's children) as it moves forward. Make it a privilege rather than a chore for your kids to be included in dates and outings, and, before you're engaged, make such excursions the exception rather than the rule. This will draw out the fun parts of the courtship—there will be plenty of time for negotiating step-sibling spats later! And it will keep your kids from getting too bonded before you're safely assured that this relationship is trending permanent. Plus, this deliberate approach prevents you from seeing one another constantly before that's a good idea, enabling you to maintain some excitement and urgency towards full commitment. As we'll see in the next chapter, you will always be the "real" parent. You don't have to figure out every aspect of the kids' relationship with your partner before the wedding; you just need to know they're safe for your kids!

DUANA C. WELCH, PhD

...

# EXERCISE 4:

## The theme park:

Let's say your new partner wants to go to a theme park, and you know your children would enjoy it. You're not yet exclusive, and you don't know whether they meet your Must-Haves. Using the guidelines above, should you ask to include your kids? What if your date asks you to bring them along? Write your answers in your Notebook, and then I'll share my response.

### OKAY, HERE'S MY THINKING, AND IT PROBABLY WON'T SURPRISE YOU:

Don't ask to bring your kids. The theme park will still be there later, when the relationship is where it needs to be to include your children.

And if your date asks you to bring your kids, don't: you can say something like,

> *"That's really kind of you to offer, and I can see the day coming when it will be fun to have the kids along. For now, I want you to myself."*

▶ **DATE OTHERS WITH KIDS?**

I sometimes meet single parents who won't date other single parents. They say it's enough taking care of their own children, and adding more complexity seems like a bad plan. And they have a point: in studies, divorce rates can be above 70% if both people bring at-home children into the union[18].

You might also consider the age and gender of a partner's kids before you get in deep. As a single mom in her 60s wanted to know, "Why is dating with teens still in the home a deal-breaker for some men?"

Plot spoiler! In research and in real life, teens can be difficult people. In fact, it can start younger than that: the hardest times to repartner are when kids are between 10 and 15[19]. Children age 9 and younger may not have as firm a concept of what life "should" be like and may be more open and flexible; and kids 16 and over often have their own lives to lead, and would rather the parent was busy with something other than them[20]. Additionally, girls may be more difficult than boys when it comes to repartnering[21]; they might be particularly jealous of their mother's attention, and moms tend to have primary custody. Of course, these patterns portray odds, not certainties, and your mileage may vary.

Yet some formerly single parents say their partner understands them and their circumstances better if both have kids. I've felt that one of many reasons Vic and I wanted a full commitment was that we each knew the other would support our parenting efforts—something we needed. Doubtless, this brought added complexity; every remarriage-with-children brings an entourage, and the more, the more complicated. But it also put us on an equal footing. And it's been comforting having a sympathetic partner who has been there, done that, too.

Regardless, I'm hesitant to advise avoiding people with children altogether. Once you already have kids, that criterion shrinks your dating pool significantly. And if the commitment and strategies in Chapters 8 and 9 are there, you can each have children and be happy anyway.

But what if you meet someone perfect for you, and you just know the kids (theirs, yours, or both) will kill your marriage? That doesn't necessarily mean you can't live happily ever after. You will need to think outside the box, though. My friends Steve and Liz are the perfect example. They met at a conference, fell in love, got engaged—and then didn't cohabit or marry for several years. They had solid reasons to suspect that their particular offspring would undermine their union. For one thing, when they announced their engagement to the then-teens, Liz recalls, "All three of the 'kids' ran from the room!" (Steve adds, "I remember it well.") So they bought houses across the street from each other and saw one another daily, and when the last one flew the coop, they married. Now, they love grandparenting together. And everyone gets along!

## PITFALL #5: CASUAL SEX?

Scientists define courtship as the interval between meeting and mating[22]. And rumor has it that most people have sex by the third date. I suspect that's true for many single parents; if memory serves, the equation goes something like:

*HORNY*

*+ STARVED FOR ADULT ATTENTION*

## + *In Need of Affirmation*

## = *You Look Good Tonight*

But science makes the case for a longer courtship. That's because although people have sex for literally dozens of reasons —curiosity, companionship, validation, variety, or to scratch an itch, to name a few[23]—the biggest of all is bonding.

Think about it: most other creatures have sex almost immediately after meeting, and then might never encounter one another again. Their offspring can run, swim, or slither right away, making two involved parents irrelevant.

Human evolution chose another path. *Sex for people is not mainly about making babies; it's about making bonds.* Our infants are born in an immature state and need the care of both parents (and, ideally, a village) for a long time if they are to survive and have children of their own. Also, human ovulation is hidden, and cavemen were never quite sure when their wives were fertile. Sex-for-bonding may have evolved in part to solve men's problem of paternity assurance: mating with one woman over and over again gave the man higher odds that the cave kids would be his[24].

*The upshot? Casual sex uses adults' most basic bonding mechanism to avoid a bond. So, casual sex is rarely as casual as people hope it will be—and it causes more problems than it solves, especially for single parents.*

Don't get hurt; get informed.

## ▶ SEX AND THE SINGLE MOM:

"Dear Duana," Jane's letter began,

> *"A sexy, trustworthy man I've got zero long-term interest in has offered me a Friends with Benefits arrangement. I'm tempted, but I'm also worried that the effects on my psyche might outweigh the pleasures and benefits. Is there any research on whether a just-sex relationship has detrimental emotional/psychological effects on women?"*

Sadly, yes—and especially for single moms. In a long-term study that followed single parents for 20 years post-divorce, 100% of the people who attempted suicide were single moms in casual sex scenarios[25]. That's not to say suicide attempts were frequent— they were actually rare. Still, it's notable that single dads never tried it, and that when single moms did, it always involved their emotional reactions to casual sex. That may be related to findings that most women who think they only want something casual end up wanting more[26]; and sex that's had very soon can actually end a relationship you'd hoped to deepen[27].

Of course, some women can have a fling and walk away whistling a happy tune. But it's not the way to bet. Emotionally risky sex is usually risky only for women, due in part to chemistry: every time women have unprotected intercourse with a man, 97% of his ejaculatory cocktail is specifically geared towards creating emotional attachment: hers, not his. He comes equipped with dopamine, oxytocin (a.k.a. Chemical Relationship Glue), vasopressin, and norepinephrine, all of which are easily absorbed into the vaginal walls and the woman's emotions[28].

Fair? No. Effective? Apparently. Most women increase their feelings for a man post-coitally—even when they intend only short-term sex. For instance, 75% of women—compared to just a quarter of men—found themselves becoming more attached than they wanted to in a friends-with-benefits situation[29].

These findings are practically an advertisement for condoms!

Yet casual sex works in reverse for men, increasing the odds that a guy will reject making a real commitment. Literally, men report losing interest, sometimes to the point of revulsion, in women they have casual sex with—often within as little as 10 seconds after the man's climax[30].

Why? Two reasons: quick sex implicitly tells guys, "She'll have you raising some other cave dude's kids in no time." *In other words, it's to his genes' advantage to ensure his paternity via her faithful attachment—and casual sex casts her fidelity potential in doubt[31].* Also, this allows men the emotional freedom to keep their options open, so they can simultaneously play the field, and pursue women they might consider more trustworthy for commitment.

Men, especially the most desirable, are biologically and psycho-logically primed to keep it casual, unless the romance builds up to the sex and not vice-versa. *This does not apply to men who have already fallen in love and already have long-term intentions towards you—but it sends up red flags if you want to remain emotionally safe and solely date men who can and will offer the long-term[32].*

### BE HARD-TO-GET:

*The take-home behind men's reactions to casual sex is, don't let him take you home!* Whether you're a gay single dad or a straight single mom, evolution has provided you the perfect way to figure out who's playing, and who's staying: make him wait.

Players are wily creatures. Women love commitment signals, and some guys have figured out that they can feign those to get sex[33]. Many men—71%, in one study—occasionally pretend to feel more than they do, or dangle commitment like a carrot[34].

Which is why waiting works: players aren't willing to fake investment for long. Men in short-term mating mode admit that if a woman poses barriers, they will leave[35]. That feels sucky, but it actually saves time and heartache wasted on He Who Was Never Committing Anyway.

Waiting not only blocks the players—it brings the stayers by increasing the stock of She Who is Hard-to-Get. Men routinely assume that women who are not easily had must be higher status and therefore worthier of their commitment[36]—and they assume the reverse, too[37]. Gay men have informed me it works the same for them. Ultimately, waiting for sex tells casual guys, "Move along to an easier target, sir," while informing commitment-minded men, "I won't put your genetic line at risk. Bet on me!"

*But wait: isn't being hard-to-get manipulative, frigid, and bitchy? Not if you're doing it right.*

▸ **FIRST OFF,** you cannot manipulate a man into loving you; being hard-to-get doesn't force men to fall, it simply jettisons players and helps men value you more if they're already inclined towards you. And I'd argue that hanging around making a guy breakfast, sending cards to his mother, and telling him he's the only one, all with an eye towards making him commit, is a lot more manipulative than giving him enough space to know his own heart and come after you.

▸ **SECOND,** the best thing any of us, male or female, gay or straight or bi, can do to win the heart of someone who likes us is to openly show that we like them[38]. Being hard-to-get does not mean being aloof, cold, distant, or lacking in enthusiasm, all of which are really bad moves. The person you attract with bitchiness is not a person you're likely to live with in happiness!

Being hard-to-get means this and only this: waiting for sex and other intimacies until you are sure of his love and commitment. It's a dance where he's leading, and you're following with enthusiasm— just a bit more slowly than he might prefer. It's a call where he dials the number, and you answer with a smile in your voice. It's a date that he planned, where you thank him and outright tell him you like him, you appreciate his planning, and you're enjoying getting to know him. It's a dinner with your children, after he has first invited you to a dinner with his.

▶ **AND THIRD**, I'm not recommending waiting to have sex until you're married. Hard-to-get means waiting until you're exclusive, but not necessarily beyond that. Sexual incompatibility is a frequent cause of infidelity and divorce[39], and having sex with a man tells you a lot about how much he loves and listens to you. I hypothesize that that's one reason women's orgasm is more difficult to achieve than men's: ancestral mothers may have used male sensitivity and intelligence in bed as a litmus test for his fitness as a permanent mate. I certainly hear from women today who agree!

*The upshot? Don't have sex until four criteria are met:*

- *you want to;*

- *your guy has asked you to be exclusive;*

- *he has told you he loves you; and*

- *he has proven it to your intuition's satisfaction!*

...

# EXERCISE 5: ▣▬▶

## *The wait-till-later speech for Seekers of Men:*

Seekers of Men, in your Notebook, write out a short speech that conveys enthusiasm for your partner, while delaying sexual intercourse. Write yours, and then I'll share one I've created for my clients to use.

......................................................................

### OKAY, HERE'S MINE:

*"I am really attracted to you, and I'm just not ready to have sex. I look forward to getting to that point though!"*

### ▶ SEX AND THE SINGLE DAD:

Guys, as we've seen, casual sex doesn't tend to be quite as rough on you. Still, it comes with some risks my male clients report, such as:

- feeling guilty when you realize she wants commitment, but you don't;

- having a hard time breaking up due to that same guilt, and because it feels weird to walk away from amazing free sex;

- getting your kids invested in a person you're with just because the sex is good and you're blind to the new partner's faults;

- setting yourself up for another divorce by marrying the wrong person, because you don't want to look at the relationship too closely once you're bonded; and

- getting excited that you may have met Mrs. Right, and then, against your will, losing interest in her if you have sex too soon into the courtship[40].

This isn't your first rodeo, so I'll keep this short: it goes against everything your male ancestors wanted, but if you're after a real thing and not a mere fling, attempt to wait for full sexual intercourse until you're deeply in love and know that this woman meets your Must-Haves. As with my advice to women, above, get fully sexual before making a permanent commitment; but don't do it right out of the gate. You can't fall in love without dopamine, and unless you're a virgin or very inexperienced sexually[41] (unlikely, if you're already a dad), your brain won't produce enough dopamine to fall in love sans waiting[42].

My male clients have found it handy to have a speech for delaying sex. Otherwise, they tell me, women wonder whether he's attracted to them. So go ahead and hug, kiss, and caress your partner, if she's willing. Be passionate—you don't want to wind up with someone who has zero sex drive, and you can tell a lot from kissing[43]. Just don't try to have sexual intercourse. And once you're past the third date, you need to tell her why you're not hurrying towards sex.

...

# *Exercise 6:* ✏️▸

## *The wait-till-later speech for Seekers of Women:*

Guys, this is such a counterintuitive ask, I'm just giving you the script my male clients have benefited from; please copy it into your Notebook, customizing it as you see fit:

> *"I'm really attracted to you and I'll bet you're used to men trying to have sex with you by this time. I'm tempted to take things to the next level physically, too, but I'm not going to yet, and I wanted to tell you why. I'm looking for the right person for a lifetime, and to do that, I've realized I need to hold off on sex until I know you really well. Just wanted you to know, I am into you!"*

Even though there are good reasons to delay sex, guys, there's a caveat: don't friend-zone yourself by hanging around hoping a woman will eventually get the idea that you are into her! *Hanging around as a friend when you want more is not attractive.* Know what is? Confidence. In the animal realm, as in ours, when males sneak around to get sex, it's because they're low-status[44]. Just as you want a high-status partner, women prefer high-status men—and one way women determine if you are high-status is through your confident behavior. So man up, show courage, and ask her out. *Women know whether or not they want you through your pursuit; there's no point in putting off this powerful signal, even if there are many points in delaying sex!*

▸ **SEX FOR ONE:**

A single dad wrote to me:

*"Are you covering any considerations about handling temporary relationships or relationships of convenience when people aren't interested in a new permanent relationship, but still have needs and desires during a period of recovery? For me it lasted more than 5 years."*

As you know by now, I view casual relationships as risky, based on the research. But this dad has raised an important issue. Our sexual needs don't end just because we got divorced. If anything, those needs may escalate: we've been accustomed to having a sexual partner, and we might hope sex will distract us from our new loneliness.

So we must handle these needs, even when we're not ready for a serious relationship. And by "handle," I mean that literally—as in, masturbation.

I felt a lot of you cringe just then. Isn't it strange that so many people find this topic far more squeamish than sex with others? Yet sex for one is the only truly safe sex there is, resulting in zero pain, harm, abuse, STI's, unintended pregnancies, or awkward hours spent wondering when you'll call, whether you'll go out with yourself again, or whether this relationship is going anywhere.

Additionally, most women have to learn to have an orgasm, and they respond more reliably with a partner if they first get in touch with themselves, by themselves[45]. And solo sex is good for you. Literally, when a man wrote me at my blog to ask how to stop masturbating in anticipation of his marriage, I researched the matter and had to respond: per the science, masturbation is such a benefit throughout your life, including after you're partnered, that there's literally no data on stopping[46]. Not only doesn't masturbation cause blindness, but it helps men last longer with a partner, it takes the edge off so guys can focus on their partner's pleasure, and it fills in the gaps during those inevitable times when one of you wants an orgasm and the other wants a nap (ProTip: nap, then orgasm, then nap).

The upshot? Masturbation isn't just for sex-crazed teens with no outlet, it's for moms and dads with electrical outlets. Take care of yourself, so you don't look to someone else to take care of you before you really know the other person or are ready for a solid relationship.

### ▶ SEX WHILE THE KIDS ARE HOME?

Folks, there's not a ton of research on how to time your adult sleepovers. We do know that the more sexual partners a mom has at home while the kids are there, the more likely the kids are to follow suit[47]. "Do as I say, not as I do," has just never played well as a parenting strategy.

Beyond limiting how many partners you bring home, and having sex when the kids are elsewhere, my opinion—in line with the rest of this chapter—is that the commitment level is key. If you wait to introduce your kids until you know this person meets your Must-Haves; if you're exclusive; and if both of you are in love and trending permanent--, that's emotionally safer for your children than bringing someone home for the night before those standards are met.

That does it for our gender—and timing—related pitfalls! Now that you've skirted those, it's time to consider what comes next. What happens when you combine families, and how can you set yourself up for success? That's in Chapter 8.

# PART III:

# Making The Choice: Getting Closer, Breaking Up, Moving Forward

# CHAPTER 8:

# There's No Such Thing As A Blended Family

T here we sat at the movies: Vic, me, and my teen. In that order. Vic held my left hand, my son held my right—and I was in the middle. It's beyond symbolic: in our day-to-day lives, they each choose me, and I choose both of them. But that does not mean they always choose each other.

A whole lot of the time, the "step" element we hope will disappear simply doesn't. As one woman in a stepfamily wrote me, "It's hard! You want to be the perfect stepparent and have them realize that they are SO LUCKY that you aren't like all those other horrible people out there." Another said, "I have been a stepparent in two different marriages. I was in no way at all prepared."

Me neither. I remember wanting so much to be the "bonus mom" for Vic's son, not the ominous-sounding "stepmother." Vic had adopted his son, and he envisioned expanding his family by adopting my child. I believe that each of our children, at ages 10 (his) and 6 (mine) when we wed, wanted our group to become a fully united family.

But that's not how things worked out, and neither I nor anyone else can factually tell you how to create a nuclear-type family unit with OPC (Other People's Children). That doesn't mean you're doomed to failure in your new life—just that it's a different life than what you or your kids may have envisioned. In this chapter we'll cover how to thrive despite the challenges of stepfamilies.

*Let's start with this: if you prepare yourself to accept what's likely, rather than what "should" be, you'll probably be much happier than believing in the myth of the blended family.*

Yes, I said "myth." In a twenty-five-year study, even when both parents permanently and happily remarried, that didn't spell nuclear-family cohesion. As lead scientist Judith Wallerstein put it, "Many of the kids say to me that, 'He's really good for my mom, but it doesn't matter for me[1].'"

The iconic *Brady Bunch* scenario, where two formerly single parents seamlessly and cheerfully bring six well-adjusted and emotionally open children into a new marriage, exists mainly on TV reruns (or perhaps in houses with motherly live-in housekeepers). In real-life families, the "step" part of parenting can be jarring. Competing alliances and agendas exist, however much we might wish otherwise. It simply is what it is. Repartnering brings an entourage, which brings complexity!

...

# EXERCISE 1: ✐
## Competing agendas:

In your view, what might stand in the way of harmony in a new family that includes stepparents, biological parents (exes, too), stepkids, and maybe stepsiblings? How do you think your remarriage might look to each of these people? What about your reactions to each of them? Put your thoughts in your Notebook, and then I'll share what I know from science.

..................................................

## OKAY, MY TURN!

The scientific consensus is: if parenting our own offspring is hard, parenting our partner's kids is harder still—for many reasons.

- **We adults naturally give our own kids more emotional leeway to make mistakes;** people love their own children more than OPC, and that love comes with a lot more forgiveness, tolerance, and patience[2]. Even when we want to love our partner's kids as much as we love our own, that's a tall order. Not only do we share genetics with our offspring (unless your children are adopted—and if so, please note that the terms "real parent" and "bioparent" apply to you in this chapter); we also share history. We were there from the start of their lives, so it makes sense that we understand our own kids better and are more bonded with them than with someone we just met.

- **Discipline-style differences can be a major source of tension even when the biological parents stay together,** nevermind when one parent is biologically related and the other is new on the scene. Sometimes, the real parent's sympathy for their kids can put them at odds with the new spouse. A new stepmom named Heather said it well: "To a stepparent, your partner's kids aren't your kids, so they feel more like roommates. And if they happen to sometimes be rude roommates, leaving messes in common areas, being loud and oblivious to other members of the house, it's much more annoying. A parent may be more inclined to forgive, overlook, or compensate for a behavior, but it'll be harder on a stepparent."

• **Moms, especially, are likely to feel protective of their children, even when they've married a good guy.** In most heterosexual marriages, Dad loves Mom above all others — but Mom usually loves the kids the most. You know the saying, "Men love women, women love children, children love hamsters"? Lotta truth there. Not only is Mom's egg and the resulting chick precious and rare relative to men's procreative power[3], but as we saw in Chapter 4, unrelated males in the home are the top threat to children's well-being and survival[4]. To the mom's evolved psychology, she might consciously love her new partner — and unconsciously fear him as a threat to her progeny, even if he's not.

• **And then, there's the kids' perspective.** *Preference for kin is a two-way street: just as parents prefer their own children, children prefer their own parents[5].* Hence why so many step-parents are on the receiving end of that painful remark, "You're not my real mom/dad!"

• **Children may be wary of their parents' new partnerships, and with good reason**. That's not only because of the abuse stats quoted earlier, but due to partner turnover. In a study that tracked the well-being of 100 kids every year for a quarter-century after their parents' divorce, only 7% had a mom and dad who remarried, happily, just once[6]. The other 93% of kids had to adjust to at least one parent's repartnering, separation, and involvement with yet another partner, again and again. No wonder many children believe each new partner spells a fresh bout of instability!

- **Also, children might fear losing Mom or Dad's love as their parent becomes obsessed with another adult.** Falling in love literally involves becoming obsessed[7] and getting high[8], and that takes attention from the children. Not surprisingly, kids may resent someone they experience as an interloper.

- **Then there's the factor of the kids' other bioparent—your or your partner's ex.** No matter how much you may dislike your ex, from a scientific standpoint, you want them to be happy in their own love life, so they don't take it out on yours[9]. The unhappy ex may be quite meddlesome in the new household, and research shows that the most troublesome of all are former wives who have not successfully repartnered[10]. Even if the children want to love you, the ex and their relatives may turn them against the new family unit in general, and the new stepparent in particular.

- **Plus, you adults got to date, fall in love, and fully choose one another**—but the kids had little say about those things, and may actively oppose or dislike the new partner or step-siblings.

When you consider all of this, the wonder isn't that stepfamilies don't blend, but that they ever get along!

But don't let this list overwhelm you. Instead, adjust your expectations. *The aim in a stepfamily is less about blending and more about coexisting, much as ingredients in a stew can go together well even though they're distinct from one another.* Ultimately, the goal is not to resemble a biological family, but to live together in peace, respect, and maybe—eventually—friendship.

It is doable! Let's see how.

# Take Care Of Your Stepmarriage And Yourself

Stepmom Heather wisely saw the challenges of stepmarriages:

*"More self-care and more relationship care are needed than with traditional couples, because the responsibilities around kids can be divisive and lopsided. If kids are a stressor on first marriages, they're more so on second ones. It's a bigger factor than most people believe it'll be when they first fall in love."*

That's for sure! Stress seldom makes things better, and kids come with stress. In bioparent couples sans stepkids, a full two-thirds remain significantly less happy in their marriage right up until the last child leaves home[11]! No wonder the stresses derived from so many competing agendas in stepfamilies can undermine your remarriage.

Don't let them. You can find a balance between your roles as step/parents and as a new couple. Whether the kids are yours or your partner's, pay extra attention to your relationship.

I recall thinking that this seems undoable. But then I remembered that when I was a super-busy single parent, I still managed to find time to date. And in nuclear families, parents also manage to plan special evenings out[12]. Step-spouses can do the same -- and they must. You fell in love by spending time together sans kids, yes? It might sound obvious, but your relationship will not perk along without continued fun and intimacy[13]. *Keep the love alive by continuing to make child-free, fun time together—and put your dates on the calendar.*

Beyond that, if there are OPC in the mix, you need to engage in self-care, since your lack of control as a stepparent can be very frustrating and in turn, hard on your marriage.

...

# EXERCISE 2:

## Stepparent self-care:

In your Notebook, write down actions you can take on a routine basis that will contribute to your well-being. You can refer to your self-care Notebook entry from Chapter 2, if you like—entering the items here that make sense to continue if you repartner with another single parent. It's perfectly fine to add stuff about time with your new mate, too: being with them counts as care and gives you a twofer because it builds your relationship. Are there other things you can think of?

My own list includes some items that don't involve my husband, such as belonging to a book club with friends; going for a walk every day to clear my head; throwing a ball for the dogs; taking a hot bath; and taking time alone to read, write, and listen to music. Other parts of my list count as taking care of myself and my marriage: having lunch with my spouse while the kids are at school (note to self: do more of this!); having specific times each day that are just for me and my mate, such as watching a series we both like after the kids' bedtimes; and locking the bedroom door while spending at least one weekend morning in bed with my husband. I also plan a week each year when my husband and I are alone together—whether or not we travel anywhere.

## STEPPARENTS: LET THE REAL PARENT
## DO THE PARENTING

Heather put it well when she likened stepkids to roommates:

> *"Imagine a rude roommate that not only has friends over and is loud
> and disruptive but insists on smoking even though they know full well
> the house rules prohibit it. You're lying in bed falling asleep when you
> notice, and now have to remind roomie of the house rules, which usually
> initiates a power struggle. How much fun is THAT before bedtime??"*

(I'm guessing: not much.)

Another stepmom inquired, "What are appropriate ways to punish
or give consequences for bad behavior when the kids aren't yours?"
And another asked, "How do I get the stepkids on board with maintaining the house so it doesn't become a source of stress? How do
I communicate expectations to them to teach responsibility and not
encourage defiance?"

Here's the super-short, science-supported answer: You don't. You
don't remind the stepkids, punish them, teach them responsibility,
or directly deal with any defiance. You don't do the real parenting—
because you're not the real parent!

This is so hard, especially if you're accustomed to parenting your
own children, and it seems easiest to jump into that role with your
partner's kids, too. But please avoid that temptation; as we'll see, the
costs are just too high. **The rule of thumb is this: the real parent
does the parenting, and the stepparent supports and voices
concerns to the real parent in private.** Write that down. Memorize
it. Consider getting it tattooed on your dominant hand. Because

it's that important. Really. If you take only one thing from this entire chapter, that's it.

*Of course, this means you've got to start with good raw material: a partner who will actually parent their biological kids, and who will take your perspective into account. Find this out before you say I Do!* If you marry someone who insists that the stepparent do the parenting, or who refuses to intervene when there are problems between the stepkids and the new spouse, that's not going to work. Scientists have long known that seriously considering a mate's opinions and needs is a rock-bottom requirement if a marriage is going to last[14].

When I asked about the stepkid/discipline issue on a Facebook post, one happily remarried single mom responded, "My advice for when you're the stepparent: I never tried to act like their mother. They have a mother." Another agreed: "Don't try to parent the other person's children, and don't let them parent yours."

Let me be the first to admit, they're wiser than I was. As I write this chapter, it's so frustrating not to be able to go back in time—I wish so much that I'd known then what I know now, with science as the guide!

When Vic and I married, he worked at an office until the evening every weekday and volunteered at a zoo on Saturdays. I mainly worked from the house, so I was the one both kids came home to; I was the one in charge of policing homework and deciding who could go to whose house, or watch what, when. Often, even on weekends, I was still the one making sure chores got done and showers got taken.

Vic and I were on the same page, having both envisioned my fulfilling much of his role while he was out of the house. And I felt like I couldn't let everything about one child slide while I definitely had to raise mine according to my vision and values.

But that didn't create peace in our home, because the "step" in stepparenting matters! My efforts didn't come off as supplementing Vic's, but as competing with the mom's—a loyalty bind for the child, and one I regret having contributed to. Nobody was happy with the results. Rather than have me play a role I wasn't meant for, it would have been far better for us to agree that Vic would do all the parenting when his son was with us--even if that meant taking his son with him on weekend volunteering and putting him in after-school and summer-camp programs. Unless your partner's ex is deceased, and maybe even then, your stepkids need you to step back and let their real parents parent.

*Yet you can't tolerate insubordinate, rude, aggressive, or otherwise disrespectful behavior.*

Take Scott, a new stepdad whose stepkids treat him with contempt—making fun of him, ignoring his requests, and rolling their eyes when he speaks. If he does nothing, it will undermine his marriage, because it's only natural to resent the partner who doesn't stick up for you. Plus, accepting the unacceptable teaches all the kids bad behavior, and sets them up for failure in their own future intimate relationships. Instead, in addition to family therapy if you can access that, here are some science-approved techniques for Scott, and you, to try.

## ▸ CATCH THE STEPKIDS DOING SOMETHING RIGHT:

The path to happiness in your home is partly in your own hands, not in terms of correcting the stepkids' behavior, but praising it. Praise the kids for what they do right. This will make their bioparent really happy (perhaps resulting in nookie for you!). And it will get you more of the behavior you want from the stepkids. As we saw in Chapter 1, all mammals naturally and unconsciously increase behaviors that get rewarded[15]. Kids are mammals, and praise is a reward. Best of all, you don't have to praise them every time; every now and then creates even longer-lasting results[16].

And show your stepkids affection and love, to the extent they can or will accept it. This is a way of loving your mate and solidifying your marriage, in addition to being kind in itself. As one stepmom told me, "I am someone who loves their father very much and always will, and I recognize that his happiness depends on them and their well-being too. So I try to do everything that supports their well-being."

You can ask the bioparent their opinion of what love means to the stepkids; it might be asking them about their day, giving hugs, listening without judgment, refraining from your own behaviors the kids dislike, attending their ball games, or going biking with them now and then. *You may or may not feel the love you show; but take the long view of life and marriage, and show it anyway.*

Again, there's no need to be perfect. And bonus! The kids will probably give you more respect when they feel accepted and appreciated.

•••

# EXERCISE 3:
## The daily-praise plan:

In your Notebook, list everything you can think of that is praise-worthy about your stepkids. Then, make it a point to praise each of them for something at least once a day. Do this for a month.

Be specific: "Jonas, you were a huge help with the dishes after supper. I really love that you pitched in without being asked. Thank you." or, "You stopped the car so smoothly at that light, it was like butter!"

*Not only will the kids gradually increase the behaviors you like—but you'll probably like the kids better, because you're actively looking for what pleases rather than irks you.*

## ▶ ENCOURAGE DATES BETWEEN YOUR MATE AND THEIR KIDS:

Children worry about being replaced in their bioparent's affections. I've literally seen kids carve messages on their door, warning the new mate to KEEP OUT—on their mom or dad's wedding day!

Instead of automatically construing this as hate, recognize it as fear. In my professional experience helping clients in stepmarriages, you can save yourself, your new spouse, and the stepkids a ton of grief by encouraging your mate to spend time alone with their kids.

For instance, maybe your new wife read to her children every night before you got married. Encourage her to keep doing that. Nurture some perspective: childhood is temporary, the kids won't always want to be tucked in, and if you keep the kids' abandonment alarms from going off, that's good for you, too.

Or, suggest that the bioparent make dates for just themselves and their kids. Maybe it's a weekly breakfast date, or a walk together each evening. You could get out of the way for an hour or so each week, saying, "I know it's important for you all to have some alone time together."

## ▶ DISCIPLINE BEHIND-THE-SCENES:

Even with the suggestions above, sometimes the stepkids may do something unkind or disrespectful. There's no need for you to live with bad behavior; you just need a disciplinary style that puts the real parent in the foreground. Here's how:

- **Broach the trouble with the stepkids' real parent when the kids, including your own, aren't in the room.**

- **Ask what your mate thinks should be done.** Remind yourself that they're the bioparent and that their say matters immensely if you want to be happy.

- **Make suggestions to your spouse, rather than demands.** It's human nature to be more compliant if people feel free to say no[17].

- **Ask the bioparent to do the actual disciplining, and back them up rather than imposing consequences.** Being the stepparent means you don't discipline—and you also don't cave when the kids dislike their real parent's corrections and try to get you to cut them some slack. You won't be the heavy, but if the stepkids try to get around the bioparent's decisions, stick with your spouse. Example: "I wish I could drive you to the skate park, but your mom said not to."

- **Complain to your spouse about the stepkids' hurtful behavior, but don't criticize[18].** In Chapter 9, we'll go into the distinction between complaining and criticizing in greater detail, but for now follow the formula:

> *"I felt [specific emotion]*
> *when [specific event happened], and*
> *I would like [specific outcome]."*

Focus solely on this exact offense, use "I" language, and avoid name-calling or slurs against anyone's character, including the stepkids'.

For example, you could say,

> *"I felt hurt and disrespected when Cheryl walked out of the room just after I suggested a family game night. Maybe she didn't hear me, but I wonder whether you might address this with her? I used to play family games after dinner with my daughter, and I'd like us to do that sometimes too, if Cheryl is okay with that. And I want us to be polite to one another, and I think she would be more open to you."*

Now, let's tackle two more examples. I'll describe each scenario, and ask you to fill in your idea of a solid reaction in your Notebook. Then, I'll share my own thoughts, based on the discipline behind-the-scenes guidelines above. Ready?

•••

# EXERCISE 4: ▭▬▶
## The cold front:

Nicole is a new stepmom whose stepkids don't give her a sense that she's welcome. Specifically, they don't make a lot of eye contact with her, preferring instead to look at their father during dinner. She tries not to take it personally, but, "It's hard not to feel a little wistful and wish to be special too."

The kids leave her out in other, probably unintentional, ways:

> *"Sometimes I notice my stepkids, when on the phone with their friends,*
> *say 'Oh I'm at my dad's house'—and I'm not mentioned. In general,*
> *there is no feeling that compares with feeling welcome. I thought this*
> *would be easy, because kids usually like me. When I go to my sister's*
> *house, her kids clamor for my attention and I feel so loved and welcome.*
> *But here, in my own home, I'm sometimes a third wheel. Luckily, I don't*
> *need a whole lot of attention, and my husband makes up for it when I*
> *do, but it's definitely a marriage-with-stepkids challenge."*

Using the guidelines above, what can Nicole do about the issue of feeling unwelcome by the stepkids? Please write your response in your Notebook.

........................................................

### OKAY, MY TURN.

Nicole might say to her husband,

> *"I know it's probably not intentional, but sometimes I feel so unwelcome*
> *by the kids, and my feelings are hurt. Tonight when we were talking*
> *about the movie, the kids made eye contact with you, but not with me.*
> *I'm wondering, do you have any ideas about that? I'm trying not to*
> *take it personally and I don't know the answer, so I'm turning to you."*

She might find that just talking to her supportive husband is soothing, and there's no further need for action. Or maybe he will ask his kids to put some effort into making more eye contact, explaining that it's important for everyone in the house to be acknowledged and seen. Either way, Nicole will have expressed her feelings to her husband, without alienating or directly confronting his kids.

...

# EXERCISE 5: ✏️
## The micromanager:

Cynthia says her stepmom was overly watchful and has a suggestion for others about that:

> *"Stepmom rule: Please don't be nosey and hover and comment on a kid's movement through the house, as in 'Oh, did you take a banana? Where are you going? What are you doing?' It would be annoying if a parent did that, so 100x more for a stepparent."*

Let's assume Cynthia snapped at her stepmom for her watchfulness. Odds are, Stepmom would feel misunderstood and hurt; most stepparents aren't willfully evil, but we don't always know how our behavior comes across with the stepkids, just as the kids don't always know how their actions look to us. It's possible that the stepmom thought it was her job to monitor the stepkids' activities, or that she worried about being neglectful if she didn't.

Should she take it up with Cynthia? What's your advice, based on the discipline behind-the-scenes guidelines above?

......................................................................

### HERE'S MY TAKE:

The stepmom, well-meaning though she may be, is best off working out her hurt feelings with her husband, not with Cynthia.

She might say something to him like,

282

*"I felt embarrassed and misunderstood this afternoon; Cynthia told me to stop hanging over her so much, and called me nosey. I guess I do need to step back, but how much? I'm never sure about the right amount of involvement, and I'm afraid to back off so much it seems like I don't care about her. Can you advise me here?"*

Maybe she can ask the biodad to talk about it with Cynthia. She can also ask her husband to encourage Cynthia to express herself in a respectful manner that avoids name-calling.

## REAL PARENTS: PRESENT A UNITED FRONT IN AN ATMOSPHERE OF MUTUAL RESPECT

Now, on to the bioparents. How should you behave towards your own children in a stepfamily? As Dave, raised by his mom and stepdad, put it, "Children typically do not like change as much as consistency. What are some tips for parents to reinforce that they respect their child, and convey where the child ranks in the parent's priorities?"

He's got several good thoughts there, including an emphasis on stability, respect, and the need for your kids to know where they stand with you, the real parent.

When the kids and the new spouse don't get along, Real Parents, who do you side with? If it's a matter of child abuse, protect the kids! But if you've chosen someone who matches the criteria from Chapters 3 and 4, and you're now at marriage-level commitment, your new partner is not a danger to your children.

In that case, be wary of siding with your kids too easily. Kids can be divisive even in a union between their bioparents, nevermind stepmarriages. *If you give your children the message that you will take their side over your mate's, the kids may try to drive a wedge between you.* The high divorce rate in stepmarriages suggests they're often successful. That's the kind of success we can all do without!

Real Parents, you need to walk a fine line in this high-stakes area. On the one hand, you need a life partner, and that's the role your new mate fills. Your kids can't and shouldn't provide the intimacy, companionship, and solace you need from another adult in a loving relationship. And when this marriage succeeds, you're giving the whole family a priceless gift: stability.

On the other hand, you need to reassure and guide your children, who may be on-edge about the impact your new spouse will have on their relationship to you. They already have parents, and they want and need you—not your spouse—to raise them.

How do you navigate between these two often-opposing camps? *Follow this critical principle: you, not your new mate, are responsible for parenting your kids, creating an atmosphere where everyone is respected, and presenting a united front with your spouse.* I can't overstate how important this is to everyone's well-being.

*The following guidelines can help you, as bioparents, prevent and deal with common problems that crop up between your kids and their stepparent.*

## ‣ SET EXPECTATIONS WITH YOUR CHILDREN:

It's never too soon to get into a routine of respect, and here's how. What follows assumes you've found a new mate, but if you haven't, just follow these guidelines on your own.

Each bioparent should meet with their kids—sans new partner—and make a list. Also meet separately with your new mate for their input, so they don't need to advocate for themselves in front of your offspring.

The list you ultimately create, based on your conversations with each party, needs to specify the exact behaviors required so each person feels respected—including how you expect your kids to treat your mate.

Your kids will abide the family rules of respect more if they have input[19], and if you frame this as a way to make sure that everyone, including them, gives and receives respect. We learn what we live, and we all need to live and learn respect.

For instance, maybe your partner construes respect as the children saying "hello," "goodbye," "good morning," "good night," and other basic courtesies that acknowledge your and your mate's presence. You might put items on the list such as, "Kids nicely say hi and bye when Stacie or Dad comes into or leaves the room, to show the respect of acknowledgment."

Or, maybe your kids decide they need to have their questions answered by you and not The Stepmom. You might add, "Dad answers all the kid questions when they need or want something, because the kids want the respect of his attention."

You, as the real parent, need to also list and enforce penalties for infractions. Here too, the kids will buy into the consequences more if they have a voice in what those are, with your guidance, rather than if you lay down the law without their involvement. For example, you might ask, "Let's say one of you is rude to Stacie when she's driving you somewhere. What do you think the consequence of that should be?" (Hint: Stacie does not drive them the next time they want to go somewhere.)

Bonus! As the bioparent, you have veto power if the kids come up with something like, "The kids need unlimited access to video games, showers once per week, and no bedtime."

...

# EXERCISE 6: ▥▬▶

## *The respect routine:*

Together with your children (but sans mate), use your Notebook to list everything you can think of that makes each one of you feel respected. Take turns.

Separately, add the items your partner requests—unless you don't yet have a partner, in which case you can add theirs once you do.

Put all items in positive language of what you do want, not stuff you're hoping to avoid. For instance, "doesn't look down at the ground when I'm speaking" is better framed as, "looks into my eyes when I'm speaking." Remember, the brain focuses on what we give it[20], so give it positives!

Also write an agreed-upon list of reasonable consequences for infractions.

When you have a list everyone agrees on (with parental veto power wielded as necessary), have adults and kids alike sign and date it, for maximum impact and compliance.

Revisit as often as your family finds necessary. *Agreements prevent problems.*

## ▶ SET EXPECTATIONS WITH YOUR SPOUSE:

Although the respect routine document goes a long way towards codifying parental-role expectations with your partner, it's not enough.

*Explicitly ask your mate to bring you all issues that relate to your kids, rather than parenting your children themselves.* Show them this chapter, to underscore that this not about distrusting your new mate, but about protecting your marriage—which requires you, as the real parent, to do the parenting.

To keep things crystal-clear, specify exactly which parental duties you're taking care of, and how you're handling the tasks you can't be present for.

It's advisable for you to do as much of the kids' daily care and guidance as you can, and to hire babysitters or involve other friends and family for much of what you can't do yourself. Offloading it to your new spouse is tempting because it looks convenient and free—but a home filled with discontented people is, in my view, expensive and highly inconvenient!

So, Real Parents, drive your children where they need to be, or get them into a carpool or bus for transit. Take them to the doctor and dentist yourself. Get help such as after-school care or tutors when you can't be there. Find summer daycamps instead of expecting your mate to become "free" daycare. And only require progress on chores, homework, and other kid tasks when you yourself are home to monitor them. Running out the door with a hurried, "Todd! Mow the lawn while I'm at work!" tacitly places your spouse in the oversight role if they're home, creating opportunities for friction.

*If you can't monitor your kids yourself or get outside help to do so, then drop expectations that your children will get stuff done while you're out.* Repeat the following: "My spouse is my partner, and I'm my children's parent. It is my job to take care of my kids, including having my kids do the things they need to. I will oversee their progress on tasks. This is good for my kids and my marriage."

•••

# *EXERCISE 7:* ✏️▬▬▷
## *The responsibility roundup:*

In your Notebook, list the various parenting tasks you do that guide and nurture your children. Include items that show emotional support and guidance, such as "giving hugs," "saying I love you," and "giving life advice." Make a deal with yourself that, even when you have a new life partner, you will continue to be the one who does these tasks.

*Once you make a commitment to someone new, show them this list and emphasize that you will continue taking care of parenting your children.*

If there are tasks, such as driving all the kids to school, which don't make sense to rigidly partition (such as because your spouse's and your kids are the same ages, and it would be odd for you to drive yours to school while your partner transports theirs)—mutually and privately decide how that specific task will be taken care of. Maybe all the kids can walk to school now, or ride bikes. Maybe they can get to a bus route. Maybe, after a time, everyone will get along well enough that you can switch off which adult hosts the daily drive.

*Whatever the agreement is, it needs to avoid putting your new mate in the parent position, and it needs to be specified between the adult partners before the bioparent tells the kids.*

## ▶ STAND BY YOUR MAN (OR WOMAN):

The road to hell is paved with letting your kids run roughshod over their stepparent. *Make sure you show and tell your mate that you have his or her back.* When you find out about rude or disrespectful behavior from your kids to your spouse, you need to be the one to deal with bringing the children back to appropriate behavior. You can revisit the respect routine document you created, to decide how to proceed.

*The keys are: you level the consequences; you be the person your mate can turn to; and you talk with the kids about expectations going forward.*

• • •

# EXERCISE 8: ▭▭▶

## *The intercession:*

In the Exercises under "discipline behind-the-scenes" in the Step-parent section, I specified some ways stepparents can talk to their mates about stepkid issues, rather than trying to guide the children directly. Now, bioparents, it's your turn. How would you respond to your mate so he or she receives your support over those issues (even if you don't ultimately see things quite the same way)? How would you respond to your kids? Write your responses, and then I'll share mine.

To refresh your memory, here's a repetition of the scenarios, but from your point of view as Real Parents:

▶ **THE COLD-FRONT:** Nicole, the new stepmom whose stepkids don't make much eye contact with her, has approached you and said she is feeling a little unwelcome by your kids. She understands that they're all adjusting and it's normal for them to prefer you, as their biodad; still, she's hurt and asks for your input. What's your response?

**Here's my thought:** Nicole might just need you to listen in a supportive way, where you don't demonize anyone, but you do acknowledge that it sucks to be left out. You might say,

> "*The guys got pretty cynical when I broke up with Samantha, and I'm afraid it may take them a while to come around. I'm here to listen, and I am so sorry they have hurt your feelings. It does feel awful to be unacknowledged. Would you like me to ask them to make more of an effort?*"

If Nicole does need you to say something, find out exactly what would help her feel acknowledged, and then express it to your kids nonjudgmentally:

*"Hey guys, at dinner, could you make a little eye contact with Nicole? She's not trying to be your mom, but she would like to have a friendly relationship with you, and I'd like you to look in her direction now and then."*

You may have to remind your kids, privately, more than once. And tell your spouse that you interceded!

▸ **THE MICROMANAGER:** Back to Cynthia, who snapped at her stepmom for being too nosey. Stepmom may be over-parenting; still, Cynthia needs a reminder to be respectful. Stepmom asked for your guidance as the real parent. What will you say?

**Here's my take:** Listen to your mate. We all need a good listening-to. That in itself will help a lot[21]! Tell her there's no need for her to feel like a neglectful parent, since she's your wife, not Cynthia's mom. You can say,

*"For everyone's good, I want to do the parenting. You're off the hook! I want you to love and cherish me, and I'll do the same for you. Part of that is making sure you are respected in our home. Would you like me to speak with Cynthia about expressing herself more appropriately?"*

Then, follow through by speaking to your child, and report back to your mate with the results:

*"I explained to Cynthia that you're trying to figure out how to be good to her, and that you've realized you can't be her mom. It's an adjust-*

*ment, and we're all going through it. I also said that mutual respect is a must—I insist on that. She agreed that she shouldn't have called you nosey, and that she will behave more respectfully going forward."*

## TWO SETS OF KIDS—TWO SETS OF RULES?

If finding peace is difficult when one adult brings kids to the marriage, it's more so when both do. To live well when two sets of kids enter the stepfamily, follow the guidelines posed throughout the chapter—with each parent in the parent position with their own kids, and the stepparent role for their partner's children.

What if you've got different discipline styles? My guess is, that was probably an issue with your former spouse, and might be an issue in your new relationship too. It's very common for one parent to be more lenient than the other when it comes to child discipline[22]. Couples often fight over these issues because we tend to see our children as our expression of the values we want to send into the world. And we'll talk a lot more about fighting fairly with your mate in Chapter 9.

That said, this doesn't need to be a tragedy. Unlike with your ex (the kids' other bioparent), you have total latitude in a stepmarriage to do it your way with your kids. *If you can't agree with your new mate on handling a given issue, you'll need to each parent only your own children, as usual—just with two sets of rules, one for each real parent's kids.*

For instance, in elementary school, Vic's son received rewards for the behaviors that led to good grades (such as keeping a daily task log), whereas mine didn't. We had different philosophies for doing that—namely, that his child didn't enjoy school and needed the incentive, whereas mine loved school and might find intrinsic motivation undermined by a bribe[23]. Of course, this seemed really unfair to my son. Along with my reasons, I had to tell my kiddo that I was the final word for my (and only my) child. It wasn't popular news, but that's the way it was. And because Vic and I presented a united front—having separate rules, but supporting each parent's authority to make and uphold them—my child knew there was little point in going around me.

Other times, there were issues where Vic and I agreed to parent the same way. Neither child was permitted to have screentime until their daily homework was done, for example. Still, the limit with each kid had to be set by the real parent.

*Although having different disciplinary styles is not as easy as having both adults on the same page, that's okay;* you and your ex probably have different rules at different homes, and most kids are flexible enough to make that adjustment. And the kids in your stepmarriage would be living by different rules if you had never gotten together. Keeping the peace by each parenting your own kids will help you stay together, especially if you won't let the kids goad you into speaking poorly of your spouse's discipline choices.

The children may well try to do that, saying the two sets of rules are not fair. Inevitably, they will compare notes and prefer one set of rules over the other. But them's the breaks: the real parent does the parenting! A stepparent setting the rules for everyone is even less fair, and works less well.

The kids can learn that each parent makes and enforces the rules for their—and only their—kids. They can also learn that the stepparent won't intervene to break the rules their bioparent made.

Bonus! This prevents the kids from pitting you and your mate against each other. When they try to get a better deal through your mate, or your mate's kids try that with you, it's no dice.

*Tell the kids this rule as often as needed, and live by it:*

> *"I make the rules for my kids, and your parent makes the rules for you."*

...

# EXERCISE 9: ✏️

## *The report card:*

Let's take an example someone presented to me while I was typing this sentence. Denise and Eli moved in together, each bringing two children spanning from elementary through high school. Report cards arrived, and all four kids performed below either adult's expectations. What should they do, according to the principles in this chapter? Take a moment to write about it in your Notebook.

........................................................

### MY THOUGHTS?

I recommend that the parents confer with each other. Ideally, they'll agree on a united plan. They then each meet only with their own kids, and deliver whatever lecture or consequence the adults agreed on. This way, there's one set of rules...but it's delivered by the parent who has authority over each specific child. For instance, Denise and Eli could each tell their kids (and only their kids) that,

*"I'm worried that these grades don't reflect the best you're capable of.
Let's try something new. For the next grading period, let's get a half-
hour of daily online tutoring in the subjects where you need help, and
show me your homework in each subject each day. You can have your
screentime every day after that's done."*

If Denise and Eli cannot agree, then they'll need to avoid undermining one another. Each of them will still meet with their kids only, and
deliver whatever plan that bioparent has come up with.

Perhaps Denise will give the speech above, while Eli will instead
tell his two kids that,

*"I don't think this is your best work. There's not going to be any more
screentime or ice cream until I see two weeks of A's on your homework."*

The kids will figure out that there are two different sets of consequences, and when (not if) the kids call that out, each parent can say,

*"Yes, each parent makes the rules for their own kids."*

## FIND PEACE TOGETHER

Using these guidelines, you can become a safe harbor for your
mate in what would otherwise be a certain storm. Will it be perfect?
No. Can it be safe, loving, and very much good-enough? Yes.

The really big idea in this chapter isn't about how tough it is to
parent OPC, or even how to each parent your own biokids. Those
are important, but they're not as vital as this:

*When you're in a stepfamily, living in peace rather than pieces means living together in mutual respect. The adults set the tone, giving an example of their love and respect in their marriage, while each parenting their own offspring.*

You may never be a real family in the traditional sense of the word. But if you embrace the positives of mutual respect while letting go of the myth of the blended family—you can be happy.

We can't be happy with just anyone, though. Sometimes, we make our Must-Haves list, check it twice—and still find out we need to break up. Other times, we get the joy of finding out we are right about this person in all the important ways—and we want to commit to them forever. In our final chapter, let's figure out endings—and launch beginnings.

# CHAPTER 9:

# Happily Ever After

Wise Readers—you've made it! You've set enough boundaries and barriers to win an Olympic hurdling event, forgiven yourself and your ex, learned who to let into and keep out of your and your kids' lives, navigated the many gender- and timing-related pitfalls of courtship, and discerned who does what in a stepfamily so everyone—kids, adults, marriage—thrives. Whew!

*You are ready for your fairytale ending. And truly, it can come true.* I was realizing just the other night that if I could re-live any part of my life again, purely for the joy of it, it would be the years I've had with Vic. Life has not been challenge-free, but let's face it—ease was never an option anyway, not for anyone. Adulting is hard. I've loved having Vic there for my challenges, and it's been my privilege to be present for his.

Real love lasts, and you can find real love. I believe it; research proves it. And you can do it!

That said, we've got just a task or two left. One is leaving. The other is staying.

# STOP KISSING THAT FROG!

Unfortunately, sometimes you might make it all the way to this point and find a deal-breaker; would-be royals can turn out to be amphibious. *If so, remind yourself that if not-good-enough worked for you, you'd probably still be with your ex. Recall that your kids are counting on you to have high enough standards to get this right. And then, please toss the frog back into the pond and resume your search.*

It's tempting not to. Ending a serious dating relationship is hard: breaking up is consistently among the five most stressful life events[1]. And you're probably not eager to add stress to your already complex life.

There are many other reasons, too. My clients, classes, and Facebook respondents have given me a wealth of explanations for why they avoided breaking up even when they knew that needed to happen. I'll share that list in a moment. But first, let's see yours.

•••

# EXERCISE 1: ▱▭▭▭▷

## *The excuse ruse:*

If you're dating someone now and you suspect or know they're not your final choice, what's keeping you from ending things? If you're not seeing anyone yet, but you've spent too much time with the wrong dating partners in the past, why didn't you end things sooner? Please take the time to write down every impediment you can think of.

## *FINISHED?*

Okay, here's that list I promised, grouped into rough categories.

### ▶ FEAR:

- "It seemed too hard."

- "I feared being alone."

- "I feared hurting the other person."

- "I was hoping they would break up with me and save me from having to end things."

- "What if nobody better comes along?"

### ▶ LOW SELF-ESTEEM:

- "What if I'm being too picky?"

- "What if I can't handle being lonely?"

- "What if I want to get back together later?" (See also: "What if I make a mistake and can't win them back?")

- "I felt like I didn't deserve better: 'Who do I think I am?!'"

- "Self-doubt, where I second-guessed my own judgment and ability to make good choices for myself: 'Maybe I'm looking at it wrong.'"

- "Blaming myself for the relationship's failure: 'It's my fault it's not working.'"

- "I'm too (old, short, tall, weird, etc.) to find someone else."

▸ DENIAL:

- "He doesn't want me now, but eventually he will see I'm right for him."

- "I told myself, 'It will get better.'"

- "I told myself, 'They'll change.'"

- "I convinced myself that I needed to change, rather than admitting that the relationship had serious problems that would never meet my needs."

▸ SUNK COSTS:

- "I've been here too long to leave now."

▸ TIRED OF LOOKING/EASIER TO STAY:

- "It was easier to afford things as a couple."

- "I wanted this one to be THE one."

- "I was too exhausted to contemplate leaving."

- "I was too exhausted to start over."

- "It was more convenient to stay than to do all the work of finding someone else."

▶ **WAITING FOR AN EVENT TO PASS:**

- "We had plans for a vacation that was coming up in two months."

- "I waited to leave until after she recovered from breast cancer."

▶ **ATTACHMENT TO OTHERS OR OTHERS' OPINIONS:**

- "My (kids, friends, dogs, cats) really liked my partner."

- "I loved my partner's (kids/family/friends/dogs/cats)."

- "I was protecting my partner's kids from my partner, who was abusive."

- "I'm afraid of others' reactions (friends, family, kids)."

- "We had so many friends in common."

- "I feared the impact on the kids."

- "I felt pressured to be in a couple, because that's more socially acceptable."

▶ **AND THE MOST COMMON REASON—BEING ATTACHED TO A BTN (BETTER-THAN-NOTHING) IS BETTER THAN NOTHING[2]:**

- "We'd had so much fun together."

- "I didn't want to give up my connection with that person."

- "At least we're compatible. Do I really need love on top of that?"

- Anything that starts with "at least," as in, "At least I don't have to live with my mom this way."

........................................................

- "There was a lot that was good about them."

........................................................

- "I didn't want to give up the good parts of the relationship."

........................................................

- "I was dickmatized (like being hypnotized, but with, you know, dicks)." (See also, "The sex was too good," and "I was ovulating.")

........................................................

- "I knew it was not working, but I felt committed or attached to this person."


## ▶ BREAKING IT TO YOURSELF:

*Folks, if you want lifetime love, no reason is good enough to settle for a relationship that's not up to the mark—even if there's a lot you like or love about this person.* Take BTN's, those unworkable lovers we settle for, at least for a time. They're actually quite a bit worse than nothing, even if your frog is one of those really pretty, colorful ones from the Amazon. You need to move on, because staying in the wrong partnership is poison.

Dead-end relationships don't build a life, they waste it—draining our time, energy, money, emotions, and motivation. They distract us from the things that really matter to us, such as being fully emotionally available to our children, which is far easier to do from the vantage point of a solid relationship than a doomed one. They mow down our mojo by eroding our self-esteem, convincing us that this is the best we can do. They kill our motivation to go look for someone else, since our itches are getting scratched at least a little bit in our part-time lover's bed; scientifically, when any need is sated, be it hunger, thirst, or sex with another person, it's a demotivator for going elsewhere to meet that need[3]. *Getting a good partner rarely happens while all our resources, emotional and otherwise, are going towards someone who doesn't fit our permanent picture!*

I know it's hard to go out into the cold world, sans even a BTN, and I've got my old diaries to prove it. It's tough to let go of people for any and all of the reasons above. I stuck around for months with a nice-but-not-for-me guy, partly because I didn't want to lose touch with his daughter. But it was my responsibility to leave a relation-ship that—for whatever reason—was not my ultimate choice. After all, it's not just my time I was wasting.

No matter what your excuses are, break up as soon as the deal is broken. You will feel grief, even though this relationship isn't workable; that's no reason to resume the relationship, but it is a reason to start looking for another, more suitable partner[4]. You, the kids, your actual prince or princess, and even that nice frog are all counting on it!

### ▶ BREAKING UP WITH YOUR PARTNER:

Okay, so you're convinced (I hope). But…how do you break up and make it stick?

First off, I'm assuming you're not ending an abusive relationship, or running away from someone your gut says is dangerous. If you are, please refer to the tips in Chapter 4 for getting help with a safe exit plan!

Now, with that scenario out of the way: studies show that people end relationships in many devious and unkind ways[5]. These include women who nix the nookie, men who cut the credit cards, and both being plain cruel—starting affairs with their partner's friends, changing their social media status to "single," and disappearing altogether in a move known as ghosting.

In a non-representative survey I conducted on breaking up[6], respondents admitted that they had sometimes ghosted others, usually because they feared causing pain and wanted to avoid witnessing its results.

Yet these same people admitted they hated being ghosted. *When you ghost someone, you are not saving them pain, but creating even more of it!* People feel disrespected and unvalued if, to you, the relationship is so unremarkable that you can't quite bring yourself to make a definitive, kind, firm goodbye. Fading out or disappearing is far from kind or respectful, and as we've seen, we need to practice kind and respectful behavior with everyone if we want our someday-kingdom to thrive.

*And don't kid yourself about being friends, either.* That's a modified BTN where men and women alike try to get the advantages of the relationship, without the relationship[7]. It's also a way that men, especially, may try to maintain sexual options[8]. *And I wish this point didn't need making, but clearly, it does: don't stalk your ex[9].* It's illegal, creepy, and keeps you stuck. If someone has said No to seeing you anymore, here's what they meant: No. Be done with this relationship, so you both have room in your lives and hearts to move on!

So if those aren't the ways to break up, what should you do instead?

*When I asked my breakup-survey respondents how they wanted to be treated, their input boiled down to this:*

- **do it in person or on the phone** (unless you think they could be violent);

- **say something you like about the person** you're leaving; and then,

- **break up definitively and kindly,** by saying that there's not enough of a match, or that your feelings haven't developed, and you're moving on.

...

# EXERCISE 2:

## *The breakup script:*

Given the criteria above, take a minute or so to write your own breakup script. Then I'll share mine.

**DONE? OKAY, HERE'S A BREAKUP SCRIPT I DEVELOPED THAT MY CLIENTS HAVE FOUND USEFUL.**

Feel free to cut-and-paste it into your Notebook, and customize it for your soon-to-be ex:

> *"I wanted to meet with you because even though I've enjoyed being with you—I just don't feel the way I need to in order to stay together. It's hard, but I've realized my feelings aren't going to change, and I'm sorry, but I am breaking up with you."*

Don't go into details, justifications, or arguments. You feel how you feel, and nobody can argue with that; or if they do, thank heaven you're leaving someone who won't respect that you know your own heart.

No matter what the person says as a follow-up, you can listen, and agree with their basic idea—and then repeatedly return to the theme that you don't have strong enough feelings to continue the relationship with them. Example:

**Them:** *"You'll never find anyone else like me!"*

**You** (even if you're thinking, "I'm counting on that."): *"You could be right, but I still don't feel like I'd need to in a permanent relationship—and I'm breaking up."*

**Them:** *"You're making a big mistake. You'll regret leaving. Nobody will love you like I do."*

**You** (even if you're dying to say, "I doubt it," and "Threats are so unattractive."): *"You could be right, but I still don't feel like I'd need to—and I'm breaking up."*

**Them:** *"After all I've done for you! You've wasted so much of my time."*

**You** (even if you're wallowing in guilt): *"You could be right, but I still don't feel like I would need to—and I'm breaking up."*

**PROTIP:** if you think your guilt, or their tears, might cause you to cave—that's delaying the inevitable. One good technique for making sure you can stick to your script? Role-play with a friend who acts as your soon-to-be-ex, throwing every argument and guilt-inducing statement they can at you!

Repeat as needed, until the other person quits objecting, leaves, or an hour is up. At which time, leave! *You can't be both the cause and cure for your now-ex's pain; the top thing that will heal each of you* is another healthy relationship[10]. So get out of the way, and start dating as soon as possible. If your grief is intense, please consider therapy or a grief group.

▶ **BREAKING IT TO THE KIDS:** Here's my opinion, which I'm extrapolating from the research in Chapter 8: the real parent does all the parenting, so *if you're not the real parent, let that person discuss the breakup with the kids.*

This can be painful if you're close to the children. I remember that when I broke off with the dad of the girl I was close to, I worried that she might feel abandoned. But she was a minor, and I felt it inappropriate to initiate any contact with her to say goodbye without her parents' unprompted invitation. As an adult, she sought me out, and we're good friends. Even if that hadn't happened, though, she was her dad's and mom's child, and I needed to let them handle delivery of what was likely to be sad news.

*If you are the real parent, clearly and kindly tell the kids the minimal information they need to know.* Here, I'm extrapolating from my breakup survey, and surmising that kids feel unhappy about being ghosted, too—not by the parent's ex, so much as by the parent who fails to tell the children that the former partner won't be coming around anymore. In my opinion, because children often assume they are at fault in their parents' divorce, it's also important to include language that reassures your children that they didn't cause your breakup.

...

# *EXERCISE 3:* ✐

## *The breakup script (for your kids):*

In your Notebook, please write out a brief, kind, clear statement you can make to your children about the ending of a relationship. Make sure to explain that your breakup is not a reflection of their worth or anything they did. I'll make a suggestion below, which you can customize according to your needs and situation.

..........................................................

### OKAY, HERE'S MY THOUGHT:

You might say something like,

> *"Sam liked you kids a lot, and I think you liked him, too. Sometimes, even when adults meet someone who has a lot of great things about them, it's still not enough of a match for them to commit to each other. It's sad, but Sam isn't going to be around anymore. Please know that he cared about you, and this didn't happen because of anything you did or didn't do."*

If your children are having a hard time dealing with the grief as or after the relationship ends, you might also consider age-appropriate bereavement groups, and counseling.

## ▸ BREAKING UP WHEN YOU LIVE TOGETHER:

It makes sense that cohabitation would help us figure out whether someone's right for us and our kids, and iron out any kinks pre-marriage, right? Most people probably agree with that sentiment, because living together before or instead of marriage is now the norm[11]. People today see cohabitation as a safer pathway to marriage, or a marriage-lite alternative that is less risky in every way[12].

I thought so too. But when I read the science, I learned that the reverse is true. *Living together offers many of the risks of divorce, with none of the safety nets of marriage.* Across the miles and decades, every study I've encountered on this subject reaches the same sad conclusion: the longer you cohabit with anyone, and the more partners you cohabit with, the more likely it is that this or any marriage you enter into will be less rather than more happy; less rather than more lasting; and less rather than more stable[13]. Your individual results could be better, of course—but it's not the way to bet.

Why? *Because, in contrast to marriage, the time horizon and commitment levels in cohabitation are sharply limited.* Making a deep investment in the partner's and their kids' well-being is simply too risky in a living-together arrangement. Sadly, that's a setup for eventual breakup—hence my inclusion of this topic here.

*All of this may be especially true when kids are in the picture:*

- **Single moms tend to become clinically depressed by cohabitation.** They assume their partner will help them bear at least the emotional burdens of childcare, and they hope a proposal is coming--but usually, it's not[14].

- **Cohabiters tend to treat arguments as possible reasons to leave** rather than to work things out, so issues linger and worsen. As I've already pointed out, kids usually come with stress, and stress comes with arguments. A primary thing co-habiters argue about is commitment itself, because most men see cohabitation as an end in itself, whereas women routinely expect it to lead to marriage[15].

- **Physical abuse rates are higher in cohabitation, too**[16]—**as is sexual infidelity**, even though cohabiters are just as likely as married people to say they expect their mate to be faithful[17]. We've already seen that the vulnerable, including single parents, are especially likely to be targeted by those who would harm them; and single moms are likelier to receive an offer to live together than to wed[18].

- **Cohabiters also get the short end of the financial stick.** Married people are far likelier to amass wealth and to share it with one another, because they feel secure enough in their commitment to take turns doing things like going to school; specializing in various home and work tasks rather than dupli-cating effort; and saving money together that they and children can benefit from in a future they anticipate sharing[19]. Cohabiters do little of this, instead using their resources almost entirely for themselves and helping each other's children very little.

- **The non-parent partner often finds that they have little idea of boundaries regarding the single parent's children:** without full commitment, the time horizon is too fuzzy to know exactly what's expected, or whether getting attached to these kids is even smart. The desire to hang in there through the inevitable slings and arrows of someone else's parenthood might not be there to begin with, or could be eroded by the uncertainty of the situation: there's evidence that the "trying it out" aspect of cohabitation has a corrosive effect on commitment that can persist after marriage[20].

········································································································································

· **And the children learn what they live[21], whether the model is commitment, or avoidance of it.**

These outcomes are tough on adults, yes—and may be even worse for kids, who prefer to have their living situation changed rarely if at all[22]!

*In short, cohabiting and marriage are separate, unequal institutions with different purposes and outcomes. Cohabiting is less about forever, and more about freedom. Marriage is exactly the opposite.* It is marriage, not cohabitation, that delivers the emotional, financial, and social goods people often hope will result from living together, because these positives arise from an infinite time horizon rather than a limited one.

"But," you may be thinking, "can't cohabitation at least help us know if this person is right for us? How better to get to know all sides of a person than by living with them 24-7?"

While that just sounds so darn logical, it's flatly untrue that cohabiting is any more helpful than wise dating; it's far less helpful, in fact. People have always had ways other than living together to discern one another's habits and characters; Chapters 3 and 4 of this book are largely about how to do just that! *It is dating done right, not cohabitation, that gives us opportunities to figure out whether we're good for one another.*

*Given the above, my main advice to you is clear: don't cohabit unless the wedding is set for a very near date, in which case marriage-level commitment is already there*[23]. The problem with co-habiting isn't the fact of sharing bed and board, but the lack of a full choice in favor of permanence, and the willingness to do what that requires—from both partners. Today's marriages that are formed between folks who didn't cohabit first—or who did live together, but only after a wedding date was set for the near future—are happier and more likely to last, compared to couples who cohabited under other circumstances[24]. The commitment is the key—not who squeezes the toothpaste from the middle!

•••

# EXERCISE 4: ▭▭▷
## *The no-cohabitation policy:*

What if your partner asks you to move in, and you're not yet engaged or married? In your Notebook, and based on what you now know of cohabitation, please write a script. Then, I'll share mine.

...............................................................

**OKAY, HERE'S MY SCRIPT, WHICH I USED AS A SINGLE MOM BECAUSE IT WAS MY TRUTH. FEEL FREE TO WORD IT TO YOUR LIKING:**

> *"If you and I work out, that will be wonderful. But I can't risk my child's security and my own on a 'maybe.' My child deserves the stability of full commitment, and I want that for myself as well. Let's keep dating and see where things go."*

The heart you save could be your own!

By the way, in case you think this script will turn partners away, every man I said this to not only fully understood my perspective — but proposed marriage. And Vic never asked me to move in first; he proposed. People who love you will not leave you over solid standards. And people who truly want a full commitment with you will make one, if you hold your ground — without getting you and your offspring into a compromising situation first.

## WHAT IF YOU'RE ALREADY COHABITING NOW, AND NEED TO BREAK UP?

Unfortunately, this information is coming much too late for some. The scientific findings are clear — but they're also counterintuitive and countercultural, and you may never have heard of them before today. I guess we can't be surprised that the cultural messages have won, and many of you may be cohabiting right now.

If you're realizing you need to exit this relationship, stomaching the breakup may be harder than if you were merely dating. You can't just meet at a restaurant, give a spiel, and move on. This breakup will take longer and involve more logistics. Who moves? Where do they go? When do they leave? How does everyone afford this? Also, there's the possibility that you and your kids have formed a really deep attachment that's wrenching to end. After all, you've lived with this other person, not just seen them a couple times a week.

*Even so, if you need to break up with your live-in partner, and either of you has children, sooner is better than later.* Follow all the directions above — factoring in your or your partner's move. You might pad the front end of the two breakup scripts above (the one for your partner, and the other for your kids) with stuff you liked about the relationship, or things your partner liked about your children. But the gist is the same, and you can basically copy those breakup scripts and customize them.

## WHAT IF YOU'RE A HETEROSEXUAL WOMAN AND YOU WANT TO MARRY THIS MAN—BUT HE'S LOST ALL HIS URGENCY TO FULLY COMMIT, BECAUSE YOU'RE ALREADY LIVING TOGETHER?

In that case, sticking around longer won't convince him, nor will begging, proposing, etc. Men want the high-status woman, and she does none of those things. So be her!

...

# *EXERCISE 5:* ✏️▷
## *The leaving speech:*

If you fit the heterosexual-woman-living-with-noncommittal-man scenario, staying won't help. But leaving might. Please copy this script into your Notebook, and use when you are ready:

*"I know we decided to move in, but it's not working out the way I'd hoped. I'm finding a place to live and will let you know what my move-out date will be."*

Don't offer further justification, but do start finding a place, and start packing. He will either realize he cannot live without you, or he won't. Either way, you're saving the heartache of continuing to invest in a relationship that is in a stalemate. But don't bluff—if you say this and don't follow through, you have lost your leverage not only now, but going forward.

Beyond that, no matter who you are, rely on your intuition to decide whether your partner will become dangerous. If you think they might, please refer to the resources and information in Chapter 4 so you can make a plan, and get yourself and your children to safety. If not, you can have the breakup discussion with your partner while the kids are elsewhere, and the breakup discussion with your kids when your partner's not in the room.

## Start Driving Into The Sunset!

Now that we've said goodbye to the storms, let's drive into the sunset of happily-ever-after.

Ask anyone what it takes to create a lasting and happy marriage, and they usually say, communication. When I've pressed folks for what kind of communication, here are three of the wisest answers:

> *"Keep the fights clean and the sex dirty. I know it sounds funny, but it is so true!! If the fights are ugly (low blows, name-calling, using things shared in close moments against you, etc.), that is damage that is never truly repaired. It is disrespect."* (single mom)

> *"Communicate frustrations instead of coping, tolerating, or giving up on addressing them. Those aren't sustainable strategies. Avoiding conflict is not the same as not having conflict."* (single dad)

*"The desired outcome needs to be kept in mind by stepparents and parents. If the desired outcome is a closer relationship, then 'winning' a fight isn't going to accomplish that, no matter how right or justified."* (woman raised by a single mom)

Science supports those statements. *Good communication drives good relationships.* But what makes for good communication and what makes for bad communication? The answers may surprise you.

### ▶ COMPLAINING VS. CRITICIZING:

Would you start your car with no oil in the engine? Well...not more than once! Yet people start arguments with their beloved in ways we now know are damaging. We're only human, after all, and we will hurt each other's feelings sometimes. Hurt often leads to anger, and anger leads to saying things we might regret. Put that together with how we may have been raised--and most of us criticize rather than complain.

Wait...there's a difference? Yep. Complaining and criticizing are nearly opposites, and their distinctions are worth memorizing.

### HERE IS THE RIGHT TOOL FOR THE JOB.

### *COMPLAINING:*

- starts with "I" or "I feel/felt";

- focuses only on this specific time/place/event;

- uses respectful language that arises from a place of goodwill; and

- focuses on the feelings of the complainer.

## AND HERE IS THE WRONG TOOL.

### *CRITICIZING:*

- starts with or implies "you";

- generalizes beyond this time/place/event, using words or concepts of "always" or "never";

- may use name-calling or character assassination, or comes from mean-spirited intent; and

- focuses on the partner's flaws.

**PROTIP:** slipping in the words "I feel" or "I felt" doesn't turn a criticism into a complaint. "I felt like you were a selfish jerk when you dragged your butt in late again, and I'd really like you to take a flying leap," is not a complaint!

*Complaining helps marriages to last happily over decades—but criticizing **always** makes your relationship run rougher.*

## ▶ THREE STEPS TO HEALTHY COMMUNICATION:

Right up until now, I've presented social science in terms of odds rather than certainties. But I've saved the most powerful information for last. In studies spanning more than 30 years, Dr. John Gottman found that each and every time someone criticized their partner, it didn't simply fail to heal a rift. It actively undermined the well-being of the marriage. Yes, 100% of the time[25]!

How do we avoid these always-toxic results? As the single dad above pointed out, it's not by avoiding conflict.

## FIRST: RELATIONSHIP MECHANICS:
## USE SOFT STARTUP.

Instead, every relationship needs a person who habitually brings up problems in the relationship, following the good communication techniques described above. In my analogy, the relationship is the car, and this person is the mechanic.

*Being a relationship mechanic is a very important job.* Just as cars don't run well without someone who attends to their needs, relationships need someone to tune them up, too. Usually in heterosexual relationships, it's the woman, but about one in five guys steps up to do this job, too[26] (Clearly, in lesbian relationships, it's always a woman, and in gay relationships, it's a guy.).

Regardless of your gender, if you're the one doing this vital work, now's the time to get good at it. In the world of cars, there are good mechanics and bad ones. Ditto for relationships. One quality of all master mechanics is that they don't ignore the weird new clunk. In fact, Gottman found that the mechanics in happy marriages complain more, not less, than the mechanics in unhappy marriages[27]! *At the first sign of disrespect or unkindness, the master mechanic takes a look under the hood, and brings up the issue with their partner.*

And when they do, they use soft startup. *Because here's another scientific "always": arguments always end on the same note they started on[28].* If they begin harshly, that's how they end, and nothing is resolved; in fact, things get worse. But if the mechanic uses a kind and gentle approach, the ride gets smoother over time.

Expert mechanics may be so kind and gentle, they don't seem to be complaining at all. For example, let's say you're feeling frustrated because your spouse used to rush home so you could spend evenings together—but now it appears they'd rather work late, be with their friends, or go do something else the moment they're in the door. It's tempting to lash out at your mate with a criticism:

- *"You don't love me anymore."*

- *"You're so selfish. You don't care about making me happy, you just do what you want."*

The trouble is, this never, ever gives the result most of us want— namely, more love and closeness. For that, we need the mother of all wrenches, something I brought up in Chapter 8, and here it is:

> **"I felt [name emotion] when [name specific event] happened, and I'd really like [name specific outcome]."**

In our example, we could say, "I felt lonely when I didn't get a hug at six o'clock, and I'd really like one now."

If possible, keep the name of the emotion neutral, not harsh; "upset" is a better choice than "infuriated," and "lonely" is better than "distraught," because the more emotionally loaded words may put your partner on the defensive. And when they're on the defensive, we again know from science that our partner cannot hear us or help meet our needs[29].

*One of the tools that master mechanics possess is an assumption of their partner's basic goodwill[30].* I was so happy to receive a note yesterday from a former client, telling me about their wedding vows. The officiant had sent them the proposed service, including a section about what to value in a marriage, and my former client told me, "I revised that whole paragraph by saying that we would build our marriage on three things: Kindness, Respect, and Charitable Interpretations of the other person's actions."

Charitable Interpretations—what a perfect encapsulation of goodwill! It's so much easier to be kind and gentle with our partner if we start by presuming they are for us rather than against us, that they want our happiness, and that a specific circumstance or moment of forgetfulness got them off-track. The good news? It's usually true. If you've done what this book suggests, you're going to choose, or have already chosen, someone genuinely healthy for you. Starting from a position of goodwill is not only very helpful for the happiness of your relationship, it's also realistic!

*Patience is another important tool of the master mechanic, because the gentle complaining they employ isn't a one-time effort.* Gentle complaints entail being specific and avoiding the temptation to bring up how this is a general problem, your spouse does this nearly every night, etc. This means the master mechanic might be complaining a lot for a while—which means they may have to find many ways to bring the point home:

> *"I missed you at dinner tonight. Remember when we used to take a walk afterwards on our own, while the kids had an hour of screentime? I'd like some more of that—maybe Friday?"*

Let's try a few examples. Don't worry if you take a while to get the hang of it. Even master couples, the happiest of the happy, criticize sometimes[31]. But they work on complaining instead. And when I first learned about this, I could not even hear the difference between criticizing and complaining, nevermind produce an answer. It's okay if it takes you time. You'll do it! As with anything, progress, not perfection, is the goal.

...

# EXERCISE 6:

## *The complaint compendium:*

For each Example here, use the information above to create a gentle complaint. Please write your answer in your Notebook, and then I'll make some suggestions.

▶ **EXAMPLE 1:** *the movie date:* Imagine that the two of you have movie plans, but your partner mis-timed the kid drop-off, and now you're going to miss the start of the show—again. You're frustrated, not only because it's happening this time, but because it happens a lot of the time. What can you say that will use soft startup and be a complaint rather than a criticism?

**Okay, here's my idea for this situation:** Wait until the kids aren't around. It makes children nervous when their parents and stepparents argue in front of them, and it doesn't give your partner a chance to save face. Then, say something like,

> *"When I miss the beginning of a movie, I feel lost all the way through the show. Would you mind if we go to a later show, and walk around the lake or have dessert beforehand?"*

Note that this response avoids pointing out the habitual pattern of the partner's less-than-stellar time management. No matter who you choose as your partner, a full 2/3 of the issues you have with them will never really go away—mainly because the issues are due to basic aspects of their nature[32]. Criticizing them for being who they are is simply going to hurt your marriage, without repairing your annoyance in the moment. Complaints stick to this time and place and event, to help you and your partner at this precise instant. (So hard to do, I know!)

Happy couples remember that their relationship is more important than their momentary anger, and although they point out that what just happened does not work for them, they don't throw their partner under the bus for it.

▶ **EXAMPLE 2:** *needling the kids:* Imagine that your partner loves to tease kids. Maybe they genuinely think it's funny, or they don't know how to talk to children, or that's how they were raised. Whatever the reason, your kids are annoyed—and you're starting to see why. This time, during dinner, your children are talking about their days at school, and your mate keeps interrupting to joke about what they're saying. "I made a B on the test," your daughter begins, and your husband interrupts with, "'B' for 'boyfriend'? Were you thinking about boys instead of school?" Your daughter then says nothing for the rest of the meal.

What can you say to your spouse that will be a complaint, not a criticism?

**My idea:** After you're alone with your mate, you might say,

> *"I noticed that when Terry was speaking about her math exam, you interrupted her with a joke. You know I love your sense of humor, but I*

*felt upset that I didn't get to hear about the rest of her day because she clammed up. Plus, I want her to listen to you seriously when you have something to say. Can you back up my parenting by listening to her all the way through without interruption next time we have dinner together?"*

Note that because this is a parenting situation, you as the parent can assert the values you're trying to teach your children, advocating on their behalf—and you can ask your mate to follow rather than lead your specific parenting efforts.

*Again, because this might be a matter of your partner's character or personality, a complaint will not permanently solve the issue.* But it is worth it. Complaining, rather than criticizing, is research-proven to de-fang issues that would otherwise get totally out of hand[33]. And criticizing never, ever helps!

▸ **EXAMPLE 3:** *Promises, promises:* Another top thing couples argue about is housework[34]. Let's say that you come home after a long and upsetting day at the office. Your partner has been working from the house, and had specifically said they would put out the trash and start a load of wash—but there it is, not even started. You're irritated, not only because you think that now, you have to do it, but because they promised and didn't deliver, and it's far from the first time. Plus, you hate nagging your partner almost as much as you hate just doing the job to begin with; can't they simply take some initiative?! What's a way for you to complain in this situation, rather than criticize?

## Here's one possibility:

*"I'm kind of upset right now. I was looking forward to just putting my feet up for a while, but now that I'm home, the trash and laundry are still undone, although you said you would take care of those chores. I*

*can't relax while the house is dirty, and I need you to follow through. Can you do them now, please?"*

Even if your partner never sees dirt and disarray in quite the same way you do, these complaints are easier for them to hear and abide by than criticisms would be. Research-guaranteed[35].

## SECOND: BOTH PARTNERS: INSURE YOUR RELATIONSHIP WITH POSITIVE INTERACTIONS.

Good mechanics realize there's a balance to everything. Yes—complaining is necessary, or the engine will slowly corrode. But to insure your relationship vehicle against theft, damage, wear, and accidents, lots of good stuff has to happen too. That's the job of both the mechanic and the copilot.

By "good stuff," I don't mean luxury vacations, expensive toys, or an endless litany of "Yes, dear's." I mean foot rubs, "I love you's," and surprise mugs of hot cocoa. How many of these positive interactions do you need?

A lot! *For every negative interaction—such as complaining—you need twenty positives[36]. TWENTY. That's the ratio happy couples maintain.*

Factually, you'll need twenty "You look amazing's," "Thank you for picking the kids up—you're the best's," "Tell me about your day's," back scratches, favorite dinners cooked, etc., for every thoughtless statement, hurtful action, failure to look up when your mate comes into the room, or promised action not taken. These positives are your cushion against the fender-benders of tomorrow.

Looking for how little you can do and still get by? There's a ratio for that, too—5:1. For a marriage to endure, you've got to have five times as many positive as negative interactions—just to hang on by your fingernails[37].

And the old message that if there's as much good as bad, you're doing okay, is totally false; all those relationships are doomed, and 1:1 never works. But again, if you want to be happy, it's 20:1.

...

# EXERCISE 7: ◖▬▬▷

## The positive portfolio:

In your Notebook, please list everything you can think of —words and actions—that would count as positive gestures in your relationship. Be as detailed as you can. If you're already partnered, feel free to ask your mate for some ideas, too—or maybe take a test together that shows which actions make each person feel loved[38]. Go ahead and commit to performing at least five of these per day— and more, as you gain practice.

### THIRD: RELATIONSHIP COPILOTS: HEED YOUR MECHANIC.

Let's assume you're more of the copilot type than a mechanic. A whole lot of men—gay and straight—fit this description, because they will perk along more or less happily for years, letting stuff slide[39].

Unfortunately, sometimes letting stuff slide is code for ignoring your partner's opinions and desires. If this is you, I have bad news:

*research consistently shows that partners who fail to account for their mate's input, tend not to keep that mate*[40]. They wind up abandoned, divorced, and confused. These are the folks who are still wondering why so-and-so left them, years after so-and-so left them. In my experience, there were warnings aplenty—but because the copilot ignored them, the whole engine went kaput.

*In other words, if you have found a good partner, take the time to listen to any complaints that partner has.* This doesn't necessarily mean you'll always agree. But it does mean you'll carefully weigh your partner's input, show them through your listening and your responses that you are doing so, and join them in what they're asking for when it's possible.

•••

# EXERCISE 8: ▭▬▭▷
## *The hearing test:*

Let's say your relationship mechanic says, "I really need you to not interrupt the kids when they're speaking. Please let them finish talking, and take what they say seriously. They feel disrespected otherwise, and I worry for your relationship with them. Plus, I'm not happy when they feel disregarded."

This is not a perfect complaint—because it goes beyond the here-and-now. But rather than focus on the imperfections in delivery, it's time for you to take the substance seriously. What can you say to prove you're doing that? Please write down your responses, and I'll make some suggestions afterwards.

..................................................................

## HERE ARE MY SUGGESTIONS:

You might say,

> *"I'm sorry, you're right. I do tend to interrupt the kids and make jokes. That's how I was raised. I will try to stop, and listen carefully instead, because I want your happiness and I want a good relationship with the kids. Maybe you can raise one finger—not the middle one!—when I'm going off the rails?"*

This is a perfect response because instead of defending yourself, or promising perfection, you're showing that you listened to your mate, you understand that this request is reasonable, and you're amenable to making a positive change. (Plus, I've yet to meet a partner who disliked being told they were right, or that their and their kids' happiness is important to their mate!)

That said, some people, men especially, tend to **stonewall** their partners[41]. You can easily tell if that's you by considering how you react when your partner expresses anger and disappointment about something you did or didn't do. Do you focus on a spot on the floor, wall, or table, cross your arms, and maintain silence until your partner is done speaking—all while hoping this will soon be over? Do you show no reaction other than that? You might not feel emotionally overwhelmed, but research consistently shows that physically, you are—and you won't be able to process anything more until your body calms again[42].

Danger! Danger! Although you probably think you're keeping the argument from escalating, your partner probably sees stonewalling as the ultimate disrespect—a silent statement that, "You're so worthless to me, you don't even deserve an answer." In studies, it's even worse for killing long-term love than criticism, defensiveness, or contempt. **Reliably stonewalling your partner is the #1 predictor of divorce, per decades-long studies of married people[43].**

**Stonewalling SOS:** I'm that charmer who not only criticized partners, I also stonewalled them. Yet after learning all about this research, I changed—and the science on healthy communication says you can, too[44]. Here's what to do, step by step.

▸ **FIRST,** notice. Pay attention to when you begin feeling overwhelmed and have the urge to tune out, cross your arms, and stare at the floor. This means you're about to stonewall, and it's time for a break.

▸ **SECOND**, call a time-out. When this happens, tell your partner, "I need a break. I'd like to come back in [name specific timeframe] and hear you out, because you and this relationship are important to me, and to do that I have to decompress." This message underscores your partner's value to you, and your commitment to joining them in making a happy marriage. Feel free to show this part of the book to your mate, so they understand what you mean when you say this!

▸ **THIRD,** take a break for 20 minutes or more. Leave the room and do something distracting that keeps your mind engaged enough that you truly let go of the problem. This is not the time to call a friend and rehearse all the ways your partner did you wrong, how right you are, etc. Distracting will lower your heart rate, so you are able to engage in the discussion when you return, and research suggests a minimum break of 20 minutes works for most people[45].

▶ **FOURTH,** return and reengage at the time you agreed on, and be open to your partner's influence by heeding your mechanic!

## NURTURE YOUR HOPEFULNESS:

When I taught college classes, towards the end of each term, I often asked students if they knew anyone who was part of a happy, functional marriage. They usually said no—yet there I was in front of them, having given them the example of my happy marriage for several months! And many of my students said they themselves were happily married, while denying they knew anyone else who was...yet my students usually knew one another.

The fact is, unhappy couples get nearly all the press—but there are far more happy couples out there than you probably think: per the stats, most older couples have said they've loved each other for their entire marriage[46], and in other research, nearly 90% of the couples who thought about divorcing described themselves as "very happy" within five years of choosing to stay together[47].

Whether you are still searching, or in an exclusive relationship, please keep this optimistic fact in mind. To help you do so, here is an Exercise—the last: the gift of a hopeful example.

...

# *EXERCISE 9:* ✏

## *The role model:*

Please write down the name of someone you know who persisted and found love that resulted in their happy marriage. This could be a friend, teacher, colleague, or other acquaintance. It's all the better if they were single parents, and/or became part of a stepmarriage, too.

Next, think of this person when you feel overwhelmed, hopeless, or unable to cope. Consider asking whether they will be a mentor to you!

Wise Readers—parents, lovers, and others: you now have the tools you need for a happy, healthy, and lasting lifetime love. Replacing ineffective behaviors with the ones in this chapter and book will not fix everything, but they will make it easier to find the right partner and to bear one another's struggles with great love.

The path of joy is not the path of ease—it does indeed take effort. But good relationships are worth it. They are the foundation of our lives, the launchpad for our children, the comfort of our days, the passion in our nights, and the security for our future.

One of my clients recently said that they didn't know if they believed in lasting or happy marriage. Later that night, I took a photo of my husband holding my hand as he fell asleep. It may not be elegant, and it may not fit some people's idea of romance. But it is love. And it is lasting. And we are happy.

*Happy marriages exist. They are, in fact, the norm. Everyone needs a hand to hold onto. This is possible. Yes, for you.*

# REFERENCES AND NOTES:

## INTRODUCTION:

1.  Cacioppo, J. T., Cacioppo, S., Gonzagia, G. C., Ogburn, E. L., & VanderWeele, T. J. (2013). Marital satisfaction and break-ups differ across on-line and off-line meeting venues. *PNAS*. You can download or view this article at http://www.pnas.org/content/early/2013/05/31/1222447110.full.pdf+html

2.  Kuhle, B. X., Beasley, D. O., Beck, W. C., Brezinski, S. M., Cnudde, D., et al. (2016). To swipe left or right: Sex differences in Tinder profiles. Paper presented at the annual meeting of the Human Behavior and Evolution Society, Vancouver, Canada.

3.  See Chandler, A. (November 1998). *Children And Families: A snapshot*. Article retrieved from https://www.clasp.org/sites/default/files/public/resources-and-publications/archive/0028.pdf

4.  For a more recent take, see: Ganong, L., and Coleman, M. (2017). *The Cultural Context of Stepfamilies*. In L. Ganong & M. Coleman (Eds.), Stepfamily Relationships: Development, dynamics, and interventions (pp. 21-36). Springer.

5.  Gottman, John M., with Silver, Nan. *The Seven Principles for Making Marriage Work: A Practical Guide from the Country's Foremost Relationship Expert*. Harmony, 2015.

6.  Hetherington, E. Mavis, and John Kelly. *For Better or for Worse: Divorce Reconsidered*. Norton, 2003.

7.  This is the projected divorce rate for first marriages, over a lifetime. See Rotz, D. (2016). Why have divorce rates fallen?: The role of women's age at marriage. Marital satisfaction and break-ups differ across on-line and off-line meeting venues. *The Journal of Human Resources*, 51, 961-1002. You can download or view this article at http://jhr.uwpress.org/content/51/4/961.short

    For any given year, the divorce rate is around .3 to .4%--that's right, a fraction of a single percent. For more information, see the chart, "Provisional number of divorces and annulments and rate: United States, 2000-2016."Article retrieved from the Centers for Disease Control and Prevention at https://www.cdc.gov/nchs/data/dvs/national_marriage_divorce_rates_00-16.pdf

8.  Buss, David M. *The Evolution of Desire: Strategies of Human Mating (Revised and updated edition)*. Basic Books, 2016.

    See also Perilloux, C., & Buss, D. M. (2008). Breaking up romantic relationships: Costs experienced and coping strategies deployed. *Evolutionary Psychology, 6*(1), 164-181.

9.  Buss, David M. *The Evolution of Desire: Strategies of Human Mating (Revised and updated edition)*. Basic Books, 2016.

10. Smith, T. J. (2002). Are Married Parents Happier Than Single Parents? In K. Anderson, D. Browning, & B. Boyer (Eds.), *Marriage: Just a piece of paper?* (p. 28). Grand Rapids, Michigan: William B. Eerdmans Publishing Company.

11. Hetherington, E. Mavis, and John Kelly. *For Better or for Worse: Divorce Reconsidered.* Norton, 2003.

12. Kreider, R. M. (August 10-14, 2006). *Remarriage In The United States:* Poster presented at the annual meeting of the American Sociological Association, Montreal. Article retrieved from http://www.census.gov/hhes/socdemo/marriage/data/sipp/us-remar-riage-poster.pdf

    See also Rotz, D. (2016). Why have divorce rates fallen?: The role of women's age at marriage. Marital satisfaction and break-ups differ across on-line and off-line meeting venues. *The Journal of Human Resources, 51*, 961-1002. You can download or view this article at http://jhr.uwpress.org/content/51/4/961.short

## *Part I: Getting Ready For Love*

### CHAPTER 1: PUT THE PAST—AND YOUR EX—BEHIND YOU

1.  Wallerstein, J. (2002). Festering. In K. Anderson, D. Browning, & B. Boyer (Eds.), *Marriage: Just a piece of paper?* (pp.96-97). Grand Rapids, Michigan:William B. Eerdmans Publishing Company.

2.  Ricci, Isolina. *Mom's House, Dad's House: Making Two Homes for Your Child (Revised edition)*. Touchstone, 1997.

    See also Ricci, Isolina. *The CoParenting Toolkit: The Essential Supplement for Mom's House, Dad's House.* Custody & CoParenting Solutions, 2012.

3. Waite, Linda J., and Gallagher, Maggie. *The Case for Marriage: Why Married People are Happier, Healthier, and Better Off Financially.* Broadway Books, 2002.

   decades in the Virginia Longitudinal Study. See Hetherington, E. Mavis, and John Kelly. *For Better or for Worse: Divorce Reconsidered.* Norton, 2003.

4. Ibid.

5. Waite, Linda J., and Gallagher, Maggie. *The Case for Marriage: Why Married People are Happier, Healthier, and Better Off Financially.* Broadway Books, 2002.

6. Wallerstein, J. (2002). Festering. In K. Anderson, D. Browning, & B. Boyer (Eds.), *Marriage: Just a piece of paper?* (pp.96-97). Grand Rapids, Michigan:William B. Eerdmans Publishing Company.

7. Waite, Linda J., and Gallagher, Maggie. *The Case for Marriage: Why Married People are Happier, Healthier, and Better Off Financially.* Broadway Books, 2002.

8. Ricci, Isolina. *Mom's House, Dad's House: Making Two Homes for Your Child (Revised edition).* Touchstone, 1997.

9. Welch, D. C. (February 2009 to present). *LoveScience: Research-based relationship advice for everyone.* Retrieved from http://www.lovesciencemedia.com/love-science-media/the-ex-files-how-and-why-to-get-along-with-your-former-mate.html

   See also Orbuch, Terri. *Finding Love Again: 6 Simple Steps to a New and Happy Relationship.* Sourcebooks Casablanca, 2012. Dr. Orbuch found that divorced people who said that they felt neutrally about their ex were significantly more likely to repartner over time than those whose feelings were more intense. So it's worth doing the work to unhook!

10. Ricci, Isolina. *Mom's House, Dad's House: Making Two Homes for Your Child (Revised edition).* Touchstone, 1997.

11. Brown, Brené. *The Gifts of Imperfection: Let Go of Who You Think You're Supposed to Be and Embrace Who You Are.* Hazelden, 2010.

    See also Dweck, Carol. *Mindset: The New Psychology of Success.* Random House, 2006.

12. Ricci, Isolina. *Mom's House, Dad's House: Making Two Homes for Your Child (Revised edition).* Touchstone, 1997.

13. Myers, David G. *Social Psychology* (12th edition). McGraw Hill, 2016.

14. Ibid

15. Ibid

16. See also Cialdini, Robert B. *Influence: Science and Practice (5th edition).* Prentice Hall, 2008.

17. Skinner, B. F. *The Behavior of Organisms.* BF Skinner Foundation, 1991.

    You can read the book at https://books.google.com/books?hl=en&lr=&id=S9WNCwA AQBAJ&oi=fnd&pg=PT20&dq=b.+f.+skinner&ots=Lltp7owEF1&sig=VvjeGXXRiz14D V-ZQyTpoRo15TI#v=onepage&q=b.%20f.%20skinner&f=false

18. Welch, D. C. (February 2009 to present). *LoveScience: Research-based relationship advice for everyone.* Retrieved from http://www.lovesciencemedia.com/love-science-media/ the-ex-files-how-and-why-to-get-along-with-your-former-mate.html

19. Jacobson, Neil S., and Gottman, John M. *When Men Batter Women: New Insights into Ending Abusive Relationships.* Simon & Schuster, 2007.

20. Bancroft, Lundy. *Why Does He Do That?: Inside the Minds of Angry and Controlling Men.* Berkley Publishing Group, 2002.

21. Jacobson, Neil S., and Gottman, John M. *When Men Batter Women: New Insights into Ending Abusive Relationships.* Simon & Schuster, 2007.

    This is my idea; for a litany of ways to protect yourself from stalking, see de Becker, Gavin. *The Gift of Fear and Other Survival Signals that Protect us from Violence.* Dell Publishing, 1997; re-released by Gavin DeBecker, 2010.

22. Gottman, John M., with Silver, Nan. *The Seven Principles for Making Marriage Work: A Practical Guide from the Country's Foremost Relationship Expert.* Harmony, 2015.

23. Ibid.

24. Page, Susan. *The 8 Essential Traits of Couples Who Thrive.* Dell, 1994.

25. See also Gottman, John M., with Silver, Nan. *The Seven Principles for Making Marriage Work: A Practical Guide from the Country's Foremost Relationship Expert.* Harmony, 2015.

26. Ibid.

    See also Orbuch, Terri. *5 Simple Steps to Take Your Marriage from Good to Great*. River Grove Books, 2015.

27. Ibid.

    See also Gottman, John M., with Silver, Nan. *The Seven Principles for Making Marriage Work: A Practical Guide from the Country's Foremost Relationship Expert*. Harmony, 2015.

28. Page, Susan. *The 8 Essential Traits of Couples Who Thrive*. Dell, 1994.

    See also Page, Susan. *How One of You Can Bring the Two of You Together*. Broadway, 1997.

29. Ibid.

    For evidence that abusive people do not respond to goodwill, see Jacobson, Neil S., and Gottman, John M. *When Men Batter Women: New Insights into Ending Abusive Relationships*. Simon & Schuster, 2007.

30. Margulies, Sam. *Getting Divorced Without Ruining Your Life: A Reasoned, Practical Guide to the Legal, Emotional and Financial Ins and Outs of Negotiating a Divorce Settlement*. Fireside, 2001.

    ACEs, otherwise known as Adverse Childhood Experiences, often wreak havoc on self-esteem, education, healthy behaviors, and longevity itself: Anda, R. (Date not Indicated). *The health and social impact of growing up with Adverse Childhood Experiences: The human and economic costs of the status quo*. Research conducted in conjunction with Adverse Childhood Experiences (ACE) Study. Retrieved from http://acestudy.org/files/Review_of_ACE_Study_with_references_summary_table_2_.pdf

31. See also Ricci, Isolina. *Mom's House, Dad's House: Making Two Homes for Your Child (Revised edition)*. Touchstone, 1997.

32. Gottman, John M., with Silver, Nan. *The Seven Principles for Making Marriage Work: A Practical Guide from the Country's Foremost Relationship Expert*. Harmony, 2015.

    See also Orbuch, Terri. *5 Simple Steps to Take Your Marriage from Good to Great*. River Grove Books, 2015.

33. Ricci, Isolina. *Mom's House, Dad's House: Making Two Homes for Your Child (Revised edition)*. Touchstone, 1997.

34.  Ibid.

35.  Ibid.

36.  Welch, D. C. (February 2009 to present). *LoveScience: Research-based relationship advice for everyone.* Retrieved from http://www.lovesciencemedia.com/love-science-media/ the-ex-files-how-and-why-to-get-along-with-your-former-mate.html

37.  Burns, David M. *Feeling Good Together: The Secret to Making Troubled Relationships Work.* Broadway, 2008.

38.  Ibid.

39.  Ibid.

40.  Myers, David G. *Social Psychology (12th edition).* McGraw Hill, 2016.

## CHAPTER 2: FORGIVE YOUR EX AND YOURSELF

1.  Anda, R. (Date not Indicated). *The health and social impact of growing up with Adverse Childhood Experiences: The human and economic costs of the status quo.* Research conducted in conjunction with Adverse Childhood Experiences (ACE) Study. Retrieved from http://acestudy.org/files/Review_of_ACE_Study_with_references_summary_ table_2_.pdf

2.  People behave differently in intimate relationships, depending on their attachment style. For a thorough look at this, see Johnson, Sue. *Love Sense: The Revolutionary New Science of Romantic Relationships.* Little, Brown, 2013.

    See also Simpson, J. A. (1990). Influence of attachment styles on romantic relationships. *Journal of Personality and Social Psychology,* 59, 971-980.

3.  Johnson, Sue. *Love Sense: The Revolutionary New Science of Romantic Relationships.* Little, Brown, 2013.

4.  Bartholomew, K. (1990). Avoidance of intimacy: An attachment perspective. *Journal of Social and Personal Relationships,* 7, 147-178.

5.  Ibid.

See also Johnson, Sue. *Love Sense: The Revolutionary New Science of Romantic Relationships*. Little, Brown, 2013.

6. Brown, Brené. *The Gifts of Imperfection: Let Go of Who You Think You're Supposed to Be and Embrace Who You Are*. Hazelden, 2010.

7. This refers to state-dependent memory, meaning that the emotional state we're in now, often colors our memory of the past and our projection of the future. For a specific study on how this impacts memory for marital happiness, see Holmberg, D., & Holmes, J. G. (1994). Reconstruction of relationship memories: A mental models approach. In N. Schwarz & S. Sudman (Eds.), *Autobiographical memory and the validity of retrospective reports*. New York: Springer-Verlag.

8. Burns, David D. *The Feeling Good Handbook*. Plume, 1999.

9. Worthington, Everett. *Five Steps to Forgiveness: The Art and Science of Forgiving*. Crown, 2001.

10. Thoresen, C. E., Luskin, F., and Harris, H. F. S. (1998). Science and forgiveness interventions: Reflections and recommendations. In E. L. Worthington (Ed.), *Dimensions of Forgiveness: A research approach* (pp. 163-189). Pennsylvania: Templeton Foundation Press.

11. Ibid.

12. This sentiment is reflected in studies as well. See Seligman, Martin E. P. *Authentic Happiness: Using the New Positive Psychology to Realize Your Potential for Lasting Fulfillment*. Atria Books, 2004.

13. Thoresen, C. E., Luskin, F., and Harris, H. F. S. (1998). Science and forgiveness interventions: Reflections and recommendations. In E. L. Worthington (Ed.), *Dimensions of Forgiveness: A research approach* (pp. 163-189). Pennsylvania: Templeton Foundation Press.

14. For a science-based exploration of how to overcome and understand betrayal, see Cole, Tim, & Duddleston, Emily. *Broken Trust: Overcoming an Intimate Betrayal and Reclaiming Your Life*. Immensus Press, 2017.

15. This is one of those quotes that's been used so often and by so many, the original source is attributed to many people and thus is not knowable.

16. Worthington, Everett. *Five Steps to Forgiveness: The Art and Science of Forgiving*. Crown, 2001.

17. Cole, Tim, & Duddleston, Emily. *Broken Trust: Overcoming an Intimate Betrayal and Reclaiming Your Life*. Immensus Press, 2017.

18. Glass, Shirley P. *Not "Just Friends": Rebuilding Trust and Recovering Your Sanity After Infidelity*. Atria Books, 2004.

19. Ricci, Isolina. *Mom's House, Dad's House: Making Two Homes for Your Child (Revised edition)*. Touchstone, 1997.

20. Myers, David G. *Social Psychology (12th edition)*. McGraw Hill, 2016.

21. Worthington, Everett. *Five Steps to Forgiveness: The Art and Science of Forgiving*. Crown, 2001.

    See also Cole, Tim, & Duddleston, Emily. *Broken Trust: Overcoming an Intimate Betrayal and Reclaiming Your Life*. Immensus Press, 2017.

22. Jacobson, Neil S., and Gottman, John M. *When Men Batter Women: New Insights into Ending Abusive Relationships*. Simon & Schuster, 2007.

23. Thoresen, C. E., Luskin, F., and Harris, H. F. S. (1998). Science and forgiveness interventions: Reflections and recommendations. In E. L. Worthington (Ed.), *Dimensions of Forgiveness: A research approach* (pp. 163-189). Pennsylvania: Templeton Foundation Press.

24. Worthington, Everett. *Five Steps to Forgiveness: The Art and Science of Forgiving*. Crown, 2001.

25. Ibid.

26. Dweck, Carol. *Mindset: The New Psychology of Success*. Random House, 2006.

27. Brown, Brené. *The Gifts of Imperfection: Let Go of Who You Think You're Supposed to Be and Embrace Who You Are*. Hazelden, 2010.

28. Ibid.

29. Ibid.

30. This is basic and science-affirmed cognitive behavioral therapy practice. See Burns, David D. *The Feeling Good Handbook*. Plume, 1999.

31.  Ibid.

32.  Daily exercise will also enhance your sex life. For research on the statements in this book, see Welch, D. C. (February 2009 to present). *LoveScience: Research-based relationship advice for everyone*. Retrieved from http://www.lovesciencemedia.com/love-science-media/exercise-this-is-a-pubic-service-announcement.html

33.  Small, D. M., Zatorre, R. J., Dagher, A., Evans, A. C., & Jones-Gotman, M. (2001). Changes in brain activity related to eating chocolate: From pleasure to aversion. *Brain, 124 (9)*, 1720-1733.

34.  Seligman, Martin E. P. *Learned Optimism: How to Change Your Mind and Your Life*. Vintage, 2006.

35.  For example, see Allen, K., Shykoff, B. E., & Izzo, J. L., Jr. (2001). Pet ownership, but not ACE inhibitor therapy, blunts home blood pressure responses to mental stress. *Hypertension, 38*, 815–820.

     Not every study finds benefits, though. For an overview of research on pet ownership and various benefits, see Siegel J.M. (2011) Pet Ownership and Health. In Blazina C., Boyraz G., Shen-Miller D. (Eds.), *The Psychology of the Human-Animal Bond* (pp. 167-177). Springer, New York, NY.

36.  Seligman, Martin E. P. *Authentic Happiness: Using the New Positive Psychology to Realize Your Potential for Lasting Fulfillment*. Atria Books, 2004.

37.  Waite, Linda J., and Gallagher, Maggie. *The Case for Marriage: Why Married People are Happier, Healthier, and Better Off Financially*. Broadway Books, 2002.

38.  Seligman, Martin E. P. *Authentic Happiness: Using the New Positive Psychology to Realize Your Potential for Lasting Fulfillment*. Atria Books, 2004.

39.  For one of many studies showing that meditation causes better health, see Lavretsky, H., Epel, E. S., Siddarth, P., Nazarian, N., St. Cyr N., Khalsa, D. S., Lin, J., Blackburn, E., & Irwin, M. R. (2012). A pilot study of yogic meditation for family dementia caregivers with depressive symptoms: Effects on mental health, cognition, and telomerase activity. *International Journal of Geriatric Psychiatry, 28*(1), 57-65.

40.  Hetherington, E. Mavis, and John Kelly. *For Better or for Worse: Divorce Reconsidered*. Norton, 2003.

41.  Ibid.

## CHAPTER 3: FACE YOUR FEARS AND FIX YOUR PICKER

1.  Hetherington, E. Mavis, and John Kelly. *For Better or for Worse: Divorce Reconsidered.* Norton, 2003.

2.  Holmberg, D., & Holmes, J. G. (1994). Reconstruction of relationship memories: A mental models approach. In N. Schwarz & S. Sudman (Eds.), *Autobiographical memory and the validity of retrospective reports.* New York: Springer-Verlag.

3.  Johnson, Sue. *Love Sense: The Revolutionary New Science of Romantic Relationships.* Little, Brown, 2013.

4.  Ibid.

5.  Wallerstein, J. (2002). Festering. In K. Anderson, D. Browning, & B. Boyer (Eds.), *Marriage: Just a piece of paper?* (pp.96-97). Grand Rapids, Michigan:William B. Eerdmans Publishing Company.

6.  Daly, Martin, & Wilson, Margo. *Homicide: Foundations of Human Behavior.* Routledge, 2017.

7.  Buss, David M. *The Evolution of Desire: Strategies of Human Mating (Revised and updated edition).* Basic Books, 2016.

8.  Ibid.

    For research into a specific culture, see Borgerhoff Mulder, M. (1985). Polygyny threshold: A Kipsigis case study. *National Geographic Research Reports, 21,* 33-39.

9.  I conducted an informal online survey and reported that outcome along with scientifically conducted research at Welch, D. C. (March 27, 2012). *Attachment styles: Overcoming fear, embracing intimacy at last.* Retrieved from http://www.lovesciencemedia.com/love-science-media/attachment-styles-overcoming-fear-embracing-intimacyat-last.html

10. There are actually three attachment styles in adulthood (Secure, Anxious, and Avoidant), but in this book there are two Avoidant style choices given. That's because of research showing that the Avoidant style is further divisible into people who fear being depended on too much, versus people who value their independence; see Bartholomew, K. (1990). Avoidance of intimacy: An attachment perspective. *Journal of Social and Personal Relationships, 7,* 147-178.

11. Waters, E., Merrick, S., Treboux, D., Crowell, J., & Albersheim, L. (2000). Attachment security in infancy and early adulthood: A twenty-year longitudinal study. *Child Development, 71*, 684-689.

See also Selcuk, E., et al. (2010). Self-reported romantic attachment style predicts everyday maternal caregiving behavior at home. *Journal of Research in Personality, 44*, 544-549.

12. Waters, E., Merrick, S., Treboux, D., Crowell, J., & Albersheim, L. (2000). Attachment security in infancy and early adulthood: A twenty-year longitudinal study. *Child Development, 71*, 684-689.

13. Ibid.

See also Selcuk, E., et al. (2010). Self-reported romantic attachment style predicts everyday maternal caregiving behavior at home. *Journal of Research in Personality, 44*, 544-549.

14. Selcuk, E., et al. (2010). Self-reported romantic attachment style predicts everyday maternal caregiving behavior at home. *Journal of Research in Personality, 44*, 544-549.

15. People behave differently in intimate relationships, depending on their attachment style. For a thorough look at this, see Johnson, Sue. *Love Sense: The Revolutionary New Science of Romantic Relationships*. Little, Brown, 2013.

See also Simpson, J. A. (1990). Influence of attachment styles on romantic relationships. *Journal of Personality and Social Psychology, 59*, 971-980.

16. Johnson, Sue. *Love Sense: The Revolutionary New Science of Romantic Relationships*. Little, Brown, 2013.

17. Ibid.

See also Levine, Amir, and Heller, Rachel. *Attached: The New Science of Adult Attachment and How it Can Help You Find—and Keep—Love*. Tarcher/Penguin, 2011.

18. Hazan, C., & Shaver, P. R. (1987). Romantic love conceptualized as an attachment process. *Journal of Personality and Social Psychology, 52*, 511-524.

19. Grieling, H., & Buss, D. M. (2000). Women's sexual strategies: The hidden dimensions of extra-pair mating. *Personality and Individual Differences, 28*, 828-963. David Buss and

Heidi Greiling did a series of four studies to assess why women mate-switch (trade up); one reason turned out to be because some women with an Anxious style are scared of losing their current partner, so they line up a back-up.

20. Ibid.

21. Ibid.

22. Levine, Amir, and Heller, Rachel. *Attached: The New Science of Adult Attachment and How it Can Help You Find—and Keep—Love.* Tarcher/Penguin, 2011.

23. Cassidy, Jude, & Shaver, Philip R. *Handbook of Attachment: Theory, Research, and Clinical Applications.* Guilford Press, 1999.

24. Levine, Amir, and Heller, Rachel. *Attached: The New Science of Adult Attachment and How it Can Help You Find—and Keep—Love.* Tarcher/Penguin, 2011.

25. This statement rests on application of cognitive behavioral psychology to attachment styles. Some claim (and I have found in my practice) that it can be shifted, intentionally, over time. For the basis for my hypothesis, see Burns, David D. *The Feeling Good Handbook.* Plume, 1999.

26. Wallerstein, J. (2002). Festering. In K. Anderson, D. Browning, & B. Boyer (Eds.), *Marriage: Just a piece of paper?* (pp.96-97). Grand Rapids, Michigan:William B. Eerdmans Publishing Company.

27. Ibid.

28. Buss, David M. *The Evolution of Desire: Strategies of Human Mating (Revised and updated edition).* Basic Books, 2016.

29. Ibid.

30. Research conducted through website HOTorNOT.com shows that people are aware of who is in their league, and they tend to ask out folks who are similar in physical attractiveness even though someone else (i.e., out of their league) is better-looking. See Lee, L., Lowenstein, G. F., Ariely, D., Hong, J., & Young, J. (2008). If I'm not hot, are you hot or not? Physical-attractiveness evaluations and dating preferences as a function of one's own attractiveness. *Psychological Science, 19,* 669-677. This choice to avoid partners out of one's league comes from realistic fears of rejection: Montoya, R. M.(2008). I'm hot, so I'd say you're not: The influence of objective physical attractiveness on mate selection. *Personality and Social Psychology Bulletin, 43,* 1315-1331.

31. Ibid.

32. Ibid.

33. Buss, David M. *The Evolution of Desire: Strategies of Human Mating (Revised and updated edition)*. Basic Books, 2016.

34. Barber, N. (1995). The evolutionary psychology of physical attractiveness: Sexual selection and human morphology. *Ethology and Sociobiology, 16,* 395-424. This article showed that unfortunately, women routinely reject shorter men for long-term as well as short-term sexual liaisons.

    See also Buss, D. M., & Schmitt, D. P. (1993). Sexual strategies theory: An evolutionary perspective on human mating. *Psychological Review, 100,* 204-232.

    And one of the *LoveScience* articles I wrote that received the most email backlash was one in which I told women to stop the height-snobbery (See http://www.lovescience-media.com/love-science-media/the-womans-guide-to-finding-love-at-midlife.html ). By overvaluing height, many women are effectively cutting themselves out of the mating market, while being angry that men bypass them for youth and beauty. It's enough to drive a LoveScientist crazy.

35. Buss, D. M., & Schmitt, D. P. (1993). Sexual strategies theory: An evolutionary perspective on human mating. *Psychological Review, 100,* 204-232.

    And see Fryar, C. D., Gu, Q., Ogden, C. L., & Flegal, K. M. (August, 2016). Anthropometric Reference Data for Children and Adults: United States, 2011-2014. National Center for Health Statistics. *Vital Health Statistics, 3(39).* Retrieved from https://stacks.cdc.gov/view/cdc/40572

36. One of many research examples of people choosing mates similar to (rather than different from) themselves is this: Botwin, M. D., Buss, D. M., & Shackelford, T. K. (1997). Personality and mate preferences: Five factors in mate selection and marital satisfaction. *Journal of Personality, 65,* 107-136.

37. Buss, David M. *The Evolution of Desire: Strategies of Human Mating (Revised and updated edition)*. Basic Books, 2016.

38. Gottman, John M., with Silver, Nan. *The Seven Principles for Making Marriage Work: A Practical Guide from the Country's Foremost Relationship Expert.* Harmony, 2015.

39. Buss, David M. *The Evolution of Desire: Strategies of Human Mating (Revised and updated edition)*. Basic Books, 2016.

40. Ibid.

41. Buss, D. M. (1991). Conflict in married couples: Personality predictors of anger and upset. *Journal of Personality, 59, 663-688*.

42. Gottman, John M., with Silver, Nan. *The Seven Principles for Making Marriage Work: A Practical Guide from the Country's Foremost Relationship Expert*. Harmony, 2015.

43. McCrae, R. R., & Costa, P. T. (1987). Validation of the five-factor model of personality across instruments and observers. *Journal of Personality and Social Psychology, 52*(1), 81-90.

    You can take the Big 5 Personality Test here: https://openpsychometrics.org/tests/IPIP-BFFM/

44. Gottman, John M., with Silver, Nan. *The Seven Principles for Making Marriage Work: A Practical Guide from the Country's Foremost Relationship Expert*. Harmony, 2015.

45. Buss, D. M. (1991). Conflict in married couples: Personality predictors of anger and upset. *Journal of Personality, 59, 663-688*.

46. Buss, David M. *The Evolution of Desire: Strategies of Human Mating (Revised and updated edition)*. Basic Books, 2016.

47. One of many research examples of people choosing mates similar to (rather than different from) themselves is this: Botwin, M. D., Buss, D. M., & Shackelford, T. K. (1997). Personality and mate preferences: Five factors in mate selection and marital satisfaction. *Journal of Personality, 65, 107-136*.

48. This is sometimes called the matching phenomenon, and many studies over decades and cross-culturally bear it out. See Myers, David G. *Social Psychology (12th edition)*. McGraw Hill, 2016.

49. OK Cupid formerly posted results of a circa-2016 series of experiments their company conducted on similarity and perceived similarity. In Experiment 3, the OK Cupid folks found something quite interesting. At random, they told users either that they were a close match with another specific user (saying they were at 90% matching when in reality the match was only 30% or 60%), or that they were not a match (saying they

were only 30% matched when really, they were 60-90%). When told they matched well, people were more likely to initiate and respond to four messages on-site. But the best odds of having four exchanges occurred when both people actually were a 90% match and were told so. Upshot? Perception matters, at least at first; people liked each other well enough to keep writing at least four times even if they weren't a match, if the site told them they were. But similarity matters too.

50. Youyou, W., Stillwell, D., Schwartz, A., & Kosinski, M. (2017). Birds of a Feather Do Flock Together. *Psychological Science 28* (3), 276-284.

Interestingly, under 10% of American married couples have opposing political party affiliations. See Rosenfeld, M. J., Reuben, T. J., & Falcon, M. *How Couples Meet and Stay Together,* waves 1, 2, and 3. Stanford University Libraries, Stanford, Ca (2015).

And the likelihood that married couples will have the same political affiliation is even stronger than the odds that they will share significant physical and personality traits. See Alford, J. R., Hatemi, P. K., Hibbing, J. R., Martin, N. G., & Eaves, L. J. (2011). The politics of mate choice. *Journal of Politics, 73*(2), 362-379.

51. Fraley, R. C. (2002). Attachment stability from infancy to adulthood: Meta-analysis and dynamic modeling of developmental mechanisms. *Personality and Social Psychology Review, 6*(2), 123-151.

Johnson, Sue. *Love Sense: The Revolutionary New Science of Romantic Relationships.* Little, Brown, 2013.

52. Fraley, R. C. (2002). Attachment stability from infancy to adulthood: Meta-analysis and dynamic modeling of developmental mechanisms. *Personality and Social Psychology Review, 6*(2), 123-151.

53. Ibid.

54. Levine, Amir, and Heller, Rachel. *Attached: The New Science of Adult Attachment and How it Can Help You Find—and Keep—Love.* Tarcher/Penguin, 2011.

55. Ibid.

56. Hetherington, E. Mavis, and John Kelly. *For Better or for Worse: Divorce Reconsidered.* Norton, 2003.

Johnson, Sue. *Love Sense: The Revolutionary New Science of Romantic Relationships.* Little, Brown, 2013.

Gottman, John M., with Silver, Nan. *The Seven Principles for Making Marriage Work: A Practical Guide from the Country's Foremost Relationship Expert.* Harmony, 2015.

57. Gray, John. *Men Are from Mars, Women Are from Venus.* Harper Collins, 2009.

58. Johnson, Sue. *Love Sense: The Revolutionary New Science of Romantic Relationships.* Little, Brown, 2013.

59. Levine, Amir, and Heller, Rachel. *Attached: The New Science of Adult Attachment and How it Can Help You Find—and Keep—Love.* Tarcher/Penguin, 2011.

60. Buss, David M. *The Evolution of Desire: Strategies of Human Mating (Revised and updated edition).* Basic Books, 2016.

61. Ibid.

62. Daly, Martin, & Wilson, Margo. *Homicide: Foundations of Human Behavior.* Routledge, 2017.

63. Jacobson, Neil S., and Gottman, John M. *When Men Batter Women: New Insights into Ending Abusive Relationships.* Simon & Schuster, 2007.

## CHAPTER 4: PROTECT YOUR KIDS AND YOURSELF

1. de Becker, Gavin. *The Gift of Fear and Other Survival Signals that Protect us from Violence.* Dell Publishing, 1997; re-released by Gavin DeBecker, 2010.

2. Daly, M., & Wilson, M. (1996). Violence against stepchildren. *Current Directions in Psychological Science, 5,* 77-81.

3. Ibid.

See also Buss, David M. *Evolutionary Psychology: The New Science of the Mind (5th edition).* Allyn & Bacon, 2014.

4. Buss, David M. *Evolutionary Psychology: The New Science of the Mind (5th edition).* Allyn & Bacon, 2014.

5. Daly, M., & Wilson, M. (1996). Violence against stepchildren. *Current Directions in Psychological Science, 5,* 77-81.

6. Daly, M., & Wilson, M. (1985). Child abuse and other risks of not living with both parents. *Ethology and Sociobiology, 6,* 197-210.

See also Daly, Martin, & Wilson, Margo. *Homicide: Foundations of Human Behavior.* Routledge, 2017.

7. Daly, Martin, & Wilson, Margo. *Homicide: Foundations of Human Behavior.* Routledge, 2017.

8. Ibid.

9. Buss, David M. *Evolutionary Psychology: The New Science of the Mind (5th edition).* Allyn & Bacon, 2014.

10. Ibid.

11. Ibid.

12. Buss, David M. *The Murderer Next Door: Why the Mind is Designed to Kill.* Penguin, 2005.

13. Ibid.

14. Ibid.

15. Buss, David M. *The Dangerous Passion: Why Jealousy is as Necessary as Love and Sex.* Free Press, 2000.

16. Buss, D. M., Larsen, R., Westen, D., & Semmelroth, J. (1992). Sex differences in jealousy: Evolution, physiology, and psychology. *Psychological Science, 3,* 251-255.

17. Ibid.

See also Buss, D. M., Larsen, R. J., & Westen, D. (1996). Sex differences in jealousy: Not gone, not forgotten, and not explained by alternative hypotheses. *Psychological Science, 7,* 373-375.

18. Buss, David M. *The Dangerous Passion: Why Jealousy is as Necessary as Love and Sex.* Free Press, 2000.

19. Ibid.

20. Buss, David M. *Evolutionary Psychology: The New Science of the Mind (5th edition)*. Allyn & Bacon, 2014.

21. Ibid.

22. Buss, D. M., & Shackelford, T. K. (1997). From vigilance to violence: Mate retention tactics in married couples. *Journal of Personality and Social Psychology, 72*, 346-361.

23. Bancroft, Lundy. *Why Does He Do That?: Inside the Minds of Angry and Controlling Men*. Berkley Publishing Group, 2002.

24. Gazzaniga, M. S. (1983). Right hemisphere language following brain bisection: A 20-year perspective. *American Psychologist, 38*, 525-537. See also Gazzaniga, M. S. (1988). Organization of the human brain. *Science, 245*, 947-952.

25. Wade, Nicholas. *Before the Dawn: Recovering the Lost History of Our Ancestors*. Penguin, 2007.

26. Any treatise on Developmental Psychology (or observation of tiny humans around age 8 months) will corroborate.

27. Ceci, S. J., & Bruck, M. (1993). Suggestibility of the child witness: A historical review and synthesis. *Psychological Bulletin, 113*, 403-439.

28. I found this in a State of Texas official memo on child abuse. For an academic take, see Daly, M., & Wilson, M. (1985). Child abuse and other risks of not living with both parents. *Ethology and Sociobiology, 6*, 197-210.

29. de Becker, Gavin. *The Gift of Fear and Other Survival Signals that Protect us from Violence*. Dell Publishing, 1997; re-released by Gavin DeBecker, 2010.

30. Welch, Duana C. *Love Factually: 10 Proven Steps from I Wish to I Do*. LoveScience Media, 2015.

31. In fact, only adultery and infertility are even more common grounds for divorce; see Betzig, L. (1989). Causes of conjugal dissolution: A cross-cultural study. *Current Anthropology, 30*, 654-676.

32. For a discussion of the research showing that partner violence is much more often committed by men against women (i.e., there are large gender differences in who engages the violence), see Buss, David M. *Evolutionary Psychology: The New Science of the Mind (5th edition)*. Allyn & Bacon, 2014.

33. Jacobson, Neil S., and Gottman, John M. *When Men Batter Women: New Insights into Ending Abusive Relationships.* Simon & Schuster, 2007.

    See also Bancroft, Lundy. *Why Does He Do That?: Inside the Minds of Angry and Controlling Men.* Berkley Publishing Group, 2002.

34. Much of this list is sourced from information available in de Becker, Gavin. *The Gift of Fear and Other Survival Signals that Protect us from Violence.* Dell Publishing, 1997; re-released by Gavin DeBecker, 2010.

35. Ibid.

36. Ibid.

37. Bancroft, Lundy. *Why Does He Do That?: Inside the Minds of Angry and Controlling Men.* Berkley Publishing Group, 2002.

38. Jacobson, Neil S., and Gottman, John M. *When Men Batter Women: New Insights into Ending Abusive Relationships.* Simon & Schuster, 2007.

39. de Becker, Gavin. *The Gift of Fear and Other Survival Signals that Protect us from Violence.* Dell Publishing, 1997; re-released by Gavin DeBecker, 2010.

40. Ibid.

41. Jacobson, Neil S., and Gottman, John M. *When Men Batter Women: New Insights into Ending Abusive Relationships.* Simon & Schuster, 2007.

42. Ibid.

43. Ibid.

    See also de Becker, Gavin. *The Gift of Fear and Other Survival Signals that Protect us from Violence.* Dell Publishing, 1997; re-released by Gavin DeBecker, 2010.

44. Jacobson, Neil S., and Gottman, John M. *When Men Batter Women: New Insights into Ending Abusive Relationships.* Simon & Schuster, 2007.

45. de Becker, Gavin. *The Gift of Fear and Other Survival Signals that Protect us from Violence.* Dell Publishing, 1997; re-released by Gavin DeBecker, 2010.

46. Jacobson, Neil S., and Gottman, John M. *When Men Batter Women: New Insights into Ending Abusive Relationships.* Simon & Schuster, 2007.

47. de Becker, Gavin. *The Gift of Fear and Other Survival Signals that Protect us from Violence.* Dell Publishing, 1997; re-released by Gavin DeBecker, 2010.

48. Ibid.

49. Jacobson, Neil S., and Gottman, John M. *When Men Batter Women: New Insights into Ending Abusive Relationships.* Simon & Schuster, 2007.

50. de Becker, Gavin. *The Gift of Fear and Other Survival Signals that Protect us from Violence.* Dell Publishing, 1997; re-released by Gavin DeBecker, 2010.

51. Ibid.

52. Bancroft, Lundy. *Why Does He Do That?: Inside the Minds of Angry and Controlling Men.* Berkley Publishing Group, 2002.

53. through 56. Jacobson, Neil S., and Gottman, John M. *When Men Batter Women: New Insights into Ending Abusive Relationships.* Simon & Schuster, 2007.

57. Page, Susan. *How One of You Can Bring the Two of You Together.* Broadway, 1997.

58. through 69. Jacobson, Neil S., and Gottman, John M. *When Men Batter Women: New Insights into Ending Abusive Relationships.* Simon & Schuster, 2007.

# *Part II: Mastering The Mechanics Of Dating*

## CHAPTER 5: BALANCE YOUR LIFE AND YOUR DATING

1. Waite, Linda J., and Gallagher, Maggie. *The Case for Marriage: Why Married People are Happier, Healthier, and Better Off Financially.* Broadway Books, 2002.

The Virginia Longitudinal Study concurs. See Hetherington, E. Mavis, and John Kelly. *For Better or for Worse: Divorce Reconsidered.* Norton, 2003.

2. Cacioppo, J. T., Cacioppo, S., Gonzagia, G. C., Ogburn, E. L., & VanderWeele, T. J. (2013). Marital satisfaction and break-ups differ across on-line and off-line meeting venues. *PNAS.* You can download or view this article at http://www.pnas.org/content/early/2013/05/31/1222447110.full.pdf+html

See also McPherson, M., Smith-Lovin, L., & Cook, J. M. (2001). Birds of a feature: Homophily in social networks. *Annual Review of Sociology, 27,* 415-444.

3.   Kalish, N. *Lost & Found Lovers: Fact and Fantasy About Rekindled Romances.* Amazon Digital Services, 1997. You can read or listen to Dr. Kalish's *LoveScience* interview at http://www.lovesciencemedia.com/love-science-media/got-obsession-rekindled-lovers-expert-dr-nancy-kalish-is-her.html

4.   This leverages the law of proximity; see Myers, David G. *Social Psychology (12th edition).* McGraw Hill, 2016.

5.   Welch, D. C. (June 19, 2013). *eBliss: Is love best begun online?* Retrieved from http://www.psychologytoday.com/blog/love-proof/201306/ebliss-is-love-best-begun-online

6.   Newcombe, Theodore M. *The Acquaintance Process.* Holt, Rinehart, & Winston, 1961.

7.   Many studies show this. See Mita, T. H., Dermer, M., & Knight, J. (1977). Reversed facial images and the mere-exposure hypothesis. *Journal of Personality and Social Psychology, 35,* 597-601. Interestingly, not only did participants prefer the mirror image of their photo (that is, the view they see each day), but their friends chose the opposite picture, preferring to see their friend from the vantage point they encounter in real life.

8.   This is true across many domains of behavior. See Dweck, Carol. *Mindset: The New Psychology of Success.* Random House, 2006.

9.   Gupta, U., & Singh, P. (1982). Exploratory study of love and liking and type of marriages. *Indian Journal of Applied Psychology, 19,* 92-97.

10.  Cialdini, Robert B. *Influence: Science and Practice (5th edition).* Prentice Hall, 2008.

11.  Smith, T. J. (2002). Are Married Parents Happier Than Single Parents? In K. Anderson, D. Browning, & B. Boyer (Eds.), *Marriage: Just a piece of paper?* (p. 28). Grand Rapids, Michigan:William B. Eerdmans Publishing Company.

12.  Buss, David M. *The Evolution of Desire: Strategies of Human Mating (Revised and updated edition).* Basic Books, 2016.

13.  Moore, M. (1985). Nonverbal courtship patterns in women: Context and consequences. *Ethology and Sociobiology, 6,* 237-247.

See also Walsh, D., & Hewitt, J. (1985). Giving men the come-on: The effect of eye contact and smiling in a bar environment. *Perceptual and Motor Skills, 61,* 837-844.

14. Ibid.

15. Ibid.

16. Abbey, A. (1982). Sex differences in attributions for friendly behavior: Do males misperceive females' friendliness? *Journal of Personality and Social Psychology, 32,* 830-838.

17. Moore, M. (1985). Nonverbal courtship patterns in women: Context and consequences. *Ethology and Sociobiology, 6,* 237-247.

18. Hatfield, E., Walster, G. W., Piliavin, J., & Schmidt, L. (1973). Playing hard-to-get: Understanding an elusive phenomenon. *Journal of Personality and Social Psychology, 26,* 113-121.

19. Moore, M. (1985). Nonverbal courtship patterns in women: Context and consequences. *Ethology and Sociobiology, 6,* 237-247.

20. Perper, Timothy. *Sex Signals: The Biology of Love.* Isi Press, 1986.

21. Ibid.

22. Mirroring facial expressions and/or "catching" the emotions of those closest to you even happens among dating couples and roommates in just one year's time; I am hypothesizing that the effect is intensified over the life of a long and happy marriage. See Anderson, C., Keltner, D., & John, O. P. (2003). Emotional convergence between people over time. *Journal of Personality and Social Psychology, 84*(5), 1054-1068.

    And making a face creates that emotion. See Levenson, R. W., Ekman, P., & Friesen, W. V. (1990). Voluntary facial action generates emotion-specific autonomic nervous system activity. *Psychophysiology, 27*(4), 363-384.

23. Hill, E. M., Nocks, E. S., & Gardner, L. (1987). Physical attractiveness: Manipulation by physique and status displays. *Ethology and Sociobiology, 8,* 143-154.

24. Ibid.

25. Buss, David M. *The Evolution of Desire: Strategies of Human Mating (Revised and updated edition).* Basic Books, 2016.

26. Bressler, E. R., Martin, R. A., & Balshine, S. (2006). Production and appreciation of humor as sexually selected traits. *Evolution and Human Behavior, 27*(2), 121-130.

27. Buss, D. M. (1988). The evolution of human intrasexual competition. *Journal of Personality and Social Psychology, 54,* 616-628.

    See also Schmitt, D. P., & Buss, D. M. (1996). Strategic self-promotion and competitor derogation: Sex and context effects on the perceived effectiveness of mate attraction tactics. *Journal of Personality and Social Psychology, 70*(6), 1185-1204.

28. In fact, if people are told someone likes them, that usually causes them to like their admirer in return. See Berscheid, E., & Walster (Hatfield), E. *Interpersonal Attraction.* Addison-Wesley, 1978.

    The effect is even better if you let the person know you like them more than you like others. See Eastwick, P. W., Finkel, E. J., Mochon, D., & Ariely, D. (2007). Selective versus unselective romantic desire. *Journal of Experimental Social Psychology, 44,* 800-807.

29. Cacioppo, J. T., Cacioppo, S., Gonzagia, G. C., Ogburn, E. L., & VanderWeele, T. J. (2013). Marital satisfaction and break-ups differ across on-line and off-line meeting venues. *PNAS.* You can download or view this article at http://www.pnas.org/content/early/2013/05/31/1222447110.full.pdf+html

30. Kuhle, B. X., Beasley, D. O., Beck, W. C., Brezinski, S. M., Cnudde, D., et al. (2016). To swipe left or right: Sex differences in Tinder profiles. Paper presented at the annual meeting of the Human Behavior and Evolution Society, Vancouver, Canada.

31. Barriers generally drive away disinterested men. See Buss, David M. *The Evolution of Desire: Strategies of Human Mating (Revised and updated edition).* Basic Books, 2016.

32. Cacioppo, J. T., Cacioppo, S., Gonzagia, G. C., Ogburn, E. L., & VanderWeele, T. J. (2013). Marital satisfaction and break-ups differ across on-line and off-line meeting venues. *PNAS.* You can download or view this article at http://www.pnas.org/content/early/2013/05/31/1222447110.full.pdf+html

33. Confer, J. C., Perilloux, C., & Buss, D. M. (2010). More than just a pretty face: Men's priority shifts toward bodily attractiveness in short-term versus long-term mating contexts. *Evolution and Human Behavior, 31*(5), 348-353.

34. Kuhle, B. X., Beasley, D. O., Beck, W. C., Brezinski, S. M., Cnudde, D., et al. (2016). To swipe left or right: Sex differences in Tinder profiles. Paper presented at the annual meeting of the Human Behavior and Evolution Society, Vancouver, Canada.

35.  Campbell, A. (2008). The morning after the night before. *Human Nature, 19*(2), 157-173.

36.  Kuhle, B. X., Beasley, D. O., Beck, W. C., Brezinski, S. M., Cnudde, D., et al. (2016). To swipe left or right: Sex differences in Tinder profiles. Paper presented at the annual meeting of the Human Behavior and Evolution Society, Vancouver, Canada.

     See Buss, David M. *The Evolution of Desire: Strategies of Human Mating (Revised and updated edition)*. Basic Books, 2016.

37.  Kuhle, B. X., Beasley, D. O., Beck, W. C., Brezinski, S. M., Cnudde, D., et al. (2016). To swipe left or right: Sex differences in Tinder profiles. Paper presented at the annual meeting of the Human Behavior and Evolution Society, Vancouver, Canada.

38.  Confer, J. C., Perilloux, C., & Buss, D. M. (2010). More than just a pretty face: Men's priority shifts toward bodily attractiveness in short-term versus long-term mating contexts. *Evolution and Human Behavior, 31*(5), 348-353.

39.  La Cerra, P., Cosmides, L., & Tooby, J. (1993). Psychological adaptations in women for assessing a man's willingness to invest in offspring. Paper presented at the fifth annual meeting of the Human Behavior and Evolution Society, Binghamton, NY (August). Seen in David M. *The Evolution of Desire: Strategies of Human Mating (Revised and updated edition)*. Basic Books, 2016.

40.  Myers, David G. *Social Psychology (12th edition)*. McGraw Hill, 2016.

41.  Rudder, C. (January 20, 2010). *The 4 big myths of profile pictures*. Retrieved from http://blog.okcupid.com/index.php/the-4-big-myths-of-profile-pictures/

42.  Myers, David G. *Social Psychology (12th edition)*. McGraw Hill, 2016. The cocktail party phenomenon, where we perk up our ears upon hearing our name but not other conversations, is a case in point.

43.  Bressler, E. R., Martin, R. A., & Balshine, S. (2006). Production and appreciation of humor as sexually selected traits. *Evolution and Human Behavior, 27*(2), 121-130.

44.  Holbrook, M. B., & Schindler, R. M. (1989). Some exploratory findings on the development of musical tastes. *Journal of Consumer Research, 16*(1), 119-124. This study indicates gelling for musical tastes by around age 24; however, newer research which I regret I cannot locate shows that we are most emotionally connected to popular music from our middle- and high-school years.

45. Myers, David G., and DeWall, C. Nathan. *Psychology (11th edition)*. Worth Publishers, 2016.

46. Holmberg, D., & Holmes, J. G. (1994). Reconstruction of relationship memories: A mental models approach. In N. Schwarz & S. Sudman (Eds.), *Autobiographical memory and the validity of retrospective reports*. New York: Springer-Verlag.

## CHAPTER 6: WATCH OUT, IT'S A TRAP! MEN, WOMEN, AND GAMES PEOPLE PLAY

1. Evolution, show 5: *Why Sex?* PBS. Retrieved from https://www.pbs.org/wgbh/evolution/sex/index.html Very much worth a watch.

2. Ibid.

3. Ibid.

4. Welch, Duana C. *Love Factually: 10 Proven Steps from I Wish to I Do*. LoveScience Media, 2015.

5. Buss, David M. *The Evolution of Desire: Strategies of Human Mating (Revised and updated edition)*. Basic Books, 2016.

6. Buss, David M. *Evolutionary Psychology: The New Science of the Mind (5th edition)*. Allyn & Bacon, 2014.

7. Jankowiak, W. R., Hill, E. M., & Donovan, J. M. (1992). The effects of sex and sexual orientation on attractiveness judgments: An evolutionary interpretation. *Ethology and Sociobiology, 13*, 73-85.

8. Smith, Brice D. *Lou Sullivan: Daring to be a Man Among Men*. Transgress Press, 2017.

9. Brill, Stephanie, and Kenney, Lisa. *The Transgender Teen: A Handbook for Parents and Professionals Supporting Transgender and Non-Binary Teens*. Clies Press, 2016.

   This identification with the psychology of one's gender orientation that exists before hormone therapy increases after hormone therapy is started, and brain changes that are aligned with transpeople's felt gender are known to increase as well. For instance, see (2015). *Research shows testosterone changes brain structures in female-to-male transsexuals*. European College of Neuropsychopharmacology. Retrieved from https://www.eurekalert.org/pub_releases/2015-08/econ-rst082815.php

See also Alter, C. (2018). Transgender men see sexism from both sides. Time. Retrieved from http://time.com/transgender-men-sexism/

10. I'm extrapolating from research showing that cisgender lesbian women who judge themselves "butch" have higher sex drives, even without hormone therapy, than women who judge themselves to be more feminine; sexual orientation and gender orientation are different things, yet the physical presentation of transmen is (as with self-identified "butch" women) often more masculine than it is for cisgender women. See Buss, David M. *The Evolution of Desire: Strategies of Human Mating (Revised and updated edition)*. Basic Books, 2016. For research on testosterone's impact on transmen, see Slrwig, M. (2017). Testosterone therapy for transgender men. *The Lancet: Diabetes and endocrinology, 5*(4), 301-311.

11. Wierckx, K., Elaut, E., Van Hoorde, B., Heylens, G., De Cuypere, G., Monstrey, S., Weyers, S., Hoebeke, P., & T'Sjoen, G. (2014). Sexual desire in trans persons: Associations with sex reassignment treatment. *Journal of Sexual Medicine, 11*,107–118.

12. Buss, David M. *Evolutionary Psychology: The New Science of the Mind (5th edition)*. Allyn & Bacon, 2014.

13. Kalick, S. M. (1977). Plastic surgery, physical appearance, and person perception. Unpublished doctoral dissertation, Harvard University. Cited by Myers, David G. *Social Psychology (12th edition)*. McGraw Hill, 2016.

14. Wiseman, R. (1998, Fall). Participatory science and the mass media. *Free Inquiry*, 56-57.

15. Langlois, J. H., Roggman, L. A., Casey, R. J., Ritter, J. M., Rieser-Danner, L. A., & Jenkins, V. Y. (1987). Infant preferences for attractive faces: Rudiments of a stereotype? *Developmental Psychology, 23*, 363-369.

16. Brown, W. M., Price, M. E., Kang, J., Pound, N., Zhao, Y., & Yu, H. (2008). Fluctuating asymmetry and preferences for sex-typical bodily characteristics. *Proceedings of the National Academy of Sciences, 105*, 12938-12943 (pnas.org).

17. Gangestad, S. W., & Thornhill, R. (1997). Human sexual selection and developmental stability. In J. A. Simpson & D. T. Kenrick (Eds.), *Evolutionary social psychology*. Mahwah, N.J.: Erlbaum.

18. Buss, David M. *Evolutionary Psychology: The New Science of the Mind (5th edition)*. Allyn & Bacon, 2014.

19. Ibid.

20. Buss, David M. *The Evolution of Desire: Strategies of Human Mating (Revised and updated edition)*. Basic Books, 2016.

21. Ibid.

22. Rozin, P., & Fallon, A. (1988). Body image, attitudes to weight, and misperceptions of figure preferences of the opposite sex: A comparison of men and women in two generations. *Journal of Abnormal Psychology, 97*, 342-345.

23. Mann, T., Tomiyama, A. J., Westling, E. Lew, A-M., Samuels, B., & Chattman, J. (2007). Medicare's search for effective obesity treatments: Diets are not the answer. *American Psychologist, 62*, 220-233.

 See also Levine, J. A., Lanningham-Foster, L. M., MCrady, S. K., Krizan, A. C., Olson, L. R., Kane, P. H., Jensen, M. D., & Clark, M. M. (2005). Interindividual variation in posture allocation. Possible role in human obesity. *Science, 307*, 584-586.

24. A study of identical twins showed that they looked younger if they weighed more and had a 4 point higher body mass index after age 40, but before age 40, they looked younger if they weighed less. After age 55, the weight needed in order to look younger was greater still, with an 8-point greater BMI yielding a younger appearance. See Guyuron, B., Rowe, D. J., Weinfeld, A. B., Eshraghi, Y., Fathi, A., & Iamphongsai, S. (2009). Factors contributing to the facial aging of identical twins. *Plastic and Reconstructive Surgery, 123*(4), 1321-1331.

25. Confer, J. C., Perilloux, C., & Buss, D. M. (2010). More than just a pretty face: Men's priority shifts toward bodily attractiveness in short-term versus long-term mating contexts. *Evolution and Human Behavior, 31*(5), 348-353.

26. Livingston, Gretchen (2014). Four in ten couples are saying "I do," again. Washington, DC: Pew Research Center (November 14).

27. Buss, David M. *The Evolution of Desire: Strategies of Human Mating (Revised and updated edition)*. Basic Books, 2016.

28. Lee, L., Lowenstein, G. F., Ariely, D., Hong, J., & Young, J. (2008). If I'm not hot, are you hot or not? Physical-attractiveness evaluations and dating preferences as a function of one's own attractiveness. *Psychological Science, 19*, 669-677.

29. Buss, D. M., & Schmitt, D. P. (1993). Sexual strategies theory: An evolutionary perspective on human mating. *Psychological Review, 100*, 204-232.

    This also applies to men: act confident, because it's associated with success and is thus inherently attractive to women. See Barkow, J. *Darwin, Sex, and Status.* Toronto: University of Toronto Press, 1989.

30. Buss, David M. *The Evolution of Desire: Strategies of Human Mating (Revised and updated edition).* Basic Books, 2016.

31. Thornhill, R., & Gangestad, S. W. (1999). The scent of symmetry: A human sex pheromone that signals fitness? *Evolution & Human Behavior, 20*, 175-201.

32. Buss, David M. *The Evolution of Desire: Strategies of Human Mating (Revised and updated edition).* Basic Books, 2016.

33. Welch, Duana C. *Love Factually: 10 Proven Steps from I Wish to I Do.* LoveScience Media, 2015.

34. Barelds, D. P. H., & Barelds-Dijkstra, P. (2007). Love at first sight or friends first? Ties among partner personality traits similarity, relationship onset, relationship quality, and love. *Journal of Social and Personal Relationships, 24*(4), 479-496. Among other things, they found that men are more likely than women to fall in love at first sight.

35. David Schmitt, who together with David Buss is a rockstar in this field of research, provides an excellent overview of the data: Schmitt, D. P. (2017). Which people would agree to have sex with a stranger? You might not. But many people would, especially men. *Psychology Today,* retrieved from https://www.psychologytoday.com/us/blog/sexual-personalities/201706/which-people-would-agree-have-sex-stranger

36. Buss, David M. *The Dangerous Passion: Why Jealousy is as Necessary as Love and Sex.* Free Press, 2000.

37. Buss, D. M., & Schmitt, D. P. (1993). Sexual strategies theory: An evolutionary perspective on human mating. *Psychological Review, 100*, 204-232.

38. Kuhle, B. X., Beasley, D. O., Beck, W. C., Brezinski, S. M., Cnudde, D., et al. (2016). To swipe left or right: Sex differences in Tinder profiles. Paper presented at the annual meeting of the Human Behavior and Evolution Society, Vancouver, Canada.

39. Buss, David M. *The Evolution of Desire: Strategies of Human Mating (Revised and updated edition).* Basic Books, 2016.

40. Cialdini, Robert B. *Influence: Science and Practice (5th edition)*. Prentice Hall, 2008.

41. Buss, David M. *The Evolution of Desire: Strategies of Human Mating (Revised and updated edition)*. Basic Books, 2016.

42. Buss, D. M. (1988). The evolution of human intrasexual competition. *Journal of Personality and Social Psychology, 54*, 616-628.

    See also Schmitt, D. P., & Buss, D. M. (1996). Strategic self-promotion and competitor derogation: Sex and context effects on the perceived effectiveness of mate attraction tactics. *Journal of Personality and Social Psychology, 70*(6), 1185-1204.

43. Schmitt, D. P., & Buss, D. M. (1996). Strategic self-promotion and competitor derogation: Sex and context effects on the perceived effectiveness of mate attraction tactics. *Journal of Personality and Social Psychology, 70*(6), 1185-1204.

44. Being sexually hard-to-get, or even being perceived that way, turns off men who have short-term agendas and intrigues men who have long-term agendas. In one study, men tipped their hand, revealing that when they seek a fling, they look for styles of dress and behavior that indicate easy sexual availability—and that they avoid these exact same styles and behaviors when they want Mrs. Right. The reverse is also true: Men seeking a fling actively avoid women who seem unlikely to give sex easily. Upshot? A man who wants sex immediately or else says he is leaving is very likely playing. See Buss, D. M., & Schmitt, D. P. (1993). Sexual strategies theory: An evolutionary perspective on human mating. *Psychological Review, 100*, 204-232.

45. Taylor, Shelley E. *The Tending Instinct: Women, Men, and the Biology of our Relationships*. Holt, 2003.

    See also Buss, David M. *The Evolution of Desire: Strategies of Human Mating (Revised and updated edition)*. Basic Books, 2016.

46. Taylor, Shelley E. *The Tending Instinct: Women, Men, and the Biology of our Relationships*. Holt, 2003.

47. Buss, D. M., & Schmitt, D. P. (1993). Sexual strategies theory: An evolutionary perspective on human mating. *Psychological Review, 100*, 204-232.

48. Rudder, C. (January 20, 2010). *The 4 big myths of profile pictures*. Retrieved from http://blog.okcupid.com/index.php/the-4-big-myths-of-profile-pictures/

49. Kuhle, B. X., Beasley, D. O., Beck, W. C., Brezinski, S. M., Cnudde, D., et al. (2016). To swipe left or right: Sex differences in Tinder profiles. Paper presented at the annual meeting of the Human Behavior and Evolution Society, Vancouver, Canada.

50. Buss, D. M., & Schmitt, D. P. (1993). Sexual strategies theory: An evolutionary perspective on human mating. *Psychological Review, 100,* 204-232.

51. Sexually experienced men (but not women, and not men who were sexually inexperienced) report a loss of sexual interest immediately following coitus. See Haselton, M. G., & Buss, D. M., (2001). The affective shift hypothesis: The functions of emotional changes following sexual intercourse. *Personal Relationships, 8,* 357-369.

52. Welch, Duana C. *Love Factually: 10 Proven Steps from I Wish to I Do.* LoveScience Media, 2015.

53. Ansari, Aziz, with Klineberg, Eric. *Modern Romance.* Penguin Press, 2015.

54. Baumeister, R. F., Bratslavsky, E., Finkenauer, C., & Vohs, D. K. (2001). Bad is stronger than good. *Review of General Psychology, 5,* 323-370.

    Another study made the same point: We like folks better if they say eight positive things than if they say eight positives and one negative. A summary of this study can be seen in Berscheid, Ellen, and Walster, Elaine Hatfield. *Interpersonal Attraction.* Addison-Wesley, 1978.

55. Buss, David M. *The Evolution of Desire: Strategies of Human Mating (Revised and updated edition).* Basic Books, 2016.

56. Buss, David M. *The Evolution of Desire: Strategies of Human Mating (Revised and updated edition).* Basic Books, 2016.

    See also Townshend, J. M., & Levy, G. D. (1990). Effects of potential partners' physical attractiveness and socioeconomic status on sexuality and partner selection. *Archives of Sexual Behavior, 371,* 149-164.

57. *Singles in America* Survey (2018). Match.com. Retrieved from https://www.singlesinamerica.com/2018/#DATINGPERSPECTIVES1

58. Buss, David M. *The Evolution of Desire: Strategies of Human Mating (Revised and updated edition).* Basic Books, 2016.

59. Ibid.

60. Welch, D. C. (November 22, 2011). *How not to suck at dating (special double issue)*. Retrieved from http://www.lovesciencemedia.com/love-science-media/how-not-to-suck-at-dating-special-double-issue.html Please see all responses to the Best & Worst Dates survey at the bottom of the post.

61. Schmitt, D. P., & Buss, D. M. (1996). Strategic self-promotion and competitor derogation: Sex and context effects on the perceived effectiveness of mate attraction tactics. *Journal of Personality and Social Psychology, 70*(6), 1185-1204.

62. Buss, David M. *The Evolution of Desire: Strategies of Human Mating (Revised and updated edition)*. Basic Books, 2016.

    See also Buss, D. M., & Schmitt, D. P. (1993). Sexual strategies theory: An evolutionary perspective on human mating. *Psychological Review, 100*, 204-232.

## CHAPTER 7: THE PARENT TRAPS: MEN, WOMEN, AND TIMING YOUR RELATIONSHIP

1. Gupta, U., & Singh, P. (1982). Exploratory study of love and liking and type of marriages. *Indian Journal of Applied Psychology, 19*, 92-97.

2. Buss, D. M., & Schmitt, D. P. (1993). Sexual strategies theory: An evolutionary perspective on human mating. *Psychological Review, 100*, 204-232.

3. Ibid.

4. For instance, men who are divorced usually seek rather than avoid remarriage. See Wallerstein, J. (2002). Festering. In K. Anderson, D. Browning, & B. Boyer (Eds.), *Marriage: Just a piece of paper?* (pp.96-97). Grand Rapids, Michigan:William B. Eerdmans Publishing Company.

5. Buss, David M. *The Dangerous Passion: Why Jealousy is as Necessary as Love and Sex*. Free Press, 2000.

6. Ibid.

7. Lies are difficult to maintain for the long-term. For research on the specific ways men and men lie to one another, see Haselton, M., Buss, D. M., Oubaid, V., & Angleitner, A. (2005). Sex, lies, and strategic interference: The psychology of deception between the sexes. *Personality and Social Psychology Bulletin, 31*, 3-23.

8.  Erikson, Erik H. *Childhood and Society.* New York: Norton. 1963.

9.  Ibid. See also research on the age at which our frontal lobes—the parts of the brain associated with personality and planning—mature: Myers, David M., and DeWall, C. Nathan. *Exploring Psychology (10th edition).* Worth, 2017.

10. Waite, L.J. (2002). Looking for Love. In K. Anderson, D. Browning, & B. Boyer (Eds.), *Marriage: Just a piece of paper?* (pp. 163-169). Grand Rapids, Michigan:William B. Eerdmans Publishing Company.

11. Baumeister, R. F., Bratslavsky, E., Finkenauer, C., & Vohs, D. K. (2001). Bad is stronger than good. *Review of General Psychology, 5,* 323-370.

12. Welch, D. C. (July 27, 2011). *Kiss-n-tell? How to time telling our (sexual and other) secrets to a new partner.* Retrieved from http://www.lovesciencemedia.com/love-science-media/kiss-n-tell-how-to-time-telling-our-sexual-other-secrets-to.html

13. This is my favorite definition of intimacy; see Page, Susan. *If I'm So Wonderful, Why Am I Still Single?: Ten Strategies That Will Change Your Love Life Forever.* Three Rivers Press, 2002.

14. La Cerra, P., Cosmides, L., & Tooby, J. (1993). Psychological adaptations in women for assessing a man's willingness to invest in offspring. Paper presented at the fifth annual meeting of the Human Behavior and Evolution Society, Binghamton, NY (August). Seen in David M. *The Evolution of Desire: Strategies of Human Mating (Revised and updated edition).* Basic Books, 2016.

15. Ibid.

16. For a general presentation of research on barriers, see Myers, David G. *Social Psychology (12th edition).* McGraw Hill, 2016.

    And for specifics on barriers and dating see, Welch, Duana C. *Love Factually: 10 Proven Steps from I Wish to I Do.* LoveScience Media, 2015.

17. Ibid.

18. Kreider, R. M. (August 10-14, 2006). *Remarriage In The United States:* Poster presented at the annual meeting of the American Sociological Association, Montreal. Article retrieved from http://www.census.gov/hhes/socdemo/marriage/data/sipp/us-remarriage-poster.pdf

19. Hetherington, E. Mavis, and John Kelly. *For Better or for Worse: Divorce Reconsidered.* Norton, 2003.

20. Ibid.

21. Ibid.

22. Miller, Geoffrey. *The Mating Mind: How Sexual Choice Shaped the Evolution of Human Nature.* Anchor, 2001.

23. Meston, Cindy M., & Buss, David M. *Why Women Have Sex: Understanding Sexual Motivations from Adventure to Revenge (and Everything in Between).* Times Books, 2009.

24. Buss, David M. *The Evolution of Desire: Strategies of Human Mating (Revised and updated edition).* Basic Books, 2016.

25. Hetherington, E. Mavis, and John Kelly. *For Better or for Worse: Divorce Reconsidered.* Norton, 2003.

26. Specifically, 44% of women, compared to 9% of men, said they had casual sex to try to get a long-term relationship; see Regan, P. C., & Dreyer, C. S. (1999). Lust? Love? Status? Young adults' motives for engaging in casual sex. *Journal of Psychology and Human Sexuality, 11,* 1-24. Another study found that after physical attraction, women's second-most-given reason for having casual sex was, "I actually wanted a long-term relationship with this person and thought the casual sex might lead to something more long-lasting." See Li, N. P., & Kenrick, D. T. (2006). Sex similarities and differences in preferences for short-term mates: What, whether, and why. *Journal of Personality and Social Psychology, 90,* 468-489.

27. Haselton, M. G., & Buss, D. M., (2001). The affective shift hypothesis: The functions of emotional changes following sexual intercourse. *Personal Relationships, 8,* 357-369.

28. Gallup, G. G., Jr., Burch, R. L., & Platek, S. M. (2002). Does semen have antidepressant properties? *Archives of Sexual Behavior, 31,* 289-293.

29. Townsend, J. M. (1995). Sex without emotional involvement: An evolutionary interpretation of sex differences. *Archives of Sexual Behavior, 24,* 173-206.

30. Haselton, M. G., & Buss, D. M., (2001). The affective shift hypothesis: The functions of emotional changes following sexual intercourse. *Personal Relationships, 8,* 357-369.

31. Ibid. See also Buss, David M. *The Evolution of Desire: Strategies of Human Mating (Revised and updated edition)*. Basic Books, 2016.

32. Haselton, M. G., & Buss, D. M., (2001). The affective shift hypothesis: The functions of emotional changes following sexual intercourse. Personal Relationships, 8, 357-369

33. Tooke, J., & Camire, L. (1991). Patterns of deception in intersexual and intrasexual mating strategies. *Ethology and Sociobiology, 12,* 345-364.

34. Unpublished study by Semmelroth and Buss, described in Buss, David M. *The Evolution of Desire: Strategies of Human Mating (Revised and updated edition)*. Basic Books, 2016.

35. Buss, D. M. (1988). The evolution of human intrasexual competition. *Journal of Personality and Social Psychology, 54,* 616-628.

    See also Schmitt, D. P., & Buss, D. M. (1996). Strategic self-promotion and competitor derogation: Sex and context effects on the perceived effectiveness of mate attraction tactics. *Journal of Personality and Social Psychology, 70*(6), 1185-1204.

36. Buss, David M. *The Evolution of Desire: Strategies of Human Mating (Revised and updated edition)*. Basic Books, 2016.

37. Hatfield, E., & Rapson, R. L. *Love, Sex, and Intimacy: Their Psychology, Biology, and History*. New York: Harper Collins, 1993.

38. In fact, if people are told someone likes them, that usually causes them to like their admirer in return. See Berscheid, E., & Walster (Hatfield), E. *Interpersonal Attraction*. Addison-Wesley, 1978.

    The effect is even better if you let the person know you like them more than you like others. See Eastwick, P. W., Finkel, E. J., Mochon, D., & Ariely, D. (2007). Selective versus unselective romantic desire. *Journal of Experimental Social Psychology, 44,* 800-807.

39. Janus, S. S., & Janus, C. L. *The Janus Report on Sexual Behavior*. New York: Wiley, 1993.

40. Haselton, M. G., & Buss, D. M., (2001). The affective shift hypothesis: The functions of emotional changes following sexual intercourse. *Personal Relationships, 8,* 357-369.

41. and 42. In making these statements, I'm putting together several lines of evidence. First, dopamine is definitely associated with testosterone, and men must have it to fall

in love; dopamine processing centers of the brain are also involved in keeping men in love. See Fisher, Helen. *Why Him? Why Her? Finding Real Love by Understanding Your Personality Type.* Henry Holt and Company, 2009. Second, dopamine levels rise in other male mammals just prior to having sex—and fall immediately after; see p. 187 of Trees, Andrew. *Decoding Love: Why it Takes Twelve Frogs to Find a Prince, and Other Revelations from the Science of Attraction.* Avery, 2009. Third, sexually experienced men (but not women, and not men who were sexually inexperienced) report a loss of sexual interest immediately following coitus. See Haselton, M. G., & Buss, D. M., (2001). The affective shift hypothesis: The functions of emotional changes following sexual intercourse. *Personal Relationships, 8,* 357-369. The conjecture on my part, then, is that when men get sex very quickly in a relationship, the loss of interest is created by an unintentional, non-conscious drop in dopamine.

43. Welch, D. C. (October 30, 2013). *Passionate kisses: Not too much to ask.* Retrieved from http://www.lovesciencemedia.com/love-science-media/passionate-kisses-not-too-much-to-ask.html

44. Buss, David M. *The Evolution of Desire: Strategies of Human Mating (Revised and updated edition).* Basic Books, 2016.

45. Meston, Cindy M., & Buss, David M. *Why Women Have Sex: Understanding Sexual Motivations from Adventure to Revenge (and Everything in Between).* Times Books, 2009.

46. Welch, D. C. (April 26, 2011). *Masturbation + marriage = ?* Retrieved from http://www.lovesciencemedia.com/love-science-media/masturbation-marriage.html

47. Hetherington, E. Mavis, and John Kelly. *For Better or for Worse: Divorce Reconsidered.* Norton, 2003.


# Part III: Making The Choice: Getting Closer, Breaking Up, Moving Forward

## CHAPTER 8: THERE'S NO SUCH THING AS A BLENDED FAMILY

1. Wallerstein, J. (2002). Festering. In K. Anderson, D. Browning, & B. Boyer (Eds.), *Marriage: Just a piece of paper?* (pp.96-97; quote is from p. 97). Grand Rapids, Michigan:William B. Eerdmans Publishing Company.

2. I'm extrapolating from the work of Daly, M., & Wilson, M. (1996). Violence against stepchildren. *Current Directions in Psychological Science, 5,* 77-81.

3. Buss, David M. *Evolutionary Psychology: The New Science of the Mind (5th edition)*. Allyn & Bacon, 2014.

4. Daly, M., & Wilson, M. (1996). Violence against stepchildren. *Current Directions in Psychological Science, 5*, 77-81.

5. Martin, Wednesday. *Stepmonster: A New Look at Why Real Stepmothers Think, Feel, and Act the Way We Do*. Houghton Mifflin Harcourt, 2009.

6. Wallerstein, J. (2002). Festering. In K. Anderson, D. Browning, & B. Boyer (Eds.), *Marriage: Just a piece of paper?* (pp.96-97). Grand Rapids, Michigan:William B. Eerdmans Publishing Company.

7. Hatfield, E., & Sprecher, S. (1986). Measuring passionate love in intimate relations. *Journal of Adolescence, 9*, 383-410. You can find out how passionately you are or have been in love by taking their test yourself: http://fetzer.org/sites/default/files/images/stories/pdf/selfmeasures/Different_Types_of_Love_PASSIONATE.pdf

8. Welch, Duana C. *Love Factually: 10 Proven Steps from I Wish to I Do*. LoveScience Media, 2015.

9. Martin, Wednesday. *Stepmonster: A New Look at Why Real Stepmothers Think, Feel, and Act the Way We Do*. Houghton Mifflin Harcourt, 2009.

10. Ibid.

11. Gottman, John M., and Gottman, Julie Schwartz. *And Baby Makes Three: The Six-Step Plan for Preserving Marital Intimacy and Rekindling Romance After Baby Arrives*. Harmony, 2007.

12. Ibid.

13. This is an extrapolation of the reward theory of attraction, where we need to be associated with good events to start and keep a great relationship. See De Houwer, J., Thomas, S., & Baeyens, F. (2001). Associative learning of likes and dislikes: A review of 25 years of research on human evaluative conditioning. *Psychological Bulletin, 127*, 853-869.

14. Gottman, John M., with Silver, Nan. *The Seven Principles for Making Marriage Work: A Practical Guide from the Country's Foremost Relationship Expert*. Harmony, 2015.

15. Skinner, B. F. *The Behavior of Organisms*. BF Skinner Foundation, 1991.

16. This is called intermittent reinforcement. See Skinner, B. F. *The Behavior of Organisms*. BF Skinner Foundation, 1991.

17. Demanding and forbidding can cause people to do the opposite; see, for instance, Brehm, S., & Brehm, J. W. *Psychological Reactance: A Theory of Freedom and Control*. Academic Press, 1981.

18. Gottman, John M., with Silver, Nan. *The Seven Principles for Making Marriage Work: A Practical Guide from the Country's Foremost Relationship Expert*. Harmony, 2015.

19. Brehm, S., & Brehm, J. W. *Psychological Reactance: A Theory of Freedom and Control*. Academic Press, 1981.

20. Shermer, Michael. *The Believing Brain: From Ghosts and Gods to Politics and Conspiracies—How We Construct Beliefs and Reinforce Them as Truths*. Henry Holt & Company, 2011.

21. Gottman, John M., with Silver, Nan. *The Seven Principles for Making Marriage Work: A Practical Guide from the Country's Foremost Relationship Expert*. Harmony, 2015.

22. Gottman, John M., and Gottman, Julie Schwartz. *And Baby Makes Three: The Six-Step Plan for Preserving Marital Intimacy and Rekindling Romance After Baby Arrives*. Three Rivers Press, 2007.

23. Lepper, M. R., Greene, D., & Nisbett, R. E. (1973). Undermining children's intrinsic interest with extrinsic reward: A test of the "overjustification" hypothesis. *Journal of Personality and Social Psychology, 28*(1), 129-137.

## CHAPTER 9: HAPPILY EVER AFTER

1. Buss, David M. *The Evolution of Desire: Strategies of Human Mating (Revised and updated edition)*. Basic Books, 2016.

2. BTN—"Better Than Nothing"—is the spot-on term coined by Susan Page. See Page, Susan. *If I'm So Wonderful, Why Am I Still Single?: Ten Strategies That Will Change Your Love Life Forever*. Three Rivers Press, 2002.

3.  This is an extrapolation of drive reduction theory; see Myers, David G., and DeWall, C. Nathan. *Psychology (11th edition)*. Worth Publishers, 2016.

4.  Hetherington, E. Mavis, and John Kelly. *For Better or for Worse: Divorce Reconsidered*. Norton, 2003.

5.  Boutwell, B. B., Barnes, J. C., & Beaver, K. M. (2015). When love dies: Further elucidating the existence of a mate ejection module. *Review of General Psychology, 19*(1), 30.

    See also Buss, David M. *The Evolution of Desire: Strategies of Human Mating (Revised and updated edition)*. Basic Books, 2016.

6.  Welch, D. C. (May 26, 2009). *Texting your breakup? Whether, when, how, why*. Retrieved from http://www.lovesciencemedia.com/love-science-media/texting-your-breakup-whether-when-how-why.html

7.  Perilloux, C., & Buss, D. M. (2008). Breaking up romantic relationships: Costs experienced and coping strategies deployed. *Evolutionary Psychology, 6*(1), 164-181.

8.  Blesky, A. L., & Buss, D. M. (2001). Opposite sex friendship: Sex differences and similarities in initiation, selection, and dissolution. *Personality and Social Psychology Bulletin, 27*, 1310-1323.

9.  Duntley, J. D., & Buss, D. M. (2012). The evolution of stalking. *Sex Roles, 66*(5-6), 311-327.

10. Hetherington, E. Mavis, and John Kelly. *For Better or for Worse: Divorce Reconsidered*. Norton, 2003.

11. In fact, the American cohabitation rate has risen 29% in the past decade. See Stepler, R. (April 6, 2017). *Number of U. S. adults cohabiting with a partner continues to rise, especially among those 50 and older*. Pew Research.org. Retrieved from http://www.pewresearch.org/fact-tank/2017/04/06/number-of-u-s-adults-cohabiting-with-a-partner-continues-to-rise-especially-among-those-50-and-older/

12. This has been true for some time. See Waite, Linda J., and Gallagher, Maggie. *The Case for Marriage: Why Married People are Happier, Healthier, and Better Off Financially*. Broadway Books, 2002.

13. Ibid.

14. Waite, L.J. (2002). Looking for Love. In K. Anderson, D. Browning, & B. Boyer (Eds.), *Marriage: Just a piece of paper?* (pp. 163-169). Grand Rapids, Michigan:William B. Eerdmans Publishing Company.

15. Ibid.

16. Waite, Linda J., and Gallagher, Maggie. *The Case for Marriage: Why Married People are Happier, Healthier, and Better Off Financially.* Broadway Books, 2002.

17. Waite, L.J. (2002). Looking for Love. In K. Anderson, D. Browning, & B. Boyer (Eds.), *Marriage: Just a piece of paper?* (pp. 163-169). Grand Rapids, Michigan:William B. Eerdmans Publishing Company.

18. Ibid.

19. Waite, Linda J., and Gallagher, Maggie. *The Case for Marriage: Why Married People are Happier, Healthier, and Better Off Financially.* Broadway Books, 2002.

20. Ibid.

21. Wallerstein, J. (2002). Festering. In K. Anderson, D. Browning, & B. Boyer (Eds.), *Marriage: Just a piece of paper?* (pp.96-97). Grand Rapids, Michigan:William B. Eerdmans Publishing Company.

22. Ibid.

23. Waite, Linda J., and Gallagher, Maggie. *The Case for Marriage: Why Married People are Happier, Healthier, and Better Off Financially.* Broadway Books, 2002.

24. Ibid.

25. to 29. Gottman, John M., with Silver, Nan. *The Seven Principles for Making Marriage Work: A Practical Guide from the Country's Foremost Relationship Expert.* Harmony, 2015.

30. Page, Susan. *The 8 Essential Traits of Couples Who Thrive.* Dell, 1994.

31. to 37. Gottman, John M., with Silver, Nan. *The Seven Principles for Making Marriage Work: A Practical Guide from the Country's Foremost Relationship Expert.* Harmony, 2015.

38. To learn what makes you (and your partner) feel loved, you can take the 5 Love Languages test at http://www.5lovelanguages.com

39. Ibid. See also Welch, D. C. (March 26, 2013). *Gay or straight: What's the difference?* Retrieved from http://www.lovesciencemedia.com/love-science-media/gay-or-straight-whats-the-difference-1.html

40. to 45. Gottman, John M., with Silver, Nan. *The Seven Principles for Making Marriage Work: A Practical Guide from the Country's Foremost Relationship Expert.* Harmony, 2015.

46. Cavanaugh, John C., and Blanchard-Fields, Fredda. *Adult Development & Aging (4ᵗʰ edition).* Wadsworth, 2002.

47. Linda J. Waite's tabulations from the National Survey of Families and Households, 1987/88 and 1992/94, in Waite, Linda J., and Gallagher, Maggie. *The Case for Marriage: Why Married People are Happier, Healthier, and Better Off Financially.* Broadway Books, 2000.

# RECOMMENDED READING:

Please visit the recommended reading section of my website at http://www.lovesciencemedia.com/the-lovescience-recommended-re/. There, you'll encounter my personal picks for books relevant to all things Love…factually.

DUANA C. WELCH, PhD

# ACKNOWLEDGEMENTS

I t takes a village to raise a book. The mayor of this particular
village is my husband, Vic Hariton, who believed in and encouraged the first *Love Factually's* existence years before its publication, and who cheered me on in the Single Parents effort too. Without
his support and his continual example that *Love Factually for Single
Parents [& Those Dating Them]* is more than hypothetical, this book
would not exist.

Among the many outstanding villagers who helped *Love Factually
[& Those Dating Them]* to come about, my family, friends, former
students, clients, and Wise Readers at LoveScience and Facebook en-
couraged this project throughout. These folks are my first-and-forever
readers, my most avid commenters, my biggest cheerleaders, and the
ones who insisted *Love Factually* and this sequel must exist. To Stanna
Welch, Gerhard Pigl, Rebekah Armstrong, Dr. Kim Fromme, Lisa &
David Gibson, Kelly Ewing, Holly Russo-Morey, Judy Sterling, Jordan
Pinson, Sarah Nichole Smiley, Silja Litvin, Evelyn Zertuche, Zack
Smith, Annette Thompson, Mary R. Dittman, M.B.A., Andrea Larson,
Diana Haroldsen, Liana A., Dave Leigh, Kristin McMahon, Melanie J.
Williams, Tiffany Yates Martin, Margie Sekulic, Carrie Lynne Pietig,
MA, Michael (who knows his full name), Katie Quinn, Ben Austin,
Monica Cooley, Rachel Sherriff, Shonna Sedgwick Butler, Marty
Idziak, Deborah Mayard, Silvia Miranda, La'Tarsha Deltrice, Amy
Francesca, James Horrigan, Barbara Barrere-Garnett, Nicole McGuire
Cuba, Patti D. Hill, Sally Piernick, Thomas Arthur ("Tom") Castle,

Scott Burkey, Adriane Myers, Rich Morey, Amanda Person, Pamela Ann Joseph Watson, Darien Sloan Wilson, Lisa Sapolis, JoAnna Stern, Sarah Hanson Vargas, Katy Siepert, Audrey Alberthal, Julia Gnida, Karl Houck, Angie Houck, Julia Gregory Poirier, Amy Azzarito, Karen Emerson, Cristina Capotorto, Ryan Estis, Belinda Belcher, Victor 'Tex' Clark, Katie Heitert Wilkinson, Griffin Cameron, Curtis Ruder, Mace Welch, David Weigle, Noelle Hunt Bennet, Dr. Scott Hanson, Dr. Randi Cowdery, Charles Simon, Joe McCully, Amy Denmon, Kari Greathouse, Kelly Conrad Simon, Dharma Kaur Khalsa of Gran Canaria, Spain, Kimberly Giunta, Dr. Dan Kee, Dr. Judy Todd, Natalie Savoy, Corey Dingman, Nanda Mugnolo--and many others too numerous to mention, or who wish to remain anonymous, I owe my deepest thanks.

Of course, this book could not exist without the scientists, authors, and scientist-authors whose work formed its basis. I am humbled by the contributions of Dr. David M. Buss, Dr. Linda J. Waite, Dr. John Gottman, Dr. Julie Schwartz Gottman, Dr. Isolina Ricci, Dr. Brené Brown, Dr. Sue Johnson, Dr. E. Mavis Hetherington, Dr. Everett Worthington, Dr. Terri Orbuch, Dr. Carol Dweck, Dr. Amir Levine, Dr. Tim Cole, Ms. Emily Duddleston, Ms. Wednesday Martin, Dr. Nancy Kalish, Mr. Gavin de Becker, Mr. Lundy Bancroft, Dr. David Burns, Ms. Susan Page, Ms. Joan Norton, Esq., and Dr. David Schmitt. I am indebted to each of them for their work, and in some cases, their direct guidance. Some of the scientific greats whose shoulders this book stands on are now deceased, including Dr. Shirley Glass, Dr. Neil Jacobson, and Dr. Judith Wallerstein.

*Love Factually's* professional team brought it to life in a way one person alone never could. Francis J. Flaherty, story doctor extraordinaire, guided my steps and understood which questions readers would want answered. His efforts and faith in me were invaluable to the final result. My sincere thanks also go to designer Erin Tyler, who ensured that people could rightly judge this book by its cover; foreign rights agent Sylvia Hayse for shepherding my work into hands around the planet in multiple languages; and Joe Davey of Crockett Sound Labs for patient, outstanding engineering of the sound for the audio version of this book. Many thanks to science writer Jena Pincott for helping Frank and me find one another; Audrey Alberthal for inspired photography; Michael Saleman, Esq., for wise counsel; and Wise Reader Holly Russo-Morey for cajoling me for many months to write *Love Factually* to begin with. She was my tipping point from uncertainty to the big plunge.

Finally, thanks to each of you for reading *Love Factually for Single Parents [& Those Dating Them]*. I hope it makes a positive difference in your love life, and that your happiness will bring peace to those around you—as much research suggests it will. Both in stats and in story, hoping for love is not just a fairy tale; love is realistic, abundant, and attainable. It is the foundation of our lives, and the springboard to all other good things. I wish it for each of you, with all my heart. Thanks for being part of the village.

Cheers,

Duana

©PHOTO BY AUDREY ALBERTHAL

## ABOUT THE AUTHOR

D
r. Duana Welch (pronounced DWAY-nah) is known for using social science to solve real-life relationship issues. She launched popular advice blog "LoveScience: Research-based relationship advice for everyone" in 2009, and has contributed to *Psychology Today* and numerous other publications, in addition to teaching psychology across 20 years at universities and colleges in California, Florida, and Texas. Her first book, *Love Factually: 10 Proven*

*Steps from I Wish to I Do*, released in 2015 in paperback, audio, and e-book, and is being published globally in five languages. *Love Factually for Single Parents [& Those Dating Them]* launched in audio, e- and paperback formats worldwide in English in 2019. Her client practice is global, via Skype and other technologies. Thanks to science and Vic Hariton, she is happily married.

You can learn more about Duana and her work at LoveFactually.co. For further information, please email her at Duana@LoveScience-Media.com.

68179129R00213